AFTERIMAGES OF MODERNITY

AFTERIMAGES

OF MODERNITY

Structure and Indifference
in Twentieth-Century
Literature

HENRY SUSSMAN

The Johns Hopkins University Press

Baltimore and London

© 1990 The Johns Hopkins University Press
All rights reserved
Printed in the United States of America

The Johns Hopkins University Press, 701 West 40th Street
Baltimore, Maryland 21211
The Johns Hopkins Press Ltd., London

The paper used in this publication meets the minimum
requirements of American National Standard for Information
Sciences—Permanence of Paper for Printed Library
Materials, ANSI Z39.48-1984.

Library of Congress Cataloging-in-Publication Data

Sussman, Henry.
Afterimages of modernity : structure and indifference
in twentieth-century literature / Henry Sussman.
p. cm.
Bibliography: p.
Includes index.
ISBN 0-8018-3887-8 (alk. paper)
1. Literature, Modern—20th century—History and criticism.
2. Postmodernism (Litererture) I. Title. II. Title:
Afterimages of modernity.
PN771.S87 1990
809'.04—dc20   89-15478

For my teachers and students

Contents

Preface

The introductory material to the present volume comprises chapters 1 and 7 and thus spans it from end to end. In this the book mimics a number of twentieth-century literary works that were similarly uncertain of where they began and ended—and of the claims that beginnings and endings assert. "The Modern/Postmodern: On the Plain of Indifference," draws together certain themes introduced locally throughout the book. For this reason its final placement is fitting; but for a general statement of the relationship between modernism and its implicit countermovement, it is also the place to start.

Of central importance to the "retrospective introduction" and the volume as a whole are a number of interrelated concerns: the notion of style as a field in which decisive conceptual issues and esthetic possibilities are articulated and played out; the fate of structuralism in twentieth-century literature, criticism, and art; a gravitation toward a certain indifference, as much as a style and a conceptual position as an affective state; and finally, in full awareness of the stultifying effect generalizations can have, a sense of the overall shape of twentieth-century intellectual experience, the complex play between certain of its major currents and undercurrents.

In one sense structuralism, viewed as a deployment of the gridwork making transdisciplinary and transepochal analogies possible, operates in every era. There is a sense of structuralism that corresponds to the Foucauldian notion of archaeology as the ongoing horizon and conditions of knowledge. Every intellectual moment may be said to distill or synthesize its own structures, which become symptomatic of its conditions of thought. Even if one accepts this sliding notion of structures and structuralism, there is also a sense in which the early twentieth century was a moment of a particularly intense structural association and ferment. Artifacts as diverse as cubist paintings, the *Cantos of Ezra Pound*, Kafka's fiction, Joyce's *Ulysses*, and early psychoanalytical theory reveled in the combinations and dislocations that structures made possible. High modernism is a consummate structuralist achievement; the yet, as I argue, the truly seminal works of modernism apprehended and resisted the oppressive impacts of their formal construction. Astructuralism is already inscribed within those few artifacts, among them Kafka's "Burrow" and Joyce's *Finnegans Wake,* straddling the watershed between modernism and the postmodern. One way that the following essays proceed, then, is to pursue the gravitation toward and resistance to structuralism in the writers whose works they read, namely Joyce, Wittgenstein, Kafka, Beckett, Adorno, and Bernhard.

The second chapter reads Joyce's *Ulysses* as an exemplary modern text. If contemporary critical theory has taught us anything, it is that generalizations, propositions, and pronouncements of any sort had best proceed from the already existing texts through which they first become possible. Though there is surely arbitrariness in assigning *Ulysses* or any work exemplary status, I do so because this text focuses and concentrates notions of the modern that have surfaced in a number of crucial contexts, literary and critical: Benjamin, Baudelaire, Poe, Proust, Adorno, Pound, Eliot, Barthes, de Man. A reading of *Ulysses* facilitates and focuses a posing of the question of the modern in general. Its role is paradigmatic in discerning that most subtle and always changing dissonance—the blur between the image and "the spontaneous afterimage"—between the modern and its implicit countermovement, called, for better or worse, the postmodern.

The fate of structures and structuralism is surely not the only axis on which certain developments in twentieth-century literature and theory may be charted. Chapter 3, "Kafka and Modern Philosophy," strives for a stylistic understanding of certain of the most distinctive experiments produced by twentieth-century art and philosophy. Style is not merely an embellishment; it articulates the stakes of the most intense intellectual engagements. Much of twentieth-century literature and philosophy hang suspended between the terse precision and minimalist expression that Wittgenstein first devised for the *Tractatus Logico-Philosophicus* and the endless prolixity and qualification found, among other sites, in Joyce's late fiction, Heideggerian phenomenology, and the discourse of deconstruction. At first glance minimalism and exaggerated prolixity could not be more antithetical. In the academic division of labor, the separation between logical analysis and Continental philosophy is founded on a similar methodological, if not stylistic divide. Earlier in the century, the chapter argues, terseness and prolixity represented complementary, not opposed, stances toward authority and the inherited intellectual baggage from the past. Kafka's "Description of a Struggle" stages a confrontation between an anorexic poet of distant (analytical) aphorism and an overweight fulminator of exaggerations. The story is not merely illustrative of the stylistic alternatives available to innovators and (intellectual) systems analysts at the turn of the century; it is prophetic of the extreme rigor and the equally extreme hyperbole at which much important twentieth-century intellectual and artistic work would be situated.

No saving or restorative synthesis ever emerges to resolve the extremes of style and expression at which the seminal works of twentieth-century literature and philosophy are situated. The implicit countermovement to modernism does not so much back off from extremes as gravitate toward a systematic indifference as violent as it is noncommittal. The indifference emerging in the wake of modernism shares neither the exuberance nor the terror with which Walter Benjamin's Angel of History addresses (backward) the inevitable future. Postmodern indifference embraces conceptual, esthetic, and sexual emanations, as well as affective ones. Chapter 7, touching on works by Beckett, Adorno, and Bernhard, suggests how an esthetic of indifference might both extend and dismantle the innovations of modernism.

Between this volume's thematic and methodological introduction ("Joyce's Musical Comedy") and its retrospective one, transpire three readings illustrative of the issues and movements at play on the shifting border between the modern and postmodern. The first of these, chapter 4, "The Circle of Exclusion," articulates a scenario common to all of Kafka's novels: the absorption of the K. of *The Castle* within an encompassing image or metaphor itself dramatizing the distortions as well as the associative potentials of language. Kafka not only begins with the premise that reality, such as it is, is a figment of language; the scenario and innumerable particular moments in his novel graphically illustrate this point. Yet the Castle, with which K. contends as both a tangible bureaucracy and a hypothesis, is a rigorous geometrical construction, a structure. In his novels, then, Kafka proceeds from the structural invention characteristic of modernist productions to a systematic derangement bespeaking a different intellectual climate and phase. Chapter 5, "The Text That Was Never a Story," explores certain of the psychological and structural implications of Kafka's unique placement. "A Country Doctor" pursues the vicissitudes of a psychological structure, the Oedipal triangle, through a narrative itself heavily structured by doubling and duplicity. This story ultimately exhausts its aging protagonist, as it exhausts the structures making it legible.

Chapter 6 approaches the *Ficciones* of Jorge Luis Borges as both a culmination and a terminus for the structural combination and bricolage characteristic of high modernism. Through careful readings of "Tlön, Uqbar, Orbis Tertius," "The Garden of Forking Paths," and "Death and the Compass," it is possible to observe Borges on the verge of major poststructuralist, postmodern apprehensions: marginality, supplementarity, duplicity, extreme idealism. The retrospective introduction both assembles a model for modernism and suggests what the egress, corresponding to the exit in a cybernetic program, from so powerful a model and fictive generation might be.

This book deploys careful literary and philosophical readings, self-contained in their own right, as a gloss or commentary on several large and for this reason dangerous topoi, including modernism, postmodernism, structuralism, and deconstruction. There are many ways for things to go wrong in such an enterprise, based as it is on difficult texts and the addressing of yet unresolved, if not problematical, issues. As vulnerable as such an exercise may be, I draw solace from two of the writers herein considered: from Wittgenstein, who never demanded perfection or immortality of the heuristic ladder of logic, which he then withdrew at the end of the *Tractatus;* and from Adorno, who stood at the intellectual home plate and took his swings even though the variegated constraints on his discourse forced him, every so often, to strike out. The following chapters assemble and elucidate a fair swathe of the literary texts that have made our century such an exuberant one. They also suggest some of the theoretical implications of these texts. If I may speak for them, they are just as happy for the exceptions to the models they hypothesize and the interpretations they offer as for any confirmation of their assertions. These chapters stand, or fall, on their suggestiveness: being definitive, in its various dimensions, is an assertion whose underlying assumptions still need further testing.

This preface strives for a snapshot of the book as a whole. It should not end without a mention of the seemingly tangential side-issues nevertheless surfacing in a wide range of contexts. I think of the process of translation, which could involve Wittgenstein, Benjamin, Joyce, and Borges; synaesthesia, curiously linking Wittgenstein to the Borges of "The Circular Ruins" and "Funes, the Memorious"; the game of chess, in which, in different ways Poe, Benjamin, Wittgenstein, and Borges are engaged. These subliminal side shows may well constitute the substantial matter at hand; may well comprise the seminal and suggestive material eluding the encompassing framework.

Curiously, the notion of the postmodern is far richer as a catalyst for discussion than as a concept in itself. The debates it has initiated have been more suggestive than any categorical or periodic definitions it has enabled. The present collection is more in the tradition of Theodor Adorno's testing of an idea—and sinking as well as swimming with it—than a comprehensive overview of the literature of modernism and postmodernity. This body of criticism is still in a vibrant state of expansion.

I feel a certain affinity between my own attempt and Ihab Hassan's *Dismemberment of Orpheus*[1] because Hassan, like myself, identifies certain traits of the postmodern esthetic or period while knowing full well the futility of such an endeavor. His work thus vacillates between the processes of hypothesis and performance. Where his own text spins away from its frameworks, it exemplifies the postmodern.

Renato Poggioli's *Theory of the Avant-Garde*[2] explores the interstice between esthetic and political radicality. Published in 1962, it is situated at the outset of the current debate, and Jochen Schulte-Sasse does well to incorporate it into his foreword to the U.S. edition of Peter Bürger's later work of virtually the same title. Poggioli assembles a broad set of traits that can be associated to some degree with avant-gardism: a profound tension with past precedent, loss of teleological orientation, a mystique of purity, stylistic and aesthetic alienation, scientificism, and, affectively, a certain disaffectation. Schulte-Sasse is right: Bürger's *Theory of the Avant-Garde*[3] demonstrates how a rigorous conceptual *Auseinandersetzung* can upgrade the quality of the models and definitions applied to avant-gardism. In this case, Bürger explores the Frankfurt school's recapitulations and critique of bourgeois and rationalist traditions as valuable sources for the discussion of the avant-garde. Bürger both extends and departs from what he finds most important in such writers as Adorno and Benjamin. By focusing on such deeply entrenched traditions as the autonomy of the artwork (and its producer), historical periodization, and individuality in esthetic production and reception, Bürger is able to reach toward a distinctly activist notion of the avant-garde: one adapted to the dynamics of mass production and reception, open to the impact of chance, characterized by *bricolage* and kaleidoscopic variation (what he terms *montage*), and not categorically opposed to political engagement. Theorization and critical exegesis enhance each other considerably in this presentation.

The Postmodern Moment,[4] edited and introduced by Stanley Trachtenberg, is precisely what its subtitle suggests: *A Handbook of Contemporary Innovation in the Arts*. Arranged by art forms and media, it presents keynote essays and useful bibliographies on the postmodern departures in such areas as art, architecture, film, and literature.

One of the strongest, although by no means universal, tendencies of this critical literature is the observation of a parallelism between the political and the esthetic. *All That Is Solid Melts into Air*, by Marshall Berman,[5] is a pleasant and informative continuation in this direction. It places the artistic innovations of its period in the context of such "real" developments as the phenomenon of development itself and the rise of such distant cities as Saint Petersburg and New York. Jean-François Lyotard's *Postmodern Condition: A Report on Knowledge*[6] is less an attempt to account for specific artifacts or the perspectives in which they arise than a theoretical extrapolation of the conditions of scholarship, institutions, and knowledge itself during an age when their conventional legitimations have undergone serious if not devastating critical questioning.

THE PRESENT volume completes a series of meditations—on modern literature, critical theory, and American literature—I undertook as a postdoctoral fellow in the Humanities Center at the Johns Hopkins University. Under the direction of Richard Macksey during the 1970s, the Humanities Center was a powerful and inspiring environment in which it was possible to discern some of the large issues surrounding literary studies. I am indebted first and foremost to Richard Macksey and the Johns Hopkins University for their formative intellectual stimulation and support.

Chapter 3 of this volume, "Kafka and Modern Philosophy," was begun under a Rockefeller Foundation Humanities Fellowship that supported the completion of a different book. I wrote the initial draft of this chapter at the request of the Kafka Society of America as a paper to be delivered at its December 1985 meeting. In addition, I am grateful to the Camargo Foundation of Cassis, France, which graciously housed me and permitted me to use its research facilities as I wrote this chapter. I received vital encouragement during the early phases of this project from Terry Cochran of the University of Minnesota Press.

The State University of New York at Buffalo has always extended me every encouragement and support in my research. I think particularly of Jon Whitmore, dean of the Faculty of Arts and Letters, and his staff, who have done much to foster the study of comparative literature on our campus as well as to facilitate my efforts. Rodolphe Gasché has played a decisive role in setting a productive tone for theoretical studies at our university and in furnishing initiative for innovative programs. The Johns Hopkins University Press, above all the humanities editor, Eric Halpern, and Irma Garlick, who prepared the manuscript, provided generous and efficient assistance in all areas of editing. Cathleen A. Carter has given freely of her time and expert assistance at a pivotal moment in her career to assure the completion of this project. Johann Pillai provided indispensable editorial assistance. As always, my family has been an inexhaustible source of encouragement and support.

Abbreviations

BBB Ludwig Wittgenstein, *Preliminary Studies for the "Philosophical Investigations" Generally Known as the Blue and Brown Books* (Oxford: Basil Blackwell, 1964).

C   Franz Kafka, *The Castle*, trans. Willa Muir and Edwin Muir (New York: Schocken, 1974). German interpolations in citations are from his *Das Schloss* (Frankfurt: S. Fischer, 1967).

CS   Franz Kafka, *The Complete Stories*, ed. Nahum N. Glatzer (New York: Schocken, 1976). German interpolations in citations are from his *Sämtliche Erzählungen*, ed. Paul Raabe (Frankfurt: S. Fischer, 1972).

F   Jorge Luis Borges, *Ficciones*, ed. and intro. Anthony Kerrigan (New York: Grove Press, 1962). Spanish interpolations in citations are from his *Ficciones* (Madrid: Alianza Editorial, 1972).

FW James Joyce, *Finnegans Wake* (New York: Penguin, 1986).

K   Thomas Bernhard, *Correction*, trans. Sophie Wilkins (New York: Vintage, 1983). German interpolations in citations are from his *Korrectur* (Frankfurt: Suhrkamp, 1985).

M   Samuel Beckett, *Molloy*, trans. Patrick Bowles (New York: Evergreen, 1955).

MM Theodor Adorno, *Minima Moralia: Reflections from Damaged Life*, trans. E. F. N. Jephcott (London: Verso, 1984).

ND Theodor Adorno, *Negative Dialectics*, trans. E. B. Ashton (New York: Continuum, 1983).

SE   Sigmund Freud, *Standard Edition of the Complete Psychological Works of Sigmund Freud*, trans. and ed. James Strachey, Anna Freud, Alix Strachey, and Alan Tyson, 24 vols. (London: Hogarth Press, 1953–74).

U   James Joyce, *Ulysses: The Corrected Text*, ed. Hans Walter Gabler (New York: Random House, 1986).

AFTERIMAGES OF MODERNITY

CHAPTER ONE

A Modern Climate

VERSIONS OF ULYSSES

It gives us an expansive and hopeful feeling whenever we equate the beginning of a book with embarking on a journey. Both the yet unturned pages and the uninitiated voyage harbor unknown discoveries. Whether it qualifies as a voyage or not, the present excursion through the twentieth century encompasses Prague, Dublin, and Buenos Aires among its ports of call. On a theoretical level, it will witness the obliteration of the very structures that high modernist literature summoned in response to its own apprehension of the primacy of language in thought.

If any twentieth-century figure is emblematic of the uncertain retracing of steps that the following chapters would accomplish, it is the figure of the Angel of History, which the German critic Walter Benjamin elaborated in thesis 9 of his "Theses on the Philosophy of History." Benjamin's Angel of History, his *Angelus Novus*, is notable in its peculiarly hesitant bearing toward the future. In its ebullient facet, the Angel of History is an adventurer. It traverses eons of time in an instant; the distances between the remotest continents, and indeed between universes, are nothing to it. The sweep of time, the entire domain of settings, historical and imaginary, in which human activity has transpired, fall under its jurisdiction. I will have occasion to return to this decisive figure of Benjamin's.

The Angel of History is always in the condition of initiating a journey, so it is perhaps no accident that the beginning of the twentieth century is one of the Angel's great moments. Sensing a monumental leave-taking, the writers of the day invoke Odysseus and other epic travelers as guides for their fictive explorations. The central books of Homer's *Odyssey* (9–12) become the narrative framework, the structural bottom line, upon which Ezra Pound grafts a bewildering array of narratives and cultural materials deriving from, among others, Chinese, Provençal, Italian, French, English, and Spanish civilizations as he pursues certain events, settings, and obsessions in the

Cantos. The *Cantos* are framed by Odysseus's encounter with the spirit of Elpenor in book II of the *Odyssey.* Elpenor's spirit demands a proper burial and memorial for the human body it has left. This encounter is emblematic of Odysseus's and hence Pound's relation to the materials, memories, and linguistic remains of the past. Modernists as diverse as Walter Benjamin, T. S. Eliot, and Wallace Stevens join Pound in the repository of discarded, if not exhausted, cultural remains. Joyce's *Ulysses* loosely inscribes the fictive, intellectual, and esthetic happenings ascribed to Dublin on 16 June 1904 within the context of the same classical epic that Pound appropriated for the *Cantos.* Kafka, in an instance of his own retrospective search for mythological settings for contemporary and everyday events, imagines Poseidon "at his desk, going over accounts. The administration of all the waters gave him endless work" (*CS*, 434).

As an explorer, the Angel of History at the beginning of the century inspires authors to engage mythological travelers as surrogate pilots for their quests. Within this overwhelming context of argosy and leave-taking, it is not completely inconceivable that the figure of Odysseus and his fellow travelers should enter and temper a wide range of twentieth-century intellectual endeavors whose writing is discursive. One could well argue that Freud, particularly the Freud of *Studies on Hysteria* and *The Interpretation of Dreams,* is an early structuralist. Such notions as drives, inhibitions, and the Oedipal complex are structures around or upon which the materials of memory, experience, and such psychic happenings as dreams can be formed. Much of Freud's work effects a translation of psychic materials, with their many sources and manifestations, into structures; and classical mythology is for Freud a particularly privileged repository of structures, the Oedipal being a case in point.

The linguistics of Ferdinand de Saussure is one of the most potent forces militating, at the beginning of the century, for a linguistic source and constitution of thought, reality, and communication, to the extent that any notion of origins applies.[1] For Saussure, there is a radical discrepancy between language and that to which it ostensibly refers. Above all, language refers to itself. The signs that comprise it are formed of an easily overlooked fusion between concepts and linguistic qualities. Languages are determined by social conventions. The signs in a language are selected arbitrarily, not by virtue of any sense inherent to them. The principle of sign selection is differential, motivated by the need for variety in signification, rather than by any identity between signifiers and what they signify.[2] Languages evolve out of a stately negotiation between the historical repository of all their possibilities, which Saussure calls the *langue*, and its conventional spur of the moment usages, the *parole*.[3] Saussure eschews mythology in his own formulations, except, as Derrida has pointed out, the myth of a distinction between oral language and writing. Language nonetheless emerges, in a post-Saussurian world, as a "new"—that is to say, nonideational and ungenealogical—source and structuring principle for the productions of intellectual activity.

The immanent close of a century presents all sorts of openings to the inevitable attempts to finalize its intellectual history. Aware of the totalistic pitfalls of this enterprise, I nonetheless hazard my own sketch of a possible version. A grandparental affinity prevails between the seminal literary works of modernism and the questioning of fundamental scientific, philosophical, and metaphysical assumptions on the part of contemporary critical theory. It may be said that the twentieth century is framed by the literary announcement and then the theoretical recapitulation of the pivotal role of language in organized human activity. Between these phases, but not in any simple sequential sense, transpires a pivotal structuralist moment: in the critical literature, substantive interests give way to the patterns, the architectural frameworks, underlying cultural artifacts and making them possible. Appreciating, with Saussure, that no reality could preempt the language in which all realities have been couched, structuralists discerned structures where prior interpreters had encountered essences and immutable truths. In structuralism a desubstantiation in the field of knowledge coincides with an isolation and variation of formal components.

It is understandable why myths and mythmaking, as an enduring and changing pretext for culture, should become a privileged topic for structuralist analysis. In a certain sense, for Western culture at least, the myths of classical antiquity have occupied a role analogous to that played by the nucleic acids in twentieth-century genetics: they have been a generative, recombinative underlying code.[4] In different ways for different structuralists, mythology has served as a way station between the finished artifacts of the past millennium and the primal code unearthed at the outset of the twentieth century by thinkers such as Saussure. Curiously, then, the fate of Odysseus as a quintessential mythical hero becomes an index to the vicissitudes of twentieth-century theory and art.

For Claude Lévi-Strauss, the figure of the anthropologist is very much a modern-day Odysseus; and myth is for Roland Barthes the preeminent model for language against itself, for a language that would, in the interest of a certain sociopolitical and economic power, restrict its nuances, sever itself from its context, and, in Barthes's own terms, "ossify" itself.[5] Particularly in such a work as *Tristes Tropiques*, Lévi-Strauss pictures himself as a traveler,[6] if not so much through space and its various geographic regions, at least through different moments and models of conceptualization and problem solving. Structures occupy in the thinking of Lévi-Strauss a role analogous to that played by inflection in Foucault's account of nineteenth-century philology:[7] without performing ethnocentric violence, they would, by gravitating toward the domain of form, account for a different culture in terms of its difference. The neutrality of structural form, a certain gentle disinterest, allows precisely for this translation. The stuctural analysis of such "primitive" phenomena as totemic classification and facial and body decorations provides for an articulation or paraphrase of their organizing principles comprehensible to Western science.[8] The sympathetic neutrality of the gravitation toward structure rather than more substantive issues would presumably protect the "other" cultures from judgment and condescension.

Within this procedural framework, the myth as a phenomenon of primitive cultures emerges as a structural matrix, a generator of narrative variables that the cultures then spin out over time. The fascination with variation and with the elements making it possible is a distinctly modernist manifestation, shared in different ways by writers and artists as distinct as Freud, Benjamin, Joyce, Proust, Kafka, and Picasso; I will consider the kaleidoscopic quality of modernism (in this case regarded as a particular historical moment) in fuller detail below.

"Our method thus eliminates a problem which has, so far, been one of the main obstacles to the progress of mythological studies, namely the quest for the *true* version, or the *earlier* one," writes Lévi-Strauss in "The Structural Study of Myth." Eschewing the quest for the aboriginal version of the myth (as he would, intentionally at least, for the pristine culture), Lévi-Strauss directs his attention toward the "gross constituent units" of myths, which he then defines as relations. "The true constituent units of a myth are not the isolated relations but *bundles of such relations*, and it is only as bundles that these relations can be put to use and combined so as to produce a meaning." Writing in a post-Saussurian world, Lévi-Strauss already knows that the myth, as a complex sign, is important almost exclusively to the degree that it produces meaning. His method would sidestep the pitfalls of originality, belief, and truth. It would focus instead on mythmaking as a production of signification.

Treating the variants of the Oedipus myth as the elements in a deck of cards—the card game, with its scientific counterpart, the index file, bearing metacritical as well as procedural significance for Lévi-Strauss's work—the structural anthropologist focuses on such tendencies as the overrating and underrating of blood relations and "difficulties in walking straight and standing upright," which become capable of linking the seemingly most disjointed phases of the myth.[9] Bundles of relations combine to form structures, and the virtue of structures is that, in a nonjudgmental way, they link apparently disparate elements and disclose meaning out of ostensible randomness. (Although it questions structuralist assumptions and operations, deconstruction shares, through its ongoing critique of the placement of language, this linkage of remote texts and cultural productions. The span of its inquiry may constitute deconstruction's closest affinity to structuralism.)

Viewed as an ensemble of relations, the myth becomes a matrix of possibilities, and mythmaking becomes an open-ended process. These redefinitions had been uncannily foreseen earlier in the century—by Joyce as he loosely grafted the episodes of Homer's *Odyssey* onto the encounters of two intertwined main characters as they meander through modern-day Dublin; and by Kafka, as he playfully demonstrated how, in keeping with its own internal logic, a contemporary adaptation could abolish the Prometheus legend itself (*CS*, 432). It is Lévi-Strauss, translating Joyce's and Kafka's knowledge into the protocol of the social sciences, who achieves a direct discursive statement of this attitude. The methodological passage cited immediately above continues:

> On the contrary, we define myth as consisting of all its versions; or to put it otherwise, a myth remains the same as long as it is felt as such. A striking example is offered by the fact that our interpretation may take into account the Freudian use of the Oedipus myth and is certainly applicable to it. Although the Freudian problem has ceased to be that of autochthony *versus* bisexual reproduction, it is still the problem of understanding how *one* can be born from *two*: How is it that we do not have only one procreator, but a mother plus a father? Therefore, not only Sophocles, but Freud himself, would be included among the recorded versions of the Oedipus myth on a par with earlier or seemingly more "authentic" versions.[10]

The overall argument here is that the disclosure of structures within an economy of signification supersedes in importance any substantive element of the myth. Freud's interpretation and use of the Oedipus myth hinges on its psychosexual content. Lévi Strauss ostensibly introduces Freud here as an earlier interpreter of—and contributor to—the myth. But he also recognizes in the founder of psychoanalysis a fellow structuralist and a fellow *bricoleur*.

There is something both elemental and irreducible—that is to say, singular—about the myth. It "grows spiral-wise until the intellectual impulse which has produced it is exhausted. Its *growth* is a continuous process, whereas its *structure* remains discontinuous." Lévi-Strauss invokes physical and chemical rhetoric to indicate the generative functions of the myth, how it produces, through invention and recombination, sequels and variants. The myth is also conditioned, however, by specificity. It runs its course, plays itself out. The myth arises in and satisfies particular conditions. As an analogy for its placement, Lévi-Strauss offers us "a crystal in the realm of physical matter. This analogy may help us better understand the relationship of myth to both *langue* on the one hand and *parole* on the other. Myth is an intermediary entity between a statistical aggregate of molecules and the molecular structure itself."[11]

Caught between structure and generality, the myth itself a hybrid creation, akin to Picasso's plastic collages and Kafka's Odradek, which looks at first glance "like a flat star-shaped spool for thread, and indeed it does seem to have thread wound upon it . . . knotted and tangled together, of the most varied sorts and colors. But it is not only a spool" (*CS*, 428). The myth is both the product and the generator of *bricolage*. It occupies an intermediary place in the Saussurian economy of linguistic evolution, between the stately *langue* and the more current *parole*. Lévi-Strauss is quite explicit about its placement in a post-Saussurian world.

All disclaimers to the contrary, Lévi-Strauss is himself a fabled traveler and a patient interpreter of the fable. In a powerful sense the space of his work, ethnographic as well as methodological, is always already inscribed in the seminal explorations of modern literature and of psychoanalysis, which happens to comprise one of literature's most concrete tangents. Joyce's *Ulysses*, the *Cantos of Ezra Pound*, and the adventures of Kafka's K. are all dedicated, in different ways, to the wanderings of Odysseus. In his ethnography, Lévi-Strauss joins these travels. He invokes the myth as a key instance of the structural model that would account for the "primitive" mind. He becomes an interpreter and spokesman for the myth that he personifies and studies.

The work of Roland Barthes arises as well in a context shaped by Saussurian considerations and terms. However receptive it was to new theoretical and psychoanalytical approaches, Barthes's work never abandoned its exploration of the sign, the process of signification, and the interplay that takes place along the axes between connotation and denotation, between paradigm and syntagm. The Barthesian myth has a different feel to it from Lévi-Strauss's: it is less a generator of signification than a statute of limitations imposed upon linguistic ambiguity and play. The attributes that Barthes assembles, relatively early in his writings, under the rubric of the myth, nevertheless serve him throughout his career as a party in the interchange between what he terms the "readerly" and the "writerly"—an allegory in which language, for a variety of sociopolitical, moral, and psychosexual reasons, erects barriers to control and contain its own unfettered meanings and associations, only to witness the eventual dissolution of these structures at the hands of its open-ended play. Barthes is critically aware of the transitoriness and limited application of the distinctions that he himself invokes. As a critic of the myth and its role as a consolidator of mainstream culture in ancient, "classical," and modern societies, he nevertheless continues in the travels of the twentieth-century Odysseus, pausing before the myth but also maintaining a critical—and metacritical—distance from it.

The myth becomes for Barthes the theater (or wrestling ring) where culture hashes out its relation to its own authority, ideology, and receptivity to improvisation. Myth is both the arena in which the plurality, discontinuity, multivalence, excess, and metonymic sliding of language disclose themselves and the setting in which these phenomena are placed under their sociopolitical constraints. His early work is marked by a fusion between modern linguistics' systematic elaboration of the sign and the Frankfurt school's attempt to furnish social critique in keeping with the complexity of twentieth-century technology, esthetics, and conceptual work. In later work, Barthes builds upon his early double enterprise by incorporating his own rhetoric of semiological concerns (for example, the fullness and emptiness of the sign; readerliness and writerliness). With exemplary receptiveness, he also opens his investigations to the innovations of Lacanian psychoanalysis and deconstruction: the fetishism of desire and the supplemental placement of writing comprise important extensions to the scenario of semiological inflation and demystification incorporated by the myth.

If any single phrase could encapsulate the course of Barthes's *oeuvre*, it would be *The Empire of Signs*, the title of his book on Japan. Barthes's early insistence that myth comprises a metalanguage, a language about language, is borne out in subsequent work. Barthes decries the repressive tolerance resulting from political uses of the myth; his own reading of the myth, however, is never neutral, focusing either on mythic thefts or on the linguistic play that the myth can never definitively suspend.

> This is a kind of *arrest*, in both the physical and the legal sense of the term: French imperiality condemns the saluting Negro to be nothing more than an instrumental signifier, the Negro suddenly hails me in the name of French imperiality; but at the same moment the Negro's salute thickens, becomes vitrified, freezes into an eternal reference meant to *establish* French imperiality. On the surface of language something has stopped moving: the use of the signification is here, hiding behind the fact, and conferring on it a notifying look; but at the same time, the fact paralyses the intention, gives it something like a malaise producing immobility: in order to make it innocent, it freezes it. This is because myth is speech *stolen and restored*. Only, speech which is restored is no longer quite that which was stolen: when it was brought back, it was not put exactly in its place. It is this brief act of larceny, this moment taken for a surreptitious faking, which gives mythical speech its benumbed look.

> What is characteristic of myth? To transform a meaning into form. In other words, myth is always a language-robbery. I rob the negro who is saluting, the white and brown chalet, the seasonal fall in fruit prices, not to make them examples or symbols, but to naturalize through them the Empire, my taste for Basque things, the Government. Are all primary languages a prey for myth? Is there no meaning which can resist this capture with which form threatens it? In fact, nothing can be safe from myth, myth can develop its second-order schema from any meaning and, as we saw, start from the very lack of meaning. But all languages do not resist equally well.[12]

Barthes's *Mythologies* of 1957 begins with a sequence of careful readings of cultural artifacts so deeply embedded in the everydayness of modern life as to have become virtually transparent. Barthes insists on treating these phenomena—ranging from margarine and laundry detergent to the new Citröen and the spectacle of wrestling—as signs of metalanguage themselves, not as things or even as simple commodites. The theory of his semiological analyses arises only in the aftermath of his engagement with these rather concrete cultural manifestations; it is generated in the course of the long essay that closes the volume, "Myth Today," from which the citations immediately above derive.

If Barthes selects a now famous photograph of a Senegalese soldier saluting the French flag from the pages of *Paris-Match* as a paradigmatic instance of mythic language, this is owing less to the obeisance to some extent constituting the subject of the image than to the mythic form of the representation itself. In this sense, Barthes anticipates McLuhan's equation between the medium and the message. And, as the above citations suggest, the form of the mythic representation, what motivates its effect, consists in its parasitism, its taking out of context, its naturalization of its contents, its avoidance of complexity, its welcoming generality, its ossification of meaning. Instrumented by twentieth-century technology and communications, the myth becomes the very form of public manipulation—political, ideological, commercial, even theological—in the contemporary world. At this moment of his career, Barthes dwells on the political implications of mythic representation: "Myth is depoliticized speech." Its "innoculation . . . consists in admitting the accidental evil of a class-bound institution the better to conceal its principal evil." Through its "neither-norism" the myth states "two opposites and balancing the one by the other so as to reject them both."[13] Under Barthes's stewardship of the myth, Odysseus has been metamorphosed from the audience's surrogate adventurer into the saluting soldier from an acquiescent army, whose image rationalizes a nation's foreign and economic policies.

In subsequent work, notably *S/Z* and *A Lover's Discourse*, Barthes will implant the totalizing and open-ended linguistic tendencies that combine to produce the mythic image within a scene of writing and an interpretative situation. What he calls, in the opening pages of *S/Z*, "the readerly" roughly corresponds to the totalizing, neutralizing, and ossifying semiological tendencies of the myth. The "writerly," on the other hand, is an attitude that emphasizes the open-endedness of texts and the plurality of their possible interpretations. From this perspective, the "text is a galaxy of signifiers" with a "plurality of entrances," dispersed "within the field of infinite difference."[14] Both texts and their interpreters fluctuate between the readerly imposition of coherence and simplicity and the writerly expansion toward the random linguistic flux underlying all efforts at systematization. Suspended between these inevitable linguistic counterattitudes, a "classical" text such as Balzac's story "Sarrazine" can join the most everyday productions of the contemporary world in the overarching enterprise of a cultural psychoanalysis. This project receives its fullest elaboration in *A Lover's Discourse*. Barthes's work maintains such fidelity to a semiological analysis of reality, whatever it may be, that even the experiences and states experienced most personally, say those of an aroused lover, can be interpreted according to linguistic situations and processes.

In the love situation as an intensification of linguistic life, everything, according to Barthes, can be placed within a wider semiological network—*tutti sistemati*.[15] Barthes's cultural psychoanalysis, as opposed to its clinical counterpart, eschews the scrutiny and incorporation of personal material (for example, dreams and memories) in favor of treating each moment in the love drama as a linguistic attitude. Jealousy, despair, and ecstasy are not only personal events: they are moments within an exchange of signs, expressions, gifts, pledges, and losses of interest. Cultural psychoanalysis, while maintaining the rigor and sensitivity to nuance characteristic of its clinical model, shifts the scene of interpretation away from the experiential and the subjective toward the plane of semiology. The disinterest and broadening of perspective allowed by such an analysis constitute its primary therapeutic effect—the only "cure" that a rigorous semiotician can allow.

Writers as diverse as Kafka, Pound, Joyce, and Proust inaugurate the twentieth century with a vertiginous sense of the provisoriness of systems, of the linguistic fluctuation held in suspense by all interpretations of reality. The dazzling adaptations of classical mythology that abound in the works of these authors correspond to the nostalgic and retrospective attitude of the Angel of History at the outset of the century. A linguistically aware Odysseus sets out in every direction, but with certain serious existential misgivings. This Odysseus informs the above all structuralist efforts arising to adapt the traditional social and natural sciences in accordance with the linguistic apprehension shared by Saussure, Kafka, Proust, and Joyce. Benjamin's Angel of History is a wiser Odysseus. Both in its linguistic adventure and in its structuralist revisions, the Angel of History exerts an influence on our century down to the present day. Both the seminal literature of our age and the theory that has qualified and extended it may be charted on the trajectory of the Angel's unfinished odyssey.

MODERNIST KALEIDOSCOPE

Structuralism and poststructuralism are not antithetical moments but concurrent phases. Structuralism makes possible a yoking or placing in tandem of diverse contexts and artifacts in which modernist esthetics take delight. Structuralism also discerns, however, the limits of its own methodology. It always already harbors the seeds of—and often rejoices in—the demolition of the structures by which it assembles and makes intelligible the incommensurate. Poststructuralism, the critique and disclosure of the conceptual underpinnings of intellectual operations, is always already inscribed in any structuralism. Any sense in which poststructuralism succeeds structuralism is therefore extremely limited.

Modernist esthetics—again—delights in the combinatorial power furnished by structures, whether characterized as forces, vortices, or vectors. Pound, for instance, can isolate the forces of political and linguistic adulteration in ancient China, Renaissance Italy, and modern America. By the same token, he can unearth esthetic value, which he regards as the pristine artifacts of a culture, in an equally diverse panorama of settings. The cultures that he appropriates and presents to his audience are charged with contradictory extremes of abysmal corruption and near-maternal purity. Esthetic mobility and political degeneracy thus comprise a structure, whose values are not unlike those associated with the Freudian Oedipal, enabling Pound to range without restriction as a cultural champion and imperialist. The Oedipal, as an elaborate allegory, comprises one, and no more than one, structure that modernists found compelling as a frame (the Heideggerian *Gestell*[16]) on which they could arrange esthetic, erotic, and social material. In the *Cantos*, Pound breathlessly assists at some of the steamiest "primal scenes" in the history of Western literature, notably the sexual war and union between Odysseus and Circe in book 10 of the *Odyssey*;[17] Joyce's Leopold Bloom muses obsessively on the business and pleasure that Blazes Boylan and Molly commingle; and Kafka's Country Doctor never quite manages to leave his Rose behind.

The Oedipal—and the triangular map of desire that it occupies—is merely one of many structures sought out by modernists. Modernists unearthed structures because they were infatuated with the combinatorial magic that structures would allow. The landscape of modern literature is hence littered with what may be best described as combination machines, matrices of permutational expansion. Among these must surely count the young Marcel's magic lantern,[18] Freud's dreamwork and "Mystic Writing-Pad,"[19] Hofrat Behrens' X-ray machine on Mann's *Magic Mountain*,[20] and Lévi-Strauss's decks of playing and index cards. One could indeed argue that the enterprise of cubism represents the incursion of the card deck into the field of the visual arts at its highest level of complexity. The scrambled image of cubism may be described as a game of "fifty-two card pick-up" played with the shards of an image whose wholeness may be imagined if not actually reconstituted. The cubism of Picasso and Braque is a visual game of combinatorial variation played with the fragments of images.

The visual counterpart to these structural generators is the kaleidoscope.[21] With a limited set of elements, it builds up a dizzying and seemingly endless sequence of images. No writer was more sensitive to the possibilities opened by these devices and to their relation to the debris of the past than Walter Benjamin. Characterizing the collaboration between the experience of the modern urban jumble and the inventions of modern technology, he writes:

> Comfort isolates; on the other hand, it brings those enjoying it closer to mechanization. The invention of the match around the middle of the nineteenth century brought forth a number of innovations which have one thing in common: one abrupt movement of the hand triggers a process of many steps. This development is taking place in many areas. One case in point is the telephone, where the lifting of a receiver has taken the place of the steady movement that used to be required to crank the older models. Of the countless movements of switching, inserting, pressing, and the like, the "snapping" of the photographer has had the greatest consequences. A touch of the finger now sufficed to fix an event for an unlimited period of time. The camera gave the moment a posthumous shock, as it were. Haptic experiences of this kind were joined by optic ones, such as are supplied by the advertising pages of a newspaper or the traffic of a big city. Moving through this traffic involves the individual in a series of shocks and collisions. At dangerous intersections, nervous impulses flow through him in rapid succession, like the energy from a battery. Baudelaire speaks of a man who plunges into the crowd as into a reservoir of electric energy. Circumscribing the experience of the shock, he calls this man "a *kaleidoscope* equipped with consciousness." Whereas Poe's passers-by cast glances in all directions which still appeared to be aimless, today's pedestrians are obliged to do so in order to keep abreast of traffic signals. Thus technology has subjected the human sensorium to a complex kind of training. There came a day when a new and urgent need for stimuli was met by the film.[22]

In this passage, from his crucial "On Some Motifs in Baudelaire," Benjamin consolidates some of the implications of the "atrophy of experience" that the essay traces. The spasmodic gestures required by modern machines comprise one manifestation of the shock esthetic presiding over a world whose cities have been overrun by crowds and deprived of spatial articulation, whose secular calendar has abolished any ritual markers. The difficult task that Benjamin assigns himself in this essay is to account in positive terms for an existential coherence and an engagement in labor and love experienced largely as loss or deprivation. In addressing the past, Benjamin adopts the nostalgic pose of his own Angel of History, held in common by the collector, the critic, who assumes the burden of memory, and the modernist. It is in this post that he can bemoan an "increasingly inhospitable . . . climate for lyric poetry."[23]

The very age that would exile the servant of memory nevertheless furnishes images for its relentless discombobulation of knowledge and community. These Benjamin groups under two major rubrics: the experience of shock and the loss of aura, the latter an imperceptible trace of handiwork, a signature of involvement in labor.[24] The shock of modernity enters into virtually every existential arena. It restructures cognition; replaces the sanctions of love with the eroticism of cruising; it defines, as I have shown, the mechanisms of tools and instruments; it is even reenacted, with the compulsion of trauma, in the leisure that people seek from their more strategic endeavors. The clock of the camera, kiddie cars, the tricks of a card game, the mechanics of film production, the lighting of a match are concrete images of the reverberation of shock in the modern world. Benjamin compares them to the "spontaneous afterimage" by which the eye both repeats and effaces perception. He can express a particular affinity for the Baudelaire who described the man of the crowd as "a *kaleidoscope* equipped with consciousness," for this formulation suggests a subordination of subjectivity to machinery, an uncanny fusion between humanity and mechanics, in which the former is not necessarily in control.

The figure of the kaleidoscope equipped with consciousness almost after the fact is illustrative of the ambivalences with which Benjamin's attitude as a writer are fraught. At once elegiac and protective toward the past, he is captivated, almost entranced, by the shock mechanism that has, almost before the fact, so radically reconfigured the conditions of thought and life. The greatest achievement of "On Some Motifs in Baudelaire," one of the seminal works of modernism and postmodernism—a contribution encompassing both concurrent movements—is the compositional performance in which Benjamin both sets the stage for and acts out the violence of shock.

It may be said of "On Some Motifs in Baudelaire" that it traces the vicissitudes of structure in twentieth-century thought. The essay is at the same time a virtuoso performance of the necessity and capability of structures and a demonstration of the inevitable self-obliteration that structures harbor within themselves. If there is to be any organization, any articulation to the barrage of sensations filtering through the "kaleidoscope equipped with consciousness," something like a structure will be necessary—to link the disparate and to posit sequences between apparently unrelated phenomena. Structural linkages between the most scattered intellectual and historical events constitute some of the achievements lauded most by Benjamin in other writers and lending the greatest distinction to this essay. However precious the crystallization afforded by structures may be, the shock esthetic of twentieth-century thought is so powerful as to deprive structures of any but the most fleeting validity. In "On Some Motifs in Baudelaire," Benjamin has composed a piece of writing setting both the inevitability and ephemerality of structures into the fullest possible relief. After assembling and linking, by means of a particularly vibrant structure, certain otherwise dispersed intellectual contributions from the beginning of the century in literature, philosophy, psychoanalysis, and historiography, Benjamin pursues the fate of his own crystallizations through the upheaval of shock.

The groundwork that the essay lays for its account of the degradation of experience in modern life largely consists in the isolation of a structure for shock. To put it better, Benjamin begins the essay by superimposing four distinct contexts whose diversity is belied by the prevalence of a common structure within them. What modern historiography (Dilthey's *Experience and Poetry*), phenomenology (Bergsonian *durée*), literature (Proust's *mémoire involuntaire*), and, not insignificantly, Freudian and Reikian psychoanalysis have in common is nothing more substantial than a common structure; yet this structure not only locates a coherence between otherwise divergent modern intellectual enterprises; it also accounts for the violence that penetrates each of these fields.

The structure of shock, wherever Benjamin discerns its operation, is characterized by an untoward paradox: the agent of activity— whether described as an organism, an individual or collective subject, or a cognitive function—is predicated by what it resists and bypasses as much as by what it asserts and incorporates. Well-being and efficiency are as much a function of negative relations as of positive ones. Dysfunctions and diseases mark not so much the invasion of an external agent as the breakdown of an already installed system of defense. A formulation that Benjamin borrows from Freud's *Beyond the Pleasure Principle* (1919) applies as well to all the intellectual settings that he yokes in tandem by structural superimposition: "For a living organism, protection against stimuli is an almost more important function than the reception of stimuli; the protective shield is equipped with its own store of energy and must above all strive to preserve the special forms of conversion of energy operating in it against the effects of the excessive energies at work in the external world, effects which tend toward an equalization of potential and hence toward destruction."[25] In this passage Freud introduces the trauma as the subjective memory piercing the psychic shield that would, under optimal conditions, deflect it. Yet the tension between opposed energy fields, and the violence erupting not from without but from within—these structural components or vectors of force go beyond the psychoanalytical subject to the operation of memory in modern literature and phenomenology, and toward the modern historiography that would disclose the violence at the roots of narrative cohesion and continuity.

The activity that Benjamin's essay incorporates is, then, complex and dialectically interesting. Benjamin initially seeks and crystallizes a structure that will account for modern shock. He then unleashes, in an instance of negative dialects, the abruptness of modern experience, in the form of the assembly line, the crowd, the camera, the roulette wheel, against his own structuring structure. His account of modern experience thus depends and founders on the structure. To the extent that it is structured by structure, "On Some Motifs in Baudelaire" must at least on one level be acknowledged as a classic of structuralist interpretation.

Within the dynamics of Benjamin's prose, shock manifests itself in the tightening of a textual knot, a conflation of strands introduced elsewhere casually. This internal condensation takes place with an unforeseen inevitability; it is the literary equivalent of the energy released through nuclear fusion. Benjamin may select certain games, processes, and contemporary phenomena as images for shock, but in its textual manifestation, shock assumes the form of a certain explosive density. Shock is tantamount to aware textuality; and the primacy of text as the basis for all logical and systematic organizations is in keeping with the linguistic apprehension, shared by Saussure, Kafka, Joyce, and Proust, with which twentieth-century linguistics and esthetics were inaugurated.

"On Some Motifs in Baudelaire" both fulfulls and dismantles its structural framework with textual convergences of dazzling brilliance and arbitrariness. One splendid example must suffice within the scope of the present discussion. Its form—and this is characteristic of Benjamin's writing—is that of a sequence of revelations set amid a single extended passage. The combination, reverberation, and dissonance that the segment in question dramatizes are characteristic of Benjamin's most striking prose:

> What the Fun Fair achieves with its Dodgem cars and other similar amusements is nothing but a taste of the drill to which the unskilled laborer is subjected in the factory—a sample which at times was for him the entire menu; for the art of being off center, in which the little man could acquire training in places like the Fun Fair, flourished concomitantly with unemployment.

> Gambling even contains the workman's gesture that is produced by the automatic operation, for there can be no game without the quick movement of the hand by which the stake is put down or a card is picked up. The jolt in the movement of a machine is like the so-called *coup* in a game of chance. The manipulation of the worker at the machine has no connection with the preceding operation for the very reason that it is its exact repetition. Since each operation at the machine is just as screened off from the preceding operation as a *coup* in a game of chance is from the one that preceded it, the drudgery of the laborer is, in its own way, a counterpart to the drudgery of the gambler. The work of both is equally devoid of substance.

> A wish, however, is a kind of experience. "What one wishes for in one's youth, one has in abundance in old age," said Goethe. The earlier in life one makes a wish, the greater one's chances that it will be fulfilled. The further a wish reaches out in time, the greater the hopes for its fulfillment. But it is experience that accompanies one to the far reaches of time, that fills and divides time. Thus a wish fulfilled is the crowning of experience. In folk symbolism, distance in space can take the place of distance in time; that is why the shooting star, which plunges into the infinite distance of space, has become the symbol of a fulfilled wish. The ivory ball which rolls into the *next* compartment, the *next* card which lies on top are the very antithesis of a falling star. The period of time encompassed by the instant in which the light of a shooting star flashes for a man is of the kind that Joubert had described with his customary assurance. "Time," he says, "is found even in eternity; but it is not earthly, worldly time. . . . That time does not destroy; it merely completes."[26]

Although made possible, facilitated, by the structure and its framework, this string of citations from a four-page passage in the Baudelaire essay, in its vertiginous tightening of strands, destroys structural coherence as well. There is already considerable art simply in the selection of the instances or data of shock: not every essayistic passage could combine Dodgem cars, the roulette wheel, and shooting stars. Yet it is the explosion of these data out of their concentration that comprises the passage's unique power. The poignancy still attached, in the age of mechanical reproduction, to the wish made upon a falling star is emblematic of the essay's relation to its own structural framework. The violence done to the wish in an age of gambling, spasmodic side shows, and demolition derbies, continues the essay's encompassing argument on the decline of experience; yet the conceptual and compositional shocks generated by the passage dismantle the structure as well. This dismantling of a structure that was a necessary foundation constitutes a pointed illustration of the relation between modernism and the movement inscribed within its margins, which I call, for purposes of this discussion, postmodernism.

The exemplary modernist instrument is the structural kaleidoscope whose crystals also happen to be particles of dynamite. The paradigmatic structure of "On Some Motifs in Baudelaire" derives from the pages of *Beyond the Pleasure Principle*. So too are the other vibrant Freudian tropes—displacement, condensation, repression, regression, denial, elaborated most suggestively in *Studies on Hysteria*, *The Interpretation of Dreams*, and *Jokes and Their Relation to the Unconscious*—structures, organizing ribs that at their best self-destruct. It has been suggested above how Saussurian distinctions furnish Lévi-Strauss and Barthes, in different ways, with the structures that their writings either confirm or delimit. (It might be argued that Lévi-Strauss's structural studies tend to reinforce their underpinnings, whereas Barthes, as he moves toward the writerly, repeats the trajectory of "On Some Motifs in Baudelaire." Lévi-Strauss's *bricolage* and the wider musings he permits himself in his retrospective works, on the other hand, constitute his own escape from structuralism.)

Structuralist adaptations remain, however, founded on the apprehension of the primacy of linguistic dynamics in systematic thought with which the twentieth century begins. It may be said of the modernist productions most distinctive of their era that they were composed under the illumination of the structuralist kaleidoscope. As an example of the development of his own *A la recherche*, Proust presents the expansion of a sonata, by Vinteuil, into a septet.[27] The inflamed Swann meanders through a *soirée* presented by the Marquise de Saint-Euverte; the setting is described as an aquarium, several of whose submarine human observers wear monocles.[28] Pound pursues a highly charged, phantasmatic conflict between cultural purity and the adulteration of esthetic and sociopolitical values through a bewildering range of settings. Cultural purity, surprisingly close to the Heideggerian notion of authenticity, is measured, masculine, ongoing. The adulteration of value is performed by bankers, Jews, war profiteers, women, Chinese emperors of dubious sexual orientation, and the most corrupt of Renaissance Italian dukes.[29] Within the setting of a counterworld to the founding presuppositions of Western thought, Borges offers us "works of fiction . . . based on a single plot, which runs through every imaginable permutation" (F, 28). What does, precisely the Wandering Rocks chapter of *Ulysses* offer us if not a kaleidoscopic view of the circulation of signs, objects, characters, and meaning in a novel whose episodes relate to one another as different turn-stops around the same structural instrument? As an antisystematic but nevertheless encyclopedic novel, *Ulysses* highlights different narrative, rhetorical, stylistic, syntactical, and etymological capabilities and moments in its various segments.

No one has been more fully initated into the mysteries and possible improvisations of the modernist kaleidoscope than Lévi-Strauss's figure of the *bricoleur*, that "jack-of-all-trades" from "primitive" cultures who devises solutions to a myriad of problems with "whatever is at hand . . . a set of tools and materials which is always finite and also heterogeneous."[30] The *bricoleur* "'speaks' not only *with* things . . . but also through the medium of things: giving an account of his personality and life by the choices he makes between the limited possibilities." The solutions to intellectual and practical problems that she or he devises "always really consist of a new arrangement of elements": they amount to a "reconstruction from the same materials." In myth and "primitive" science the *bricoleur* "builds up structures by fitting together events, or rather the remains of events."[31]

Himself a *bricoleur*, Lévi-Strauss first devises and then employs this figure in unraveling the workings of "la pensée sauvage." Although he recognizes in cubist collage an instance of *bricolage* in twentieth-century art,[32] the suggestiveness of this attitude in accounting for modernist theory and esthetics extends well beyond the scope of his anthropological explanations. The scenario of *bricolage* is in fact one of the most useful discursive expositions of the attitude toward materials, the cohesion between disparate elements, and the improvisation of new variations characteristic of the distinctive productions of high modernism. The citations above underscore the strategic role played by structure in these activities. The kaleidoscopic organization and themes I have touched upon in the works by Joyce, Proust, Mann, and Borges arise in the "spirit" of *bricolage*—as does the emphasis on and construction with cultural waste products in a vast range of artifacts, extending from the poetry of Pound, Eliot, and Williams to the plastic creations of Picasso and Duchamp, to the music of Charles Ives.[33]

Music, with its themes and variations, is itself a combinatorial art-form. In the rage of creative improvisation within the pictorial and plastic arts between 1900 and 1920, images of guitars, violins, and other musical instruments played an emblematic role in dramatizing the kaleidoscopic fragmentation and proliferation of visual material. The subject matter of musical instruments and notes enabled the visual arts to express certain vital aspects of their implicit theory and esthetic program. The work of Picasso, Braque, and other artists during this period overflows with images of musical instruments. These exist both in cubist forms of visual disfiguration and in more self-evident representational modes. Wallace Stevens, hoping to introduce a pronounced element of musicality in his poetry and fascinated by the work of Picasso, appropriates the latter's *Old Guitarist* (1903) as the visual point of departure for "The Man with the Blue Guitar" (1937). The visual field of cubism is littered with musical instruments, their fragments, and their notes, as is amply attested to by such works by Picasso as *Violin* (1912), *Violin Attached to Wall* (1912–13), *Violin* (1912–13), *Bottle, Guitar, Pipe* (1912–13), *Violin and Clarinet* (1913), and *Harlequin Playing a Guitar* (1914–19); and by Braque as *Musical Instruments (Guitar)* (1908), *Still Life with Pitcher and Violin* (1910), *Duet for Flute* (1911), *Still Life with Playing Cards* (1913), *Musical Forms (Guitar and Clarinet* (1916), and *Woman with a Mandolin* (1917).

Wallace Stevens's dump and T. S. Eliot's wasteland may be privileged waste-sites for modernist improvisation, but *bricolage* has no more profound discursive counterpart than the "mosaic technique" by which Walter Benjamin accounted for the omnivorous incorporation of citations from other authors into the setting of his own prose.[34] Modernism can still delight in the curatorial feat of finding use and even creative solutions in debris. When one leaves its precincts behind, the origination of language and other productions does not even matter. The materials are simply there. The distinction between "self" and "other" production is inapplicable, and the kaleidoscope has lost either its capability or its interest in spinning out discernible new patterns. Poundian vorticism still discloses the form of activities by tracing out their force lines.

The distinctive climate of modernism is, then, combinatorial, structural, variational, and retrospective—with an emphasis on gathering and recycling discarded materials. The twentieth-century

Other of this vital esthetic is indifferent, resigned, subversive, and endlessly accepting. Although often unmarked, the frontier between these climates is always tangible when crossed. The truly enduring creations of twentieth-century theory and art—such as Kafka's and Joyce's fiction and Benjamin's prose—stand on both sides of the modern/postmodern.

CHAPTER TWO

Joyce's Musical Comedy:
Ulysses as an Exemplary
Modern Text

A MUSICAL NOTE AND THE ANGEL OF HISTORY

Et seule la musique me paraît aujourd'hui supportable, consonnante, à la mesure de ce qui nous rassemble dans la même pensée. . . . Je me suis alors aperçu que Paul, qui ne me l'avait jamais dit, avait une expérience d'instrumentiste et que la musique avait aussi été pour lui une pratique. Et le mot qui me le fit savoir, ce fut le mot "âme," quand Pierre, mon fils, et Paul parlèrent familièrement de "l'âme" du violon ou de la basse et m'apprirent que "l'âme" de ces instruments, c'est en français le nom de la pièce de bois, petite et fragile, toujours très exposée, menacée, qu'on place dans le corps de l'instrument pour soutenir le chevalet et mettre en communication les deux tables. Je ne savais pourquoi j'en fus si bizarre-ment ému sur le moment même, obscurément bouleversé par la conversation à laquelle j'assistais—sans doute à cause du mot "âme," qui nous parle toujours à la fois de vie et de mort et nous fait rêver d'immortalité, comme l'argument de la lyre dans le *Phédon*. Et je regretterai toujours, parmi tant et tant d'autres choses, de n'en avoir reparlé à Paul. —Jacques Derrida, "In Memoriam," *The Lesson of Paul de Man*

It may be said of James Joyce as of scant few writers that he composed a musical accompaniment to his own fiction. The question, movement, form, and theme of music quite tangibly infuse his work, shaping its affect and texture. Music, in its turn, is not merely an art form, an activity, or an index of esthetic distinction; whether the Misses Morkans' beloved preoccu-pation or the occasion for Molly and Boylan's earthy romance. Music is a form of language that both sets in relief and delimits the claims and functions of language in general. It is no accident that the ques-tion of music fascinated Nietzsche as he set about the task of expos-ing and defining the illusions that Western thought, over its long course, fabricated for itself in order to enforce its codes of morality and logic. The refrains of music not only sweep the reader, by the author's design, along a sequence of affective states toward a predeter-mined end; they also raise the question of the author's medium, tools, presuppositions, and motives.

The question of music arises at the outset of the philosophical inquiry, whether situated in Schopenhauer or Nietzsche, that issues forth in the improvisations of modernism. Music is the first of the ancient and primordial arts whose departure from the mission and metaphysics of representation is freely acknowledged. As Nietzsche noted in *The Birth of Tragedy*, musical notation waives its "right" to simultaneous translation into discourse.

In this sense we may discriminate between two main currents in the history of the language of the Greek people, according to whether their language imitated the world of image and phenomenon or the world of music [je nach dem die Sprache die *Erscheinungs-* und *Bilderwelt* oder die *Musikwelt* nachahmte]. . . . I here call attention to a familiar phenomenon of our own times. . . . Again and again we have occasion to observe that a Beethoven symphony compels its individual auditors to use figurative speech [*Bilderrede*] in describing it, no matter how fantastically variegated and even contradictory may be the composition and make-up of the different worlds of images produced by a piece of music. . . . The poems of the lyrist can express nothing that did not already lie hidden in the vast universality and absoluteness that compelled him to figurative speech [*Bilderrede*]. Language can never adequately render the cosmic symbolism of music, because music stands in symbolic relation to the primordial contradiction and primordial pain. . . . Rather all phenomena [*Erscheinung*], compared with it, are merely symbols [*Gleichnis*]: hence *language* [*Sprache*], as the organ and symbol of phenomena, can never by any means disclose the innermost heart of music; language, in its attempt to imitate it, can only be in superficial contact with music.[1]

In this seminal and justly famous passage, Nietzsche's reasoning is circuitous. Musical expression cannot be represented symbolically, for analogies are inadequate to it; yet language is the set of manifestations of which music comprises one instance or part. By delving into music, Nietzsche thus liberates one form of language from a representational imperative while relocating the scene of pain and apprehension, of experience itself, away from the drama of subjectivity to the linguistic sphere encompassing all communicative acts.

Nietzsche flags music as the anomaly, the exceptional case, that ultimately redirects the rules. Through the instance of music is revealed the dominion of a grammar hitherto concealed and forgotten, the code of language itself. The notion of music, however—as early in modernism as Schopenhauer and Nietzsche may have released it from the functional and metaphysical constraints of representation—also shares another status, with Ishmael of the Pequod, that of the last survivor. No longer quite *of* the representational contract or the subject, music nevertheless survives these metaphysical illusions whose dominion is limited by their linguistic nature. Music becomes the most efficacious and poignant afterimage of that to which it is alien. Often described as haunting, music inhabits, occupies, or takes over an empty house. As the art whose initial note dispatches the superstructures of representation and metaphysical illusion, music retains, by its analogies to emotional variation and cognitive noise, the most intense possible traces of that which it has displaced. Mourning the loss of Paul de Man, Jacques Derrida turns to music as the only sphere in which the feelings of separation and loss and the notions of life and death have some validity in the aftermath of deconstruction. Only the very tangible music producer known as the violin and its fellow string instruments retain their souls, which combine a wooden concreteness and a pronounced fragility. The haunting refrains of music comprise the graveyard of afterlife of metaphysics.

For modernism as well as for language, then, the play of music is a highly duplicitous message. Music may break with bravado the conventions of the representational code, yet it also imposes harmony and restraint. The text of Joyce's fiction is impregnated with citations of lyrics from songs. Songs exist by virtue of a superimposition of melodic and poetic texts. When sung, lines of poetry are assigned, and one might say confined, to specific moments of time. In their aural evanescence and the continuity of their performance, songs throttle and squelch the linguistic play of verse. The melody of songs thus resolves the tensions of language at the same time that music, in the Nietzschean tradition, radically resists translation into a naïve symbolic script. By the same token, the most memorable phrases of songs, those quoted in a wide variety of contexts, become generalizations for or abstractions of experience. A particularly insistent musical catchword or phrase, such as "Love's Old Sweet Song" or "Those Lovely Seaside Girls" in *Ulysses*, becomes emblematic of a complex matrix of associations. Singular signifiers, through literary as well as musical repetition, consolidate their logical power and thus augment their weight. In *Ulysses* as in "musical" works by other authors (Mann, but not Proust), the musical catchphrase perfects its method of summing up experience, or its claims to do so, as it pursues, very much by design, the course of its reprises.

Music predominates within *Ulysses* at two extremes of its register: microscopically, from line to line, music annotates the limits of representation in language; in the larger progressions between structural units and at the level of the framework, music becomes the house organ and implement of resolution, progression, and consummation, whose effect is that of the all-covering snow that closes, in more senses than one, "The Dead."

The double message of Joycean music may serve as a talisman for the mixed emotions with which the experimentalists of modernism addressed the future and the distortions that they discovered in their own work. The past is closed, its certitudes and etiquettes outmoded, its access recently but inextricably barred. The winds of futurism are frigid and uncertain. Modern technology lends innovations a scale and totalizing force rarely confronted before. The winds of futurism have gathered an insurmountable force. The question is not whether to resist them, but when the capitulation will take place. If there is a pause before the onslaught of the future, empirically and metaphysically, it is merely an instant, the second during which a drowning man sees all of life go by. And what are the themes and images that occur to the great bellwethers of modern innovation as they imagine their immanent submersion in an irresistable historical maelstrom? They think of their mothers, and childhood, and the preservation of natural and esthetic states of purity that may never have existed. They seek the furtive musical refrain that could lend both inevitability and completion to a fictive work, or a totalistic image, say the snow, that could encompass the frailties, regrets, and social and sexual tensions released by a Dublin party set at a particular moment but also timeless.

Whereas the postmodernist undertakes the attack against nostalgia and harmony as the primary and encompassing task, the seminal figures of modernism assume the double posture ascribed by Walter Benjamin to *Angelus Novus*.

> An angel looking as though he is about to move away from something he is fixedly contemplating. His eyes are staring, his mouth is open, his wings are spread. This is how one pictures the angel of history. His face is turned toward the past. Where we perceive a chain of events [*eine Kette von Begebenheiten*] he sees one single catastrophe which keeps piling wreckage upon wreckage and hurls it in front of his feet. The angel would like to stay, awaken the dead, and make whole what has been smashed. But a storm is blowing from Paradise; it has got caught in his wings [*der sich in seinen Flügeln verfangen hat*] with such violence [*und so stark ist*] that the angel can no longer close them. The storm irresistibly propels him into the future to which his back is turned [*der er den Rücken kehrt*], while the pile of debris before him grows skyward. This storm is what we call progress.[2]

If progress may be said to prevail in an age of "mechanical reproduction," it does so not without resistance. Borrowing an image from Klee, Benjamin sets a historical stage for the events of our century that may be paradoxically described as regressive progress. Not only the angels but also the modernists have their eyes fixed on the past. They advance not out of desire but under constraint (if not under arrest). The paradise that they remember and for which they yearn is a tinderbox of violence (hence Proust's Montjouvain is but a stone's throw away from the tranquil garden where the family awaits Swann).[3] The honor of first breeching the walls of a *terra incognita*, of first understanding and improvising hybrid forms, falls to the modernists, but they accept it in terror, resisting every step of the way.

The stance of the modernists is thus nostalgic. Indeed, the more audacious their departures from their inherited codes and esthetic stockpile may be, the more poignant are the expressions of their regressive yearning. It is in the context of a very specific modernistic nostalgia that Proust frames his epic *A la recherche du temps perdu* at both of its extremities, in a sentimental rhetoric of recollection and returning home. The Oedipal fascination and anxiety cutting a large swathe through the writings of modernist male writers from Proust and Kafka to Pound and Joyce is yet another manifestation of this peculiarly backward forward stance. *Hamlet*, particularly in the imperatives enunciated by the ghost of the protagonist's father and the psychosexual issues they raise, is the most sustained literary backdrop to Joyce's *Ulysses*. Ezra Pound's enraged invective against usury and political corruption goes hand in hand with his highly motivated assistance at the love scene between Circe and Odysseus. At the same time that he champions and promotes, among other causes, vorticism, Gaudier-Brezeska, and James Joyce, Pound rails against the defilement of language and economic value, which he invests with a near-maternal purity and innocence. The intellectual endeavor of composing personae, one that continues throughout the *Cantos*, is to capture and preserve cultures in the pristine state of their poetic articulation.

The ambivalent posture that the Angel of History assumes at the innovative leave-taking of modernism is not an aberration; it is at the heart of approaching the modern as a theoretically responsible category. The modern demands at least two intuitive definitions, but these are dissonant at the same time that they are mutually necessary. On the one hand, a notion of the modern as a sliding frame of reference situated at the open-ended frontier of innovation is essential; on the other hand, certain obsessions and technical achievements make it possible, from different points of view, to situate the modern, or the rise of modernity, at specific moments of time.

No one has demonstrated greater sensitivity to the tension within the modern itself than Paul de Man, who, while insisting on the need to find rigorous terms for the avant-garde or what he calls, in "Literary History and Literary Modernity,"[4] the generative, also considers it essential to avoid the impulse to sever the leading edge of improvisation from history. "Literary History and Literary Modernity" is precisely an exercise in thinking through the connection between the cutting edge (a sliding perspective, because there is always an open-ended space of improvisation) and its inevitable historical context. This essay, although ostensibly a theoretical discussion of literary history, is at the heart of de Man's political thought, because he clearly associates the Fata Morgana of a totally ahistorical new order with fascist thought and politics.

De Man's discussion sets out from the tension between regarding modernity as "an attempt at self-definition, as a way of diagnosing one's own present" and as "a set of values that exist independently of their modernity." He too is struck by the splaying out of this concept between sliding and time-specific dimensions. He appeals to Nietzsche as a model for the definition of modernity as the radical potential already installed in the open-endedness of the present.

> Modernity exists in the form of a desire to wipe out whatever came earlier, in the hope of reaching at last a point that could be called a true present, a point of origin that marks a new departure. This combined interplay of deliberate forgetting with an action that is also a new origin reaches the full power of the idea of modernity. Thus defined, modernity and history are diametrically opposed to each other in Nietzsche's text.[5]

Without in any way diminishing the radical potential of modernity—and in the above passage modernity's absorption in an all-encompassing present is reminiscent of the Angel of History's Angst—de Man indeed goes on to challenge the severing of history from modernity. The dynamic that de Man discovers to prevail between these two terms is both synthetic and radically asymmetrical: it belongs to the other process of mutural reading, say between symbolism and allegory in "The Rhetoric of Temporality," that placed de Man's own work at a cutting edge in discerning both the transference and miscues constitutive of interpretation.

A major logical as well as rhetorical task to which de Man sets himself in this essay is isolating the historical element within the "generation" that for him exemplifies modern innovation. "As soon as modernism becomes conscious of its own strategies—and it cannot fail to do so if it is justified, as in this text, in the name of a concern for the future—it discovers itself to be a generative power that not only engenders history, but is part of a generative scheme that extends far back into the past."[6] De Man's insistence in this essay—and insistence may well comprise its predominant performative gesture—is that regardless of how radical modern generativity may be, modernity plays a role in structuring history and does not achieve any decisive rupture from it.

For de Man, literature is dumbfounded, or blinded, by the radical appeal of its invention. "The appeal of modernity haunts all literature. It is revealed in numberless images and emblems that appear at all periods—in the obsession with a *tabula rasa*, with new beginnings—that finds recurrent expression in all forms of writing. No true account of literary language can bypass this persistent temptation of literature to fulfill itself in a single moment."[7] This radical moment of modernity, in its inherent blindness to itself, would situate itself outside history, but viewed from another perspective, this sliding perspective of debunking and departure can be viewed as *constituting* a temporally aware model for literary history and history in general.

As is often the case in his work, de Man ultimately eschews choosing between a completely floating notion of modernity and an inherently time-bound model of history. The most radical literary modernity is situated between history and modernity's blindness to itself. History and interpretation are not mutually exclusive but rather exist in a complex relation of supplementarity to each other.

Could we conceive of a literary history that would not truncate literature by putting us misleadingly *into* or *outside* it, that would be able to maintain the literary aporia throughout, account at the same time for the truth and the falsehood of the knowledge literature conveys about itself, distinguish rigorously between metaphorical and historical language, and account for literary modernity as well as for its historicity? Clearly, such a conception would imply a revision of the notion of history, and, beyond that, of the notion of time on which our idea of history is based. . . . To become good literary historians, we must remember that what we usually call literary history has little or nothing to do with literature and that what we call literary interpretation—provided only it is good interpretation—is in fact literary history. If we extend this notion beyond literature, it merely confirms that the bases for historical knowledge are not empirical facts but written texts, even if these texts masquerade in the guise of wars or revolutions.[8]

Modernity is less a literary-historical category to be defined in its own right than an occasion or an arena for observing the manner in which history and generation read each other. In this respect, de Man's allegory is theoretically beyond my own approach. In attempting to come to terms with both modernism and postmodernism (the latter of which I treat as the radical, destructured flank of the former), I would like to have things both ways, to treat these categories as both shifting and time-specific categories. I would on the one hand argue, echoing de Man, that certain of the features most typical of modernism and postmodernism can also be observed at the frontier of other historical moments, that the perspective of modernity floats through history. At the same time, certain of the common motifs and interests placing modern productions in communication with one another do seem to coalesce at a particular moment, and it does seem worthwhile to assemble the common factors and revel in their variations. It is a remarkable historical moment indeed in which Kafka, Joyce, Picasso, and Braque can engaage in kaleidoscopic variations, and in which Freud and Proust can pursue the meanderings of the involuntary in symbolic processes. The moment that serves as the occasion for this study is, then, both shifting and time-bound—in de Man's terms, both generative and historical. If I myself cannot choose between floating and time-bound notions of my subject or period, I can at least make this indecision an integral part of the discussion.

In a cultural pale far removed from such figures as Joyce, Pound, Eliot, and Lewis, the Polish writer Bruno Schulz evokes the endlessly inclusive familiarity of childhood spring nights as the setting where violence and distortion erupt. Initially, a stamp album documents the existence of far-away and exotic lands, whose concrete traces it neatly orders. By the end of Schulz's *Sanatorium under the Sign of the Hourglass* (1937), however, uncanny characters and events materialize from the pages of the stamp collection, which the nostalgic narrator dubs "the Book." The evenings of spring in childhood inspire and encompass the first stirrings of love, but they also harbor the seeds of familial disintegration—whose fullest extension will be the bizarre afterlife known as the sanatorium, where the narrator finds and confronts his father. The world of the sanatorium is a cracked mirror of life. It contains, for example, a near-double of the fabric shop that the narrator's father operated during his lifetime "proper." Distortion and delay, however, configure the afterworld rooted in the generous and harmonious evenings of spring. "Don't worry," Dr. Gotard of the sanatorium reassures the narrator, who has come on a visit to his father. "'The whole secret of the operation,' he added, ready to demonstrate its mechanism on his fingers, 'is that we have put back the clock. Here we are always late by a certain interval of time of which we cannot define the length. The whole thing is a matter of simple relativity. Here your father's death, the death that has already struck him in your country, has not occurred yet.'"[9] Bruno Schulz extends the narrator's family drama by appending to it a future: a finite and brief one, as opposed to the afterworlds of Greek and Roman mythology, a future in which the anomalies of domestic life are granted expression. Like the Angel of History, Schulz travels forward facing the past, the idyllic nights of spring. The future to which he is propelled is "organized" by a minimal, but for that reason devasting, distortion. In light of the tangible threats confronting Schulz's community and personal existence, his sense of living on borrowed time is an apt one.

Bruno Schulz would deposit us at his sanatorium, with its almost nauseating anomalies derived from the life of familiarity, as a final station on the train of his fictive thought; whereas James Joyce would punctuate the Sirens episode of *Ulysses*, set in a hotel pub dominated by its barmaids' golden sexuality, with musical refrains lending the hour and scene an aura of lyrical pathos. Some of the music in this episode is sung by Simon Dedalus, progenitor of the Artist as a Young Man and member of a phantasmatic list of Molly's lifetime lovers. Bloom assists at the scene, during which he is, at several points, confronted by Boylan. Herein lies a fictive allegory and intimation of the subtle frontier between the modern and postmodern. The sanatorium, like Kafka's Castle, represents a pitiless endpoint for the expectations of recollection and nostalgia. In *Ulysses*, Joyce addresses the impacts of print technology, hype, and sexual freedom. Yet he laces the volume, literally and figuratively, with the binding refrains of musical lyrics. Resolutely aware of his gifts, sources, and destiny, Joyce confronts his mission as a modernist head-on. *Ulysses* may be regarded as a full-scale exploration of the textual, literary, esthetic, psychological, and cognitive resources and operations of its time, but it is composed in the Angel of History's retrospective posture.

Music may be the most prevalent and weighty art form incorporated into *Ulysses*, but it by no means stands alone. If *Ulysses* constitutes an encyclopdedic work obsessed with drama and lyric poetry as well as music, this is not merely to demonstrate its author's erudition and to consummate the esthetic traditions out of which it arises. Each art form appropriated by this novel makes an appearance on its stage for a specific purpose: to demonstrate the particular qualities with which it endows literary texts. If *Ulysses* practices a certain esthetic imperialism, it is less in the interest of providing gratuitous advertising for successful art forms than of composing a detailed and highly specific allegory of textual configuration and performance. As has been obliquely suggested above, music serves as an efficacious figure in characterizing the flow and repetition of phrases, in the text and in the texture of the psyche. Music helps to explain the very local generalization that goes on in the interpretation of any sequential text: how some phrases or units of meaning achieve, through condensation as well as repetition, a talismanic status, by which they "account for," "explain," or even "represent" other signifiers.

Drama penetrates as close as music to the core of *Ulysses'* textual configuration. On the thematic level, the drama serves as an invaluable index in indicating the work's central concerns. *Ulysses*, to the degree to which it must gloss *Hamlet* (among many of Shakespeare's plays) and Goethe's *Faust* in order to ensure the aptness of its allusions, may be regarded as a highly successful, and, incidentally, comparative work of literary criticism. (Indeed, the richness of the interplay between the newly emerging discipline of comparative literature and the seminal productions of modernism is a subject meriting full treatment in its own right. *Ulysses, The Cantos of Ezra Pound*, and Proust's epic novel are as much comparative studies couched in literary forms as they are contributions to their respective formal genres.) The ongoing discussion of *Hamlet* in *Ulysses* underscores its Oedipal concerns, its dallying "between conjugal love and its chaste delights and scoptatory love and its foul pleasures" (*U*, 165). The discussion of *Hamlet* in the novel may in a sense be regarded as its powerhouse, situated on the sutures linking its compulsion to innovate with its Oedipal anxiety and nostalgia. *Faust* introduces and explains, procedurally as well as thematically, that particular dramatic pleasure in a work of art that consists in the derangement and obliteration of the structures that the work has erected in the interest of its own legibility. Through quite specific citations, the Nighttown or Circe episode of *Ulysses* becomes its *Walpurgisnacht* scene, allowing the split levels of action and meaning that enrich Goethe's masterwork.

Even more significant, however, than the coherence that *Ulysses'* dramatic allusions may seem to lend this art form in the West is the manner in which drama acts out certain fundamental forms of textual configuration. Specifically, the high points of drama in *Ulysses* demonstrate the accretion of text through the internalization and disfiguration of textual material. This uniquely dramatic function within a work of art has been traditionally known as the play-within-a-play or, more recently, the *mise en abîme*.[10] One of the ways in which texts grow, or expand their range, is through self-cannibalizing acts of parasitism. Two foci of dramatic concern in *Ulysses*, the Skylla and Charybdis episode, set in the director's office of the National Library, and the Nighttown scene, prominently internalize and disfigure textual material from the novel in question and Joyce's prior works. This process of irony—splitting levels, whether described as of action or consciousness, and framing or staging the text—nonetheless plays a decisive role in the configuration of virtually every episode in the work. It is obviously in the context of the *mise en abîme* that the National Library episode, which harbors the most complete fusion of literary knowledge, Oedipal nostalgia, and textual sensibility in the novel, at one point breaks off into a script for a play in which its central characters are assigned lines. The scene, in other words, that agonizes most explicitly about Hamlet's predicament, the sexual activity of Anne Hathaway during the bard's prolonged absence, and the reason why he willed her only his second-best bed, also issues forth in, or gives birth to, an internal play. The parturition, transcending the boundaries of gendrification, the birth of text within text, bears striking similarities to the miracle of Bloom's childbearing in Nighttown.

In addition to staging its own discourse as a play, the National Library or *Hamlet* episode originates the practice of allegorical naming or suggestive name distortion that will henceforth pervade the novel. Within the confines of this scene, a Mr. Best becomes "Mr. Secondbest Best" (*U*, 167), and "Best of Best brothers" (173), while a John Eglinton becomes "Eglintoneyes" (171) and "Eglinton Johannes, of arts a bachelor" (175). The name of a character is a hypothesis; and any text that ironizes the system of character equivalencies it has posited also elaborates its implicit corollaries. The devices of internal dramatization, allegorical naming, and dramatic distortions such as the transformation of catchphrases and objects into characters not only define the uniqueness of certain theatrical climaxes in the novel; they are also instrumental in describing the generation of the novel's episodes and developments.

Drama, or better put, theatricality, the sensibility of dramatization, rivals music as the most prevalent esthetic model for textual production and performance in the work.[11] In a narrative work, the citations of lyrical poetry that Joyce incorporates share roughly the same status as song lyrics. By the same token that words deprived of the music with which they are customarily coupled attain the qualities of text, lines of verse repetitively cited by Joyce, such as those from Yeats's "Who Goes with Fergus?" (*U*, 8–9, 41, 474, 496–97)[12] attain the talismanic power of a musical refrain. Joyce's grafts of musical notation into the text of *Ulysses* (162, 566–67) may be regarded as the fullest extension of an attempt to compose a phonic text, to limit the severing of sound from word in the process of citation.

The arts of *Ulysses* exist in a supplementary relation to one another, each demonstrating something of textual activity specific to its sphere.[13] Joyce's citations of lyrical verse may be said to demonstrate the compression and condensation effected by carefully designed linguistic phrasing, a shorthand destined to stand out amid the novel's exchange of signifiers. Though verse does not attain the prominence as an art form in *Ulysses* that it achieves in *Portrait of the Artist as a Young Man*, there is an ongoing strand of allusions to its works and practitioners, including Wordsworth, Keats, Blake, Shelley, Byron, Whitman, and A.E., in addition to Yeats. If Joyce designed *Ulysses* as a custom house of the classical verbal arts, capable of rendering a certain retrospective overview, each medium functions as an esthetic and semiological model: drama illustrates the accretion of text through *mise en abime* and disfiguration; music exposes the compositional principles of the work's ephemeral and elusive unities; lyric epitomizes the condensation by which literary language generates its exceptional force.

Joining these venerable art forms in *Ulysses'* esthetic economy are two of more recent origins and perhaps more modest claims: journalistic reportage and the "gentle" art of advertising. Journalism, whose compositional principles are both elaborated and dramatized in the segment of the Aeolus episode set in the Dublin *Evening Telegraph* office, combines lyrical compression with modernist bricolage. In its mass audience, to which it is able to communicate information with hitherto unequaled speed, modern journalism represents the culmination of what McLuhan, Ong, and others would call print culture.[14] The discussion at the *Evening Telegraph*, joined by such characters as J. J. O'Molloy, Myles Crawford, Ned Lambert, O'Madden Burke, and Lenehan in addition to Bloom and the two Dedaluses, displays the qualities of polished journalism: a close juxtaposition of heterogeneous subjects, a fine memory for historical detail (the Childs murder; John F. Taylor's speech), and brilliant turns of phrase ("Muchibus thankibus"). The often hilarious headlines devised by Joyce for the breaks in this discontinuous dialogue divert the reader from its train and its subject matter as often as they render service as labels. At a moment when modern journalism is merely consolidating its powers and when advertising has not yet begun to exploit its own, Joyce discerns the powerful affinity between by-lines, jingles, and catchy lyrics and the very specific interactions between signs on the page and in the mind. Bloom does not master "the Great Tradition" in art and thought in any rigorous sense of the words. He is, however, an avatar of a communications design that will operate on practical and applied levels.

Journalism, as characterized by *Ulysses*, along with advertising, its commercial derivative and instrument, is above all a comic art, rejoicing in the anomalous collision of heterogeneous signifiers. Much later in the century, Marshall McLuhan will draw attention to the tremendous thematic and modal "give" on the first page of a major newspapaper. The novel pays ample tribute to the ponderous and tragic "bitter" mysteries that Stephen traces through the Western tradition (in works such as the *Odyssey, Hamlet,* and *Faust*)— and weighs. *Ulysses* is not reticent in acknowledging the overwhelming semiological and psychosexual crises triggered by incestuous, adulterous, and murderous desire. It is, however, the comical path— whether pursued by a catchword between songs and conversations or by individuals through a city—that ultimately tempers and directs the novel's direction. *Ulysses'* closest and most sustained esthetic analogon is musical comedy. Its tragic motives and *Walpurgisnächte* of the soul are contained and surrounded by a sea of semiological association in which, precisely, no signifier is ever lost, destroyed, or wasted. The musical organization of *Ulysses* allows no sign ever to achieve singularity, to die having been articulated alone, so to speak, without relatives. The musical refrains that issue from a variety of singers during the Sirens episode ultimately encompass the novel. A work celebrating the minor arts and misfortunes of a little man is set within the form of a musical comedy. Its reduced stage may well furnish a more acute sounding board for the mysteries and torments of love than the epic arenas of opera and tragedy. The notion of an ongoing linguistic play of signifiers nonspecific in origin or end, whether applied to literature or to the psychoanalytic field, shifts the emphasis away from tragedy as a model for the stages and separations of life and toward comedy.

Ulysses may be characterized as a musical notation played on a minor, comic scale. The work ironically downscales its encyclopedic, encompassing pretensions, making itself the butt of a joke. Much of Joyce's fiction falls under the sway of this self-reducing confusion. The snowfall at the end of "The Dead" seems to finalize the tragic waste of Michael Furey's lost love, the banality of Gabriel Conroy's pained pretensions, and the stunted hopes of all segments of the Irish community. In form, however, this passage is musical. Thematically, the all-encompassing snow bespeaks the necessity and democracy of death. But the snow, as the forerunner of *Ulysses'* binding and protective musical reprise, leaves us with a comical reassurance, that death will be contained, refrained.

> Yes, the newspapers were right: snow was general all over Ireland. It was falling on every part of the dark central plain, on the treeless hills, falling softly upon the Bog of Allen and, farther westward, softly falling into the dark mutinous Shannon waves. It was falling, too, upon every part of the lonely church yard on the hill where Michael Furey lay buried. It lay thickly drifted on the crooked crosses and headstones, on the spears of the little gate, on the barren thorns. His soul swooned slowly as he heard the snow falling faintly through the universe and faintly falling, like the descent of their last end, upon all the living and the dead.[15]

Thematically speaking, this is a humbling scene for one of the rising champions of a modern Ireland, a man who would count total possession of his wife among his prerogatives. The snow is falling, on the living and the dead, on the graveyard whose crown of thorns weaves messianic tragedy into an already uncomfortable meteorological outlook. Not only is the snow falling, but so is Gabriel Conroy's soul. Virtually everything falls in this passage except the musical cadence, which beats out metrical finality, contains the torment that Gabriel has forced, and combines distinct narrative under the sign of the "general." It is to the repetitive framework of musical comedy that *Ulysses'* outrageous puns, stylistic *pastiches*, and novel-exploding experiments are grafted.[16] The shock of the modern, registered on a set of musical belongings, looks lovingly backward toward the "general."

The least heralded genre incorporated into *Ulysses* may well be that of discursive prose. It is, however, the medium of the crucial Ithaca episode, leading from the havoc of "Nighttown" to Molly's closing epiphany. It is in discursive prose, the language of criticism, that Joyce chooses to frame some of his crowning writerly achievements: the cosmic descriptions of the Dublin water supply (*U,* 548–50) and the constellations (573–75); and the legalistic inventory of Bloom's house (575–78). Like the astronomical nova, such passages explode through intensification: they dissolve the constraints of prose by exaggerating its qualities. Joyce's discursive prose reaches toward the bournes of the universe just as a humble bicycle ride may attain continental scope. Joyce's reliance on discursive prose as a fictive medium installs a scholarly and critical dimension in his work. Where the language of fiction devolves upon discourse, fiction incorporates a critical assessment of itself. In this sense, *Ulysses* both retrospectively configures and exemplifies a new genre: the critical novel, the novel of criticism. A Freudian joke within the history of the novel, *Ulysses* releases the critical potential discerned by few of Joyce's forerunners and contemporaries, among them Rousseau, Sterne, Proust, and Musil. The purpose of the following remarks on the novel is as much to place it within the wider movements and paradoxes characterizing the modern and the postmodern as it is to enlarge an already splendid literature of Joycean criticism.

A RING OF KEY(E)S

Like the other great densely written texts in the history of literature, *Ulysses* resides at the point where its seemingly arbitrary signs and signifiers achieve a pronounced weight in coding and design and where, conversely, their overdetermination verges on playful whimsy. Alexander Keyes is the name of a merchant and a business whose extended advertisement Bloom is trying to secure for the *Evening Telegraph* in the course of *Ulysses.* As an instance of the model of the circulation of signifiers in language and the mind that Joyce hypothesizes in *Ulysses,* however, *Keyes* does not merely descend upon the text with the standard arbitrariness of family names. *Keyes* is as such a metasignifier, referring to the intense process of the novel's encoding and decoding and the circulation of its other key (overdetermined) signs, as it is the haphazard designation of a character and a firm.

The text of *Ulysses* repeatedly dramatizes the arbitrariness, slipperiness, and confusion of signs and the unpredictable trajectories they follow. Haphazardly meeting Bantam Lyons outside the chemist's at the end of the Lotus Eaters episode, Leopold Bloom unwittingly gives rise to such a misunderstanding, one that resounds throughout the novel. Lyons literally mistakes Bloom's statement that he was "just going to throw . . . away" the racing sheet (*U*, 70) for an informed endorsement of Throwaway, a horse running in the race whose eventualities he ponders. Lyons disseminates the advice he "takes" from Bloom (without Bloom's having offered it) to the circle of acquaintances he encounters during his perambulations in the city that day. Bloom is thus the unintentional cause of much disappointment to an arbitrary set of characters, including Boylan.

While it may be the name of a fictive horse, *Throwaway* is also a sign in the novel, one exemplary of the principles of dissemination, circulation, displacement, and confusion pursued by other signs. "Key" signs in *Ulysses* circulate and produce and disfigure meaning with the haphazardness of a horse race. In certain processes, such as betting and other speculative endeavors, signs may produce tangible results, but this outcome can never be substantially related to the essence or nature of the sign.

A throwaway is also, however, an announcement of brief time value, a medium reflecting the ephemeralities of taste and the marketplace in an age of advertisement. *Throwaway* and its yellow coded signs in *Ulysses* circulate within the text with the seeming freedom and chance of a "real" throwaway. Animals, music, and Shakespeare comprise the three most prevalent motifs in the novel. *Throwaway* is also the locus where the ritualistic, mythical, and totemic resonances of animal imagery join the action of the plot and the semiological circulation of the text.

It is not altogether unanticipated, then, that other signs, whether characters, objects, or animals, should move through the novel with the arbitrariness, indirection, and unpredictable results of "throwaway." The more obvious parallels include the appearances — and name — of one Cashel Boyle O'Connor Fitzmaurice Tisdall Farrell (*U*, 131, 177, 200, 205, 209, 235, 419); the trajectory — and tapping — of the "blind stripling" who, upon arrival at his destination, undertakes his work as a piano tuner (148, 205–6, 209, 216, 236–38), and, of course, "Keyes," the man, the house, and the advertisement (10, 17, 27, 68, 88, 99, 118, 120, 386, 399, 478, 559, 638). No more graphic illustration of the procession of signs through the novel is furnished than the parade of sandwich boards (127, 187–88, 208, 596) spelling out the name H.E.L.Y.S., which designates a store, a merchant, a former locus of Bloom's employment, and one in the array of Molly's phantom lovers that Bloom imagines to himself — specifically described as a strand or series (601–2). (Wisdom Helys, the character, is also linked, by homonymy, to philosophy, or Greek — Hellas — knowledge.) The coded signs in the text of *Ulysses* march through it in calculated disorder, copulating with one another by design and intertwining various chains of association.

The Rose of Castile, by the same token, an opera by Michael William Balfe (1808–70),[17] is the most prominent in the novel's references to Spain, and also bears, in complex fashion, on Molly Bloom: her origins in Gibraltar, her musical vocation, her beauty, the flowers (or blooms) littering the scenes of her earliest sexual experiences. By the outrageous punning of Lenehan in the Aeolus episode, "The Rose of Castile" is also "like a railway line. . . . See the wheese? Rose of cast steel. Gee!" (*U*, 110–11). The displacement effected by the joke intertwines a cluster of sensuous associations, in their esthetic, geographical, botanical, and corporeal dimensions, with the motif of railroads and the trams that cross and interconnect throughout the Dublin region; the tangible and even pedestrian "rows of cast steel" become the pathway leading a cluster of esthetic, "purple" images (if not pink ones) into the lexicon of the novel. The novel's tramlines, like its key(e)s, are metatextual instruments of reference and suggestion. Tramlines are to a map of the novel's movements what key(e)s are to its enigmatic symbolic codes: a potential entry and occasion for illumination.

Ulysses' pregnant signs—and here again Bloom's childbirth is not so much perverse as apt—are, precisely, the key(e)s to its codes and its constitution as a text. They relate to one another by indirection rather than by controlled traffic patterns. Certain elements in the novel's semiological code, such as Denis Breen with his ledger (*U*, 131, 198, 208) and Stephen's uncle, Richie Goulding, and his legal bag (207, 217), recur in patterning that can only be described as random. Other images tend to form associative clusters, so that when one surfaces, its "relatives" are at least in the vicinity. Three passages, for example, one at the beginning of the transitory Lestrygonians episode (124), one at the end of the "Oxen of the Sun," set in the maternity hospital (348–49), and the parodic rendition of the biblical *begats* in the midst of the Nighttown scene (404–5), assemble diverse strands of the novel's messianic rhetoric.[18] These passages mark a convergence of the novel's motifs of prophesy and evangelism, animal sacrifice, and the return to Zion. At the pork butcher's in search of his famous kidney, Bloom picks up a prospectus for a "model farm at Kinnereth on the lakeshore of Tiberias" (48) showing a "young white heifer." The name for the collective is Agendath Netaim ("bowl of seedlings" in Hebrew), and its European business office is situated at Bleibtreustrasse 34, Berlin W. 15. A minor but persistent preoccupation on the part of Bloom with the Jewish homeland is thus associated, from the outset, with the broader motif of cows and sacrifice, which extends to the vast range of animal references in the novel. Cows, in *Ulysses*, are not merely animals that were sacrificed at the Temple in Jerusalem; they are the source of the milk delivered in the introductory episode (12), the flowering Molly Bloom, described by Bannon as "a skittish heifer, big of her age and beef to the heel" (325), the animals infected with hoof-and-mouth disease that Mr. Deasy would like to save from extermination (27), and a source of the meat that Bloom finds so repugnant at midday, prompting him to switch restaurants (136, 138–40). Just after purchasing his pork kidney, Bloom hopes to catch up with the preceding customer, in order to profit from her "moving hams" and "prime sausage" (49). Women, through their associations with cows, direct and indirect, are bovine and comprise a sexual manifold ("the grey sunken cunt of the world" [50]), but they also arouse humane sympathy and a protective instinct. Through their ritualistic associations, cows evoke the communality of primitive religions and belief.

By elective affinity, the notion of primitive belief easily lends itself to another imagistic strand in the novel, that related to modern evangelism, whose claims parallel those advanced by the biblical prophets. So it is that later in the novel, one Alexander J Christ Dowie, who announces the coming of Elijah, twice coincides with the collective Agendath Netaim, sacrificial animals, and, perhaps because Joyce designates the United States as the homeland of hype, with the cartoon vagabond Dusty Rhodes (346–49, 404).[19] Elijah is not merely the name of the preeminent prophet of the Old Testament (282–83); a "crumpled throwaway" for Dowie, tossed into the water, becomes a "skiff" sailing "eastward by flanks of ships and trawlers" (197, 205).

The above elaboration of the meaning that accrues to the elements in two image clusters in *Ulysses* should suggest the density of the text's coding, the speed and weight with which it gathers meaning. The perfectly obvious connection between messianism, Zionism, and evangelical fervor loops twice back to women (as animals and fetishes) and extends toward advertising language and chance (the horse, Throwaway). Not far into the novel, the reader reaches the point where it is no longer possible to retain the variegated associations that its images set off. The novel's textual density instigates a crisis of compulsive memorization on the part of its author as well as its readers.

It is for this reason that *Ulysses* abounds in lists and other compendia, whose purported result is comprehensiveness—in scope and substance. The Shakespearean command, "List!"—which recurs in the text of *Ulysses* with the insistence of Hamlet's ghost—refers as much to the mnemonic devices necessitated by compulsive association as it does to the indignities suffered by Hamlet (*père*). Were it possible, a truly comprehensive list would encompass all the nuances of meaning triggered by a signifier, all the directions in which it verges, all the couplings that it makes. This compulsion to comprehensiveness, on the part of both the author and the aware reader, is fated to the frustration of its wish. A mood of mock-heroic futility thus pervades the discursive prose of the Ithaca episode, whose recurrent questions often elicit lists in response. Recounting the series of Molly's lovers is a trivial task in comparison to charting the flow of Dublin's water supply from its sources to its users (*U*, 548–50) or recapitulating the comprehensive legal description of Bloom's property (585–86). *Ulysses* interrupts its own flow not only with lists but also with rhetorical fulminations, such as the seemingly endless Hibernian digressions and qualifications in the Cyclops episode (242–47, 252–55, 260, 265, 268–69, 272, 277–79). The text of *Ulysses* accentuates rather than muffles the fragmentariness of its individual images in opening up this "encyclopedic" dimension.

In the density of its texture, then, *Ulysses* spins out a vast array of signs and meanings that it then tries to make accessible through key(e)s and at least containable in lists. The novel treats the reader to a vertiginous proliferation of images, paths of association, and levels of meaning. At the same time, the novel incorporates a statute of limitations to this expansion. What prohibits *Ulysses* from lapsing into an unbounded semiological morass is nothing more formidable than "love's sweet melody," a phrase or phrasing that restricts the possibility of a unique, and hence unqualified, sign.

NEVER OFF-KEY

Though one key may be sufficient to open a lock, one instance of a signifier is inadequate for its decipherment and deployment within a semiological code. At the same time that *Ulysses* is remarkable for the variety of its semantic elements and the inventiveness with which it combines them, it is every bit as fervent in its insistence that no key word appear only once, that there be at least one recurrence of every signifier of any significance. The novel, in keeping with its musical form and mission, strategically stabilizes and domesticates its "outstanding" signs, those dense enough to leave a trace, by attaching their "original" occurrence to at least one repetition. In geometrical terms, of course, the second occurrence of the sign constitutes the condition sufficient for a line. In *Ulysses* the nature of this line is unambiguously musical. Compulsive semantic repetition sweeps every potentially singular element into a nostalgic melody.

From a semiological point of view, the Nighttown episode is not defined primarily by its negativity. It functions not so much as a mythic Hades, a Miltonic or Goethean pandemonium or a Freudian unconscious—but rather as a junkyard or automobile graveyard where virtually every moving part is eventually bound to show up. Among the many charming qualities of this "definitive" play-within-a-play is its transformation of key words and objects into characters or dramatic subjects. Within this *mise en abîme* that nonetheless owes many of its operating principles and distortions to the *Walpurgisnacht* interlude in *Faust*, dramatic lines are assigned to, among others: the piece of soap purchased earlier by Bloom at the chemist's (*U*, 360), Adonai (489–90), a waterfall, issuing forth in the word "Poulaphouca," the name of a source of Dublin's water and the site of a hydroelectric plant (446, 448, 450, 590), the Navvy, who re-cites "The Boys from Wexford" (368–69), and a cap (384, 411–12). The Nighttown episode provides a reprise for many of the song lyrics incorporated prior to it in the novel, including "Love's Old Sweet Song" (363, 464), and "My Girl's a Yorkshire Girl" (469). It is a setting where minor characters, lost amid the vastness and complexity of the novel's "stream of life" (71, 128, 135), or characters who have never entered the action proper achieve some prominence. Within the world of "Nighttown," dancing master Denis J. Maginni rises above the cursory attention accorded him elsewhere in the novel (181, 208, 469–71); Bloom's grandfather, Lipoti Virag, comes to life (417–24); and "Kevin Egan of Paris," Alexander J Dowie, and Elijah the prophet are transformed from allusions into characters (483, 401, 404).

This process of recycling, however—this compulsive reprise of potentially singular elements—is by no means limited to the Nighttown episode. The entire novel may be said to transpire within a rhythm of semiological dispersion and gathering. Though the collation of elements disseminated from a vocabulary as rich as *Ulysses* could never be comprehensive, the energy and desire invested in the extension of the semiological point into a line, in the binding of signifiers through recurrence, is nevertheless a prominent feature of the text.

No invention is apparently more frivolous, playful, and extraneous than one that appears during the Lestrygonians episode, after Bloom, having settled on Davy Byrne's for lunch, has partaken of his bread, cheese, and wine. The "mild fire of the wine" (*U*, 143) stimulates Bloom's (and the narrative's) associative tendencies. The subject at hand is, naturally at such a moment, food.

> White hatted *chef* like a rabbi. Combustible duck. Curly cabbage *à la duchesse de Parme*. Just as well to write it on the bill of fare so you can know what you've eaten. Too many drugs spoil the broth. I know it myself. Dosing it with Edwards' dessicated soup. Geese stuffed silly for them. Lobsters boiled alive. Do ptake some ptarmigan. Wouldn't mind being a waiter in a swell hotel. Tips, evening dress, halfnaked ladies. May I tempt you to a little more filleted sole, miss Dubedat? Yes, do bedad. And she did bedad. Huguenot name I expect that. A miss Dubedat lived in Killiney, I remember. *Du de la* French. Still it's the same fish perhaps old Micky Hanlon of Moore street ripped the guts out of making money hand over fist finger in fishes' gills. (*U*, 143–44)

Like any coded passage of the text, this one functions as a key to other passages and themes implicated by its language. In the present case, the foods that Bloom ponders extending from his meal run to poultry and seafood. Stylistically, the passage suggests a free asociation reaching full gear: by the last sentence, Bloom's thoughts have achieved the sudden halts and shifts in subject matter unmarked by pauses or punctuation, which characterizes Molly's undisciplined stream of consciousness at the end of the novel.

The passage above is a highly active one. While sliding from ducks to geese in the poultry cuisine to lobsters and sole on the side of seafood, Bloom conjures an imaginary scene in which, as a waiter in a "swell hotel," he invites a Miss Dubedat to a second helping of fish. The chaining of foods gives way to an exploration of the etymological, semantic, and phonic dimensions of this name, which at this point in the text ranks as one of the most frivolous, least determined ornaments in the novel. By alliteration, the name is associated with doing and its past tense, and with feminine volition. The imaginary Bloom-as-waiter exhorts Miss Dubedat to "ptake" of more fish: this invention spins off from the superb logical-alliterative game, "Do partake of some ptarmigan." The name intensifies sexual ambiguity. We simply cannot know whether Miss Dubedat does or doesn't. Her name appeals to a missing certainty that might be furnished, under ideal circumstances, by "dad," or perhaps "God." Etymologically, the name is exotic, French, but is also associated with religion, foreshadowed in the passage by the image of a rabbinic chef's hat, and with a slightly troubled theology at that, French Protestantism.

At first glance, that is to say in its first instance, the signifier "Miss Dubedat" seems to be nothing more than a whimsical knot teased into the fabric of *Ulysses*, as frivolous as the "tips, evening dress, half-naked ladies" of the imaginary hotel restaurant. As I have shown, the name communicates with several of the novel's ongoing themes and functions as a copula linking them. But as one encounters it for the first time, "Miss Dubedat" is largely unmotivated, an obstruction to the stream of consciousness as much as a catalyst, an oddity to be lost or forgotten amid the proliferation of meaning.

The recurrence of this name amid the contrived Goethean frivolity of the Nighttown scene imposes, however, a certain weight and compulsion not evident at the time of its first occurrence. "The lady Gwendolen Dubedat bursts through the throng" celebrating Bloom's coronation as Lord Mayor of Dublin, "leaps on his horse and kisses him on both cheeks amid great acclamation" (*U*, 396). The same character joins a list of personages that Bloom passes as he makes his definitive exit from the Nighttown scene. The final instance of the name consummates the linguistic play that had been seeded during the Lestrygonians episode, "the bookseller of *Sweets of Sin*, Miss Dubedatandshedidbedad, Mesdames Gerald and Stanislaus Moran of Roebuck" (*U*, 479). The reappearances of the whimsical name may be taken as manifestations of the novel's impossible volition to control and direct its elements. Not every character, event, and weighted image from the beginning of the novel reappears in "Nighttown"; nor can the author fix its meaning. Only one ptarmigan in the course of the novel, for instance, is "ptaken." The reinscription of the "potentially singular," as William Beatty Warner has developed this term, is nonetheless highly suggestive of an anxiety about the "floating" of signifiers accompanying a *jouissance* in their play.[20] The repetitive line of music furnishes an anchor for the otherwise dizzying flight of signs. As the Citizen might say, "Signs needs whatever base they can get begob and bedad."

HAMLET'S MATERNAL GHOST

She was no more: the trembling skeleton of a twig burnt in the fire, an odour of rosewood and wetted ashes. She had saved him from being trampled underfoot and had gone, scarcely having been. A poor soul gone to heaven: and on a heath beneath winking stars a fox, red reek of rapine in his fur, with merciless bright eyes scraped in the earth, listened, scraped up the earth, listened, scraped and scraped.

Sitting at his side Stephen solved out the problem. He proves by algebra that Shakespeare's ghost is Hamlet's grandfather. Sargent peered askance through his slanted glasses. Hockeysticks rattled in the lumberroom: the hollow knock of a ball and calls from the field.

Across the page the symbols moved in grave morrice, in the mummery of their letters. (*U*, 23)

During his brief stint as tutor to a benighted nation, the Artist as a Young Man straightens the accounts of an ugly student and remarks how even he had been loved. The love bestowed upon even the frail and unworthy turns his thoughts to his own recently absented mother. As at the very end of "The Dead," a broad perspective, here a nocturnal heath, frames the ephemeral and personal dimensions of loss. The heath is populated by a predatory fox, made more ferocious by the alliterative rolling of *r*'s. The mother, purified by pain and sacraments, is relinquished to and ravished by a bestial nature, repeating Antigone's torment at Creon's injunction against her brother's burial. At the moment when Stephen expresses his epiphany of pain, however, he also gives himself over to an Oedipal calculus of filiation and an absorption within the overall field of symbols: he engages in a Kafkan and Borgesian speculation on the priority of Shakespeare or his demon (Hamlet); and he meditates on the nature of language.[21]

Death in *Ulysses* is a general condition, as it is in Hegel's *Phenomenology of Spirit*, not a biological fact. Death is the existential correlative to music, devouring but also absorbing and resolving all. In a work obsessed with the filial, causal, and sexual questions raised by Shakespeare's *Hamlet*, the fact that the most poignant confrontation of death draws Stephen Dedalus to the ghost of his mother is nothing short of breathtaking.

The passage above moves from metaphysical and existential loss, the death of a mother, to the calculated and uncontainable play of signs in language. As a teacher, Stephen's thoughts wander from the regimen of the classroooom to the universe of signs; as a child at Clongowes, his musings had slipped from arithmetic exercises to the calculation of his position within the astronomical universe.[22] Shakespeare and his works become, in *Ulysses*, the dramatic stage upon which Stephen observes and expounds the quantum mechanics of language: its effects upon causality and paternity, upon the metaphysics of first causes and retrospective yearning, upon the matrix of human affairs.

Bloom is "visited" by a thwarted father, an unrealized son, and an impossible grandfather. He is almost surrounded—in all directions but one—by the general limit imposed by death: the only path open to him, one already complicated and cluttered, is the one leading into his wife's body. Within the pages of *Ulysses*, Hamlet's ghost, detached from the Shakespearean text and appropriated, becomes a character in its own right. Bloom confronts no less than three emanations of this figure in the course of the novel. Paddy Dignam, buried late in the morning, appears to Alf Bergen in the afternoon (*U*, 247). The ghost of Hamlet in the text of *Ulysses* thus evokes hilarity as well as pathos. In all cases but one, however, Hamlet's ghost staggers through the novel in the figure of a man.

Stephen is the character whose Hamlet's ghost is a woman, or mother. He is the fictive surrogate for whom the universe of signs has opened most widely and with the greatest vertigo. These two statements serve as corollaries of each other.

A modernist work, *Ulysses* is constituted by *bricolage* and superimposition. Situated on complementary gyres, Bloom is the wanderer coming home, Stephen the wanderer setting out. As Joyce explicitly spelled out for his audience, Bloom is Odysseus; Stephen, Telemachus. By appropriation and superimposition, Shakespeare, and his demon Hamlet, are drawn into the Odysseus-Telemachus cycle as well. "But all those twenty years what do you suppose poor Penelope in Stratford was doing behind the diamond panes?" (*U*, 166). The narrative overtly specifies the connection: Shakespeare is Odysseus. Behind Bloom and Stephen, Shakespeare and Hamlet, Joyce and Stephen, however, lurks another silent and beckoning figure, Oedipus. Oedipus is the consummate Hamlet's ghost of *Ulysses*: the reason for Stephen's glancing reference to Freud and "the new Viennese school" (169); the direction in which Stephen's curiosity about Anne Hathaway's intramural activities and Bloom's pained preoccupation with Molly tend. Stephen's recurrent remorse about his mother also takes place under the sign of Oedipus.

As an exemplary modern work, *Ulysses* remains subject to the thrusts of nostalgia, recollection, and remembrance. Yet the linguistic facts of life that Stephen has discovered, partially through his sensitive reading of Shakespeare, will no longer sustain the standard model of paternity and influence in which the son is both compelled toward and barred from the mother (or origin) by a terrifying and vanquished father. In setting out on the adventures of love and writing, Stephen addresses a ghost (or *Geist*) who is feminine. This situation is emblematic of the compelling need in a romantico-modernist work for a radically revised Oedipal model. The retrogressive tug lingers, but the Artist as a Young Man must confront a linguistic uncertainty figured as a woman in order to complete his esthetic mission—not the hierarchical, militaristic terror of the masculine imaginary. The maternal ghost that Stephen faces in the pages of *Ulysses* epitomizes the disfigured Oedipal model for writing and sexuality that modernism assembles.

The Shakespearean discussion in the Skylla and Charybdis episode (and elsewhere) thus serves as the novel's theoretical motor, linking its ongoing thematic concerns to the conceptual categories under which they may be subsumed. While other episodes are more indicative of *Ulysses'* musical composition ("Sirens," "Penelope") and its theatrical structure ("Circe"), no segment is more vital in articulating and allegorizing the novel's self-generating theory of itself.

Stephen is the dominant figure in the Shakespearean conversations. Despite his fictional youth, his expression during these discussions achieves the intensity and graceful chaining of Joyce's writing in its most memorable moments. A climatic moment in this filament of the novel occurs when Stephen describes the production of texts and the backward posture of ghosts.

—As we, or mother Dana, weave and unweave our bodies, Stephen said, from day to day, their molecules shuttled to and fro, so does the artist weave and unweave his image. And as the mole on my right breast is where it was when I was born, though all my body has been woven of new stuff time after time, so through the ghost of the unquiet father the image of the unliving son looks forth. In the intense instant of imagination, when the mind, Shelley says, is a fading coal, that which I was is that which I am and that which in possibility I may come to be. So in the future, the sister of the past, I may see myself as I sit here now but by reflection from that which then I shall be. (*U*, 159–60)

—That may be too, Stephen said. There's a saying of Goethe's which Mr Magee likes to quote. Beware of what you wish for in youth because you will get it in middle life. Why does he send to one who is *buonaroba*, a bay where all men ride, a maid of honour with a scandalous girlhood, a lordling to woo for him? He was himself a lord of language and had made himself a coistrel gentleman and he had written *Romeo and Juliet*. Why? Belief in himself has been untimely killed. He was overborne in a cornfield first (a ryefield, I should say) and he will never be a victor in his own eyes after nor play victoriously the game of laugh and lie down. . . .
They list. And in the porches of their ears I pour.

—The soul has been before stricken mortally, a poison poured in the porch of a sleeping ear. But those who are done to death in sleep cannot know the manner of their quell unless their Creator endow their souls with that knowledge in the life to come. The poisoning and the beast with two backs that urged it King Hamlet's ghost could not know of were he not endowed with knowledge by his creator. That is why the speech (his lean unlovely English) is always turned elsewhere, backward. Ravisher and ravished, what he would but would not, go with him from Lucrece's bluecircled ivory globes to Imogen's breast, bare, with its mole cinquespotted. He goes back, weary of the creation he has piled up to hide him from himself, an old dog licking an old sore. But, because loss is his gain, he passes on towards eternity in undiminished personality, untaught by the wisdom he has written or by the laws he has revealed. His beaver is up. He is a ghost, a shadow now, the wind by Elsinore's rocks or what you will, the sea's voice, a voice heard only in the heart of him who is the substance of his shadow, the son consubstantial with the father.
—Amen! was responded from the doorway.
Hast thou found me, O mine enemy?
Entr'acte. (U, 161–62)

As a weaver of language, the literary artist is more of Penelope's camp than Odysseus'. The Artist-Son slays not so much the Father as the ordered concept of Time. Hamlet and Joyce's Artist possess as Young Men the knowledge disclosed to ordinary fathers either too late or not at all. They know to sidestep the desires whose realization will only be too full (Fulle) "in middle life." The Artist comes by his crucial knowledge early. The young Shakespeare "was overborne in a cornfield first" by the older woman who became his wife. Ordinary men attain their knowledge late, which is to say never. The Shakespearean stage machinery represents this hopeless and belated quest through the device of a walking, or sleepwalking, ghost. The Artist's knowledge is prodigious and prescient: Shakespeare represents it as a retrospective search for an "agenbite of inwit" that momentarily flared but then was lost.

Shakespeare and Hamlet's ghost have, then, assumed the retrospective posture of the modernist Angel of History. But this groping backward is founded on the Artist's preemptive insight, the violence he does and embodies to the temporality of standard time. Stephen's interpretation of Hamlet pivots on the notion of esthetic time. He welds the various emanations—ghosts, spirits, shadows—proceeding from the conventions of the theater and the rhetoric of poetry to his standard and esthetic temporal progressions. Hamlet père never learns his lesson, as Stephen elaborates, even when it is incorporated into the text of Shakespeare's play. It is in this sense that he is an "old dog licking an old sore. . . . He is a ghost, a shadow now, the wind by Elsinore's rocks or what you will."

The textual composition of literary art demands a deviant temporality, a sexuality capable of incorporating "inwit," a world attuned to the monstrous knowledge of prodigy. The figure of the father and the notion of paternity constitute the primary scene on which the violence of esthetic time is registered.

> Hurrying to her squalid deathlair from gay Paris on the quayside I touched his hand. The voice, new warmth, speaking. Dr Bob Kenny is attending her. The eyes that wish me well. But do not know me. —A father, Stephen said, battling against hopelessness, is a necessary evil. He wrote the play in the months that followed his father's death. If you hold that he, a greying man with two marriageable daughters, with thirtyfive years of life, *nel mezzo del cammin di nostra vita*, with fifty of experience, is the beardless undergraduate from Wittenberg then you must hold that his seventy year old mother is the lustful queen. No. The corpse of John Shakespeare does not walk the night. From hour to hour it rots and rots. He rests, disarmed of fatherhood, having devised that mystical estate upon his son. Boccaccio's Calandrino was the first and last man who felt himself with child. Fatherhood, in the sense of conscious begetting, is unknown to man. It is a mystical estate, an apostolic succession, from only begetter to only begotten. On that mystery and not on the madonna which the cunning Italian intellect flung to the mob of Europe the church is founded and founded irremovably because founded, like the world, macro and microcosm, upon the void. Upon incertitude, upon unlikelihood. *Amor matris*, subjective and objective genitive, may be the only true thing in life. Paternity may be a legal fiction. Who is the father of any son that any son should love him or he any son? (*U*, 170)

The text of *Ulysses* once again marks the coincidence between Stephen's loss and the vigils of a supernatural character assumed to be, throughout the history of literature, masculine. As "conscious begetting," fatherhood is hopelessly arbitrary and banal. Fatherhood resounds with meaning and force only as a construct in the imaginary, where it loses its gender and changes the nature of its procreation. Fatherhood, as it engenders text, is a mothering. From the perspective of the imaginary, the Nighttown episode is endowed with a fine realism. The legal, theological, and existential havoc that textual production throws into fatherhood is catalogued in the passage quoted above. It is in this sense that the heresy of "Sabellius, the African," who "held that the Father was Himself His Own Son" (*U*,

171) is not merely an abberation; it is, rather, a possibility crucial to the text's constitution, a theological analogon to language's engendering itself out of itself.

If, of all characters in *Ulysses*, Stephen Dedalus is visited by a female emanation, if his Hamlet's ghost is a mother, not his father, this paradox merely crowns the accommodations that the novel makes for esthetics and the esthetic enterprise: the temporality that it demands and the filiation that it determines. The maternal ghost of Hamlet emerges from a compositional process in which textual displacement usurps any first cause; in which a prodigiously premature knowledge collides into a hopelessly unresponsive world. The maternal ghost of *Ulysses* may be said to realize a sexual ambivalence already inscribed between the lines of *Hamlet*. Stephen's Shakespearean explorations are situated at the crossroads, the points of transfer linking its thematic obsessions, its formal innovations, and the epistemological drama of its characters. The maternal ghost consulted by Stephen hints at both the revisions of philosophical and narrative forms demanded by modernist thought and the nature of a subsequent neutral domain that will be released from the multifaceted sway of nostalgia.

DRAMATURGE OF THE ABYSS

Ulysses was very much conceived and written as an episodic work, whose various segments would build toward a polyphony of modes and voices. Joyce made considerable efforts to install a pronounced locality within each episode. Although no segment exhausts a particular formal innovation or an esthetic sphere of reference in *Ulysses*, it may be said that stylistic *pastiche* reaches a crescendo in "The Oxen of the Son," that "Sirens" is the most comprehensively musical chapter, that "The Wandering Rocks" most fully explores modernist techniques of *bricolage*, cutting, and *montage*.

Joyce designed the discrete episodes of *Ulysses* both as separate compositions and as contributions to the larger work. The most significant element common to the episodes is the practice of internalizing or framing material from elsewhere in the text that I described earlier as the *mise en abîme*. In its fullest extension, the practice of the *mise en abîme* implicates the concept of repetition. Any reiteration of distortion of signifiers or images may be treated as a recycling from inside. For the purposes of the present discussion, however, I prefer thinking of the Joycean *mise en abîme* in a slightly more specific way: as the manner in which episodes and the larger work both consolidate and question their positions through the absorption and digestion of their own contents. An overall survey of the work suggests that this process and figure are the most prevalent forces linking its diverse episodes.

As vital and constitutive as the *mise en abîme* may be to the novel's uniqueness and composition, this metastructure of process is itself highly differentiated within the framework of *Ulysses*. Some episodes, and I think here particularly of "Circe" and "Penelope," may be treated as *abîmes* or abysses of the work as a whole, as structural units primarily devoted to the combination, summation, and distortion of thematic and semantic strands scattered throughout other episodes. The Circe episode, not only in its explicit Goethean references but also in its obsessive collation of the material prior to it in the text, is specifically fitted out to function as an internal phantasmagoria, whether considered as an underworld, an unconscious, the imaginary, or a purgatory. More than one critical study of *Ulysses* has been devoted to the particular theatricality that "Circe" manifests and develops. Once isolated, however, the particular combinations, mutations, and distortions lending "Circe" its unique mood emerge in other episodes under slightly different guises. "Penelope," for instance, gathers and reshapes the novel's themes, characters, events, and concepts in the form of a runaway diatribe, where units of thought flow unbounded into one another and thematic compartmentalization dissolves. "Penelope" provides not only another example of the *mise en abîme*, supplemental to "Circe": the final segment of the novel also manifests the specific qualities and resources available to the abyss at that moment in its development. The *abîme*, the homothetic generator of meaning and distortion placed within the text itself, is not merely a whimsical play zone or escape to which the novel may tend at will. It is an ongoing metastructure of signification whose functions include the violent juxtaposition of semantic units and the derangement of structural patterns, including itself.

In other segments, textual dramatization or theatricality may be said to take place locally: out of the syntactic, stylistic, and formal devices specific to a particular setting emerges a condensed rendition of the process. The characters of "Skylla and Charybdis," for example, after a spirited Shakespearean discussion, find themselves within the dramatis personae of a brief internal play. The climactic act of voyeuristic-exhibitionistic love that Bloom and Gerty MacDowell consummate from afar both extends and violates the naïve, domestic rhetoric making "Nausicaa" unique. ("Madcap Ciss with her golliwog curls," [*U*, 290]; "–O my! Puddeny pie! protested Ciss,"

[297]). The Cyclops and Ithaca episodes explode under the weight of the—respectively—verbal fulmination and obsessive collation that make their rhetoric possible and epitomize their operation.

The *mise en abîme* of *Ulysses*, then, is both systematic and local. Yet a third form of internal dramatization ensues from the floating of signifiers from episode to episode tht carry with them complex associations or arcs of thinking. Such privileged and heavily coded figures as flowers, Elijah, and Bloom's piece of soap circulate through the text and dramatize the trajectories of signifiers on the page and possibly in cognitive life. Episodes such as "Aeolus" and "The Wandering Rocks," with their truncated segments and jarring juxtapositions, in turn dramatize the operation of texts composed of such floating signifers. *Ulysses'* internal *mise en abîme* is systematic, episodic, and "floating." Through the composition of *Ulysses*, Joyce proclaims himself and acts the role of the modern dramaturge of the abyss. This textually constituted domain emerges as the compelling compositional principle of *Ulysses* and of the modern literature that pursued it in a concerted way.

Walter Benjamin, assessing the contribution of Proust's *A la recherche*, wrote that "great works of literature found a genre or dissolve one."[23] The role of the Joycean *mise en abîme* inscribes the work within a counterpoint between recollection and destruction. To exemplify the *mise en abîme* of *Ulysses* would require the reproduction of the work as a whole. As an instance of this function, I forcibly truncate one swathe of text from the overall texture. Out of the controlled question-and-answer format of the Ithaca episode emerges a description of water that overflows the limits of measure—but also dramatizes the novel's generation of meaning, association, nuance, and force.

What in water did Bloom, waterlover, drawer of water, watercarrier, returning to the range admire?

Its universality: its democratic equality and constancy to its nature in seeking its own level: its vastness in the ocean of Mercator's projection: its unplumbed profundity in the Sundam trench of the Pacific exceeding 8000 fathoms: the restlessness of its waves and surface particles visiting in turn all points of its seaboard: the independence of its units: the variability of states of sea: its hydrostatic quiescence in calm: its hydrokinetic turgidity in neap and spring tides: its subsidence after devastation: its sterility in the circumpolar icecaps, arctic and antarctic: its climatic and commercial significance: its preponderance of 3 to 1 over dry land of the globe: its indisputable hegemony extending in square leagues over all the region below the subequatorial tropic of Capricorn: the multi-secular stability of its primeval basin: its luteofulvous bed: its capacity to dissolve and hold in solution all soluble substances including millions of tons of the most precious metals: its slow erosions of peninsulas and islands, its persistent formation of homothetic islands, peninsulas and downwardtending promontories: its alluvial deposits: its weight and volume and density: its imperturbability in lagoons and highland tarns: its gradation of colours in the torrid and temperate and frigid zones: its vehicular ramifications in continental lakecontained streams and confluent oceanflowing rivers with their tributaries and transoceanic currents, gulfstream, north and south equatorial courses: its violence in seaquakes, waterspouts, Artesian wells, eruptions, torrents, eddies, freshets, spates, groundswells, watersheds, waterpartings, geysers, cataracts, whirlpools, maelstroms, inundations, deluges, cloudbursts: its vast circumterrestrial ahorizontal curve: its secrecy in springs and latent humidity, revealed by rhabdomantic or hygrometric instruments and exemplified by the well by the hole in the wall at Ashtown gate, saturation of air, distillation of dew: the simplicity of its composition, two constituent parts of hydrogen and one constituent part of oxygen: its healing virtues: its buoyancy in the waters of the Dead Sea: its perservering penetrativeness in runnels, gullies, inadequate dams, leaks on shipboard: its properties for cleansing, quenching thirst and fire, nourishing vegetation: its infallibility as paradigm and paragon: its metamorphoses as vapour, mist, cloud, rain, sleet, snow, hail: its strength in rigid hydrants: its variety of forms in loughs and bays and gulfs and bights and guts and lagoons and atolls and archipelagos and sounds and fjords and minches and tidal estuaries and arms of sea: its solidity in glaciers, icebergs, icefloes: its docility in working hydraulic millwheels, turbines, dynamos, electric power stations, bleachworks, tanneries, scutchmills: its utility in canals, rivers, if navigable, floating and graving docks: its potentiality derivable from harnessed tides or watercourses falling from level to level: its submarine fauna and flora (anacoustic, photophobe), numerically, if not literally, the inhabitants of the globe: its ubiquity as constituting 90% of the human body: the noxiousness of its effluvia in lacustrine marshes, pestilential fens, faded flowerwater, stagnant pools in the waning moon. (*U,* 549-50)

This passage is both a tribute to the aquatic medium and a geological survey of the language it has generated. It is at the same time philosophically rigorous—pursuing water through such Aristotelian categories as extension, form, quality, and quantity—and free, in the sense of free association. Bloom's admiration ramifies through the manifestations, attributes, and uses of water. This passage assembles in the interest of breadth (if not comprehensiveness) and at the expense of the continuity or flow of the narrative. What it combines is far more a rhetoric of water (or an etymological network around it) than the thoughts of a fictional character. In extension, the passage provides a "peaceable kingdom" for the diverse elements in this language:

hydrostatic	currents	hydraulic
hydrokinetic	gulfstream	canals
subsidence	courses	rivers
multisecular	waterspouts	loughs
(multiform)	torrents	bays
basin	freshets	bights
luteofulvous	eddies	sounds
(tawny-yellow)	spates	fjords
soluble	whirlpools	minches
homothetic	maelstroms	anacoustic
(self-contained)	inundations	photophobe
alluvial	rhabdomantic	lacustrine
lagoons	(like a divining	flowerwater
tarns	rod)	pools
confluent	hygrometic	
tributaries	(fluid-measuring)	

The Ithaca episode as a whole may be said to effect a translation of the events and circumstances narrated prior to it into discursive prose and thus to constitute an internal redramatization of the text. Within this exploration of discursive prose, however, with the effect both of parodying its neutrality and marveling at the linguistic precision it affords—the "water" passage elaborates its subject and performs its subject's aquatic qualities. Like water, the passage overflows and overwhelms the conduits of narrative and logical progress. The digression on water constitutes, then, an abyss in and of the abyss.

The Joycean *mise en abîme* is itself protean, or multisecular. Its form at any particular moment is strongly influenced by the local particularities of setting, style, and formal experimentation. This internal staging or framing of the text nonetheless transpires with a persistence that one cannot afford to overlook. The *mise en abîme* and the disfiguration it effects become the preeminent principles by which Joyce's works generate text, meaning, and nuance out of themselves.[24]

During the bleary sequel to his revelry and confrontation with the law, over coffee in a cabman's shelter, Stephen expresses a repugnance to knives that is surprising in its intensity but consistent with an ongoing strand of references to swords and cutlery: "—Liquids I can eat, Stephen said. But O, oblige me by taking away that knife. I can't look at the point of it. It reminds me of Roman history" (*U,* 519). While both Stephen and Joyce may have experienced some aversion to bathing, their instinctive hatred of knives, the closure they figure, and the power of violence they implement are even greater. A similar hesitation about knives runs through Kafka's fiction, from "A Country Doctor," which I explore in chapter 5, to *The Trial.*

In the aftermath of *Ulysses,* Joyce's writing achieved the liquid state and quality anticipated in the digression on water that I explored in the preceding section. Molly's monologue, in "Penelope," stands at the land's end in Joyce's writing, at the juncture between a certain solidity and fluidity, between modernism and postmodernism.

The fluid discourse that gathers in such settings as Barney Kiernan's, the maternity hospital, and 7 Eccles Street—where, respectively, Bloom confronts the Citizen, drinks and converses with the doctors, and takes Stephen after a long night—overwhelms the narrative line in the text ascribed to Molly, and establishes its dominance in Joyce's writing. Henceforth, writing itself will be a liquid medium, gathering and dissolving, blurring distinctions of logic and causality, combining textual remains into a random and varied detritus.

Ulysses' consummate statement, its terminus but also the setting-off point for Joyce's postmodernist discourse, is placed in the hands (or perhaps the mind, or even the feet) of that adventurous housewife, Molly Bloom. A feminine mind or language thus becomes the human emanation of water, the fluid medium. There has even been some critical speculation, based on such lines as "who knows is there anything the matter with my insides" (*U,* 633), that Molly is in the process of menstruating during her monologue.[25]

The conceptual state of fluidity is that of limited generalization: the overview that emerges in the end without claiming priority; abstraction or oversight as alluvial deposit or trace, what Benjamin called the afterimage.[26] Fluidity affords completion with indifference; the increase that occurs independently of striving. "Fluid" generalization is not yet speculation or systematic thought; it is nonetheless contrived, and hence beyond any random state of interaction between signifiers.

Molly Bloom, as the "Rose of Castile," or even as the "rows of cast steel," is repeatedly linked to music. Molly's musicality is a mode of thought and articulation as well as her esthetic medium, her vocation; and the occasion for her affair with Boylan. Music is the genre emblematic of the state of fluidity.[27] Molly's interior monologue assumes the form of a musical writing and notation. It functions on the level of aspecific indifference.

In devising a style for Molly's nocturnal ruminations, Joyce places less emphasis on generic clarity and the units of logic and statement than on concocting a distinctive "stuff" or material of linguistic activity. In this regard, Joyce joins such writers as Proust, the Pound of the *Cantos*, and T. S. Eliot, whose contributions are measured less in specific passages or sections than in the crystallization of an encompassing poetic medium in which textual ramifications, cognitive ties, and existential obsessions are registered. I shall return to this point when the discussion addresses several exemplary postmodern texts, including ones by Samuel Beckett and Thomas Bernhard. The statement of "Penelope" is a forerunner of the discourse of *Finnegans Wake*. Its distinctive qualities include an extreme dearth of markers between sections (paragraphs) and "units of thought" (sentences); a lack of proper nouns, enabling key pronouns to be polyvalent; and, in keeping with the absence of markers, a jarring juxtaposition of thematically unrelated elements. The product of this poetic stuff, which I have discussed elsewhere in relation to Pound and other modern poets,[28] is a less finished art object than an open-ended linguistic matrix or generator. In the case of Joyce, the combinatorial matrix out of which language articulates itself is nothing other than a musical clef or key. Molly's epiphany may be regarded as a musical coda in which the text recombines its dispersed motifs for one last time and assesses the possibilities left for a musical discourse of fiction.

It is in the nature of modernist productions moving toward an emphasis on texture of stuff rather than discrete finished works that, to quote Williams, "anywhere is everywhere," any moment is as indicative of key concerns and processes as any other. As an instance of the final human music that Joyce selects as a last accompaniment to a still-modern work of art, indicating the remaining hopes for nostalgia and recollection, I choose the following:

frseeeeeeeefronnnng train somewhere whistling the strength those engines have in them like big giants and with water rolling all over and out of them all sides like the end of Loves old sweeeetsonnnng the poor men that have to be out all night from their wives and families in those roasting engines stifling it was today Im glad I burned the half of those old Freemans and Photo Bits leaving things like that lying about hes getting very careless and threw the rest of them up in the W C Ill get him to cut them tomorrow for me instead of having them there for the next year to get a few pence for them have him asking wheres last Januarys paper and all those old overcoats I bundled out of the hall making the place hotter than it is that rain was lovely and refreshing just after my beauty sleep I thought it was going to get like Gibraltar my goodness the heat there before the levanter came on black as night and the glare of the rock standing up in it like a big giant compared with their 3 Rock mountain they think is so great with the red sentries here and there the poplars and they all whitehot and the smell of the rainwater in those tanks watching the sun all the time weltering down on you faded all that lovely frock fathers friend Mrs Stanhope sent me from the B Marche paris what a shame my dearest Doggerina she wrote on it she was very nice whats this her other name was just a p c to tell you I sent the little present have just had a jolly warm bath and feel a *very* clean dog now enjoyed it wogger she called him wogger wd give anything to be back in Gib and hear you sing Waiting and in old Madrid. (*U*, 621)

These lines are situated at one of the six paragraph breaks in the extended passage—at the third, to be exact. Thematically, the citation encompasses a passing train and Molly's railroad associations, old magazines she discarded that day, including copies of the one that Bloom had earlier read in the outhouse, and reminiscences of her youth in Gibraltar, particularly its rocks and the music she sang there. Like the wider movement of "Penelope," then, this passage moves between her dramatic sexual encounter with Boylan (somewhere behind the train images), her status and cares as a housekeeper, and a nostalgia for the past, viewed as a utopia of freedom and fulfilled desire.

If these points may be regarded as privileged coordinates in Molly's geography, the passage between them is anything but smooth or orderly. The narrative that Joyce fashions for Molly and *Finnegans Wake* comprises a discursive counterdomain to the world delimited by Western grammar, just as Jorge Luis Borges' Tlön, in a story that I examine in chapter 6, becomes an alternate model for Western science.[29] Molly's monologue abounds with the most egregious violations of grammatical order: run-on sentences, sentence fragments, and whimsical interjections. The first four signifiers of the passage quoted above, for example, are bound by no order save a rough temporal sequence: "frseeeeeeeefronnnng train somewhere whistling."

The first word is, of course, a neologism recognizable largely because of its pairing with *train*, whose sound it presumably imitates. The triad "train somewhere whistling" could be recombined in any sequence.

Arising in a random and nonsequential minitext, the passage, like a train, is off to a delayed start. Its first "legitimate" sentence might be punctuated, "the strength those engines have in them like big giants, and the water rolling all over and out of them all sides," but even this "sentence" consists of two exclamations, the second of which has no verb and ends with two dangling prepositional phrases. For Molly's discourse, this is an admirably formed sentence, yet it is separated from the next thought about trains, specifically about the men separated from their wives in the engines by "the end of Loves old sweeeetsonnnng," which bears some similarity to the sloshing locomotive. The absence of the grammatical closure that would be furnished by punctuation is particularly appropriate to the jarring shifts in the subject matter.

The passage turns between the unbridled energy of the train, the finitude of domestic economy, and the prissiness of civil society, the last exemplified by the dress and note Mrs. Stanhope, an acquaintance from the Gibraltar days, sent Molly from Paris. Beyond the limited domain demarcated by Molly's preoccupations (and her grammar) looms, however, the vast, expansive backdrop of the past. The past, not coal, or steam, powers the locomotive that thunders through Molly's discourse in the form of a train whistling in the night and Boylan's phallus.

The thrust of this train is retrospective. It points, like the arrow in a Klee painting.[30] The panorama that it opens is populated with archetypal images, rocks and flowers, images with long and complex histories in the novel. The episode, and the novel, devolve upon another rock, Howth head, and not Gibraltar, "among the rhododendrons." Rocks furnish a certain solidity, a bedrock, for the delirious expansiveness of perfume and sexual awakening. Molly's discourse performs an act of expansion, the release of grammatical, logical, and moral underpinnings—for *Ulysses*, the body of Joyce's writing, and postmodernism.

Music is the form of this release; it furnishes the rhythm for the chorus of affirmative "yeses" with which the volume of *Ulysses* drowns itself. Music literally surrounds and penetrates the limits of *Ulysses*, the self-imposed constraints of modernism. It even enters Molly's musings on rag-and-paper collecting, in the form of Mrs. Stanhope's admiring reminiscences of her singing. The name of this correspondent suggests that music is the "standing hope" for the domestic wasteland.

Modernism is a backward and time-dated address to the future that although always uncertain, attains specific technological and sociopolitical contours in the twentieth century. Some of the images for nostalgia in the seminal literary works of modernism are unforgettable: Marcel's nightly maternal kiss in Proust's *A la recherche,* Amalia's pathetic (in the full sense of the word) wedding in Kafka's *Castle,* the Homeric fascinations of Pound's *Cantos* and Joyce's *Ulysses.* Modernism knowingly harbors the seeds of its own antiquation and its own deconstruction. The address of modernism's totalistic yearnings in a postmodernism of indifference and capitulation is the seminal and archetypal instance of deconstruction in the century. In a sense the struggle between modernism and postmodernism, their reciprocal implication, has not yet ended. This interplay is described in chapters 3 and 7 of this book as a play of styles, an alternation between exaggerated spareness and prolixity. I shall pursue this deconstructive counterpoint in a decisive text by Kafka and between the enterprises of logical positivism and deconstruction.

Music is the sole survivor, the ongoing residue of the release that empties modernistic nostalgia into postmodernism. It survives the stripping away of metaphysical delusions surrounding language and subjectivity that is the repeated performative gesture of deconstruction. Music is both the limit of representation and its metaphysics, and the limit of conceptual dismantling. It is not by accident that Joyce seized upon music as the preeminent form for his exemplary modernist novel. In the wake of modernism, as of deconstruction, there remains a haunting, all-too-human music. By its own particular temporality, music sets off and continues always in the wake (and in the *Wake).*

Positioned squarely in the posture of the Angel of History, Benjamin's *Angelus Novus, Ulysses* is an exemplary modern work. In its intricately written pages it anticipates and weighs the fate of twentieth-century intellectual and artistic life.

CHAPTER THREE

Kafka and Modern
Philosophy: Wittgenstein,
Deconstruction, and the Cuisine
of the Imaginary

ALLEGORY OF THE FATHER, OR HAMLET'S GHOST
AMONG THE PRECISIONS OF WITTGENSTEIN

Among the many emanations of
the father: he who can never give enough, who is limited, obtuse,
sparing—but whose gift, when bestowed, handed down, arrives with
arbitrariness and almost foreboding. The child awaits the gift,
expects it, but, when she or he receives it, experiences it as an imposition; the juridical term would be *a sentence.* What children discover in themselves to combat the inherent blindness and finitude
of the father is their special gifts. One's gifts or giftedness are the
alternatives one discovers to counteract the arbitrariness and base-
ness of the father. But giftedness has always already been conditioned by the arbitrariness of one's patrimony. Hence, as one grows
and struggles, one is in the paradoxical position of always increasing
one's gift—reaching out for more—and at the same time struggling
with the gift and its structure.

The time-honored theaters of Western thought, settings of communal expression, legitimate release of inner images and feelings, legitimized "acting out." What are these theaters? Theologically, the
temple with its altar or pulpit; esthetically, the dramatic stage; ped-
agogically, the classroom. All are invested with a certain sacredness
in Western thought. The settings allow for a certain subject/audience
opposition but also for collective acknowledgment of what is
known, and for what can only occasionally be admitted. All contain
an authority structure but are programmed for the sharing, if not the
disbanding, of that authority.

Psychoanalysis, like the stage, is a gestic theater. Both afford the
gesture free play. The gesture is to the stage what numeration is to

the text of Wittgenstein's *Tractatus Logico-Philosophicus:* a marginal countertext, a counterpoint. The gestures need to be read like the involuntary subjective acts of psychoanalysis.

In psychoanalysis there is some danger that the serial narration of the "subject" will obscure the matter at hand, the danger that the patient will obfuscate the telling points of pain through the continuity of the unfolding story. The creative therapist may hence divert attention to phenomena seemingly remote from the matter at hand: that is, to the telling gestures.

The violation of narrative continuity is hence in the paradoxical position of comprising the straightest access and line in the direction of the node of pain. The notorious Lacanian "seven-minute hour" may be regarded as one therapeutic device among many whose impact is to break a possibly too easy continuity and to point— indicate — in the obverse direction of the slight detail that really matters, to the unassuming tip of the iceberg.

A text is, among other things, a performative act, or rather a complex of performative gestures at different levels. Text is asubjective — that is, divorced from the intention and history of its producer or compositor — but its gestures are as significative as the telling involuntary acts of psychoanalysis.

Hence, in reading Wittgenstein, in the *Tractatus Logico-Philosophicus* and less pointedly in later works, one confronts a series of significant gestures whose place is beyond the narrative, that is, beyond the specific contemporary problems and issues within the history of philosophy that Wittgenstein is addressing. Among these metalinguistic acts may be numbered the following:

1. A pronounced spareness or economy of expression.
2. The devising of a numerical code ostensibly indicative of conceptual priority, order, derivation, and subordination.
3. A careful and economic adding of conceptual complexity along the sequence of the text.
4. An unmarked transition from proposition to proposition one of whose effects is to undermine the super- and subordination instrumented by the numerical code.
5. A rigorous distinction making whose purpose is to separate the linguistic wheat from the linguistic chaff, an obstinate residing within the pale of what can be rigorously said.

These are spare but stiff gestures. If one attends to them as a low aside in the wings of the Wittgensteinian stage, one perceives that they mount into an encompassing speech act of refusal, repudiation, dissociation. Wittgenstein renounces the metaphysical and psychological patrimony of his philosophical tradition as in "real life" he signs over his inheritance.

> 5.5421 This shows too that there is no such thing as the soul—the subject, etc.—as it is conceived in the superficial psychology of the present day.
> Indeed a composite soul would not be a soul.[1]

If we discern the ghost of a father on the ramparts of Wittgenstein's text, we do so in violation of his studied admonitions not to speculate or psychologize. We infer a certain conflict, a near-life-and-death struggle from its telling absence, as the soon to be liquidated sinologist in Borges' "Garden of Forking Paths," specifies: "To eliminate a word completely, to refer to it by means of inept phrases and obvious paraphrases, is perhaps the best way of drawing attention to it." (F, 99–100). Readers are entitled to make this inference, in the manner of the therapist who is often in the position of selecting the patient's eye movements as a phenomenon of attention rather than the contents of the unfolding story.

An even more minimalist theater than the psychoanalytical office is the bed of sexual love, for at least on many occasions in this drama, costumes aren't necessary. This is, of course, an observation on minimalism and a sexual joke. Notably missing from Wittgenstein's discourse is not only the baggage and rhetoric of psychology but also the affect and thrust of desire.

To discern in the margins of Wittgenstein's work the ghosts of fathers, the embers of unfulfilled desire, is to go directly counter to its explicit program, which is to say no more than can be rigorously said, without ghosts or chimeras. Wittgenstein's discourse is hence in the tradition of Newtonian precision and Humean skepticism. At the same time, Wittgenstein's acuity with regard to the decisiveness of language as the medium of thought brings him to the point where language constitutes its own reality, or rather, where language can *say* irrespective of logical or empirical limits. This point is situated at the Saussurian watershed between the signifier and the signified, where the sign is disclosed in its arbitrariness. The distressing thought of a fire in King's College may have no basis whatsoever in reality, and yet the sentence (*Satz*) or proposition (*Satz*) describing the conflagration may be in perfect keeping with grammar. The famous King's College fire in *The Blue Book* is a nonexistent phenomenon whose existence is rendered possible by the internal logic of language. It shares the status of a flaming tuba among Magritte's images,[2] and of the man-insect in Kafka's *Metamorphosis*. In the

Tractatus Logico-Philosophicus, Wittgenstein reaches toward the continental divide between actuality and linguistic possibility among the corollaries to propositions 2 and 3. It may be said, then, that there are ghosts in Wittgenstein's philosophy as well as on the Shakespearean stage and in the storage closets of metaphysics. Wittgenstein's ghosts, however, surface in the anomalousness of "impossible figures,[3] Moebius strips, and grammatical possibility, not out of the vagaries of some communally held supernature.

EXPANSION TOWARD FINITUDE

There have become increasingly fewer ways of dying in the twentieth century, a phenomenon that was already evident at its outset. From the perspective of the uneasy stalemate that has prevailed in world politics for the past thirty years, an Orwellian phenomenon in which war can be identified as peace, a situation in which conflict between the so-called major powers is displaced to secondary or tertiary regions—it may be difficult to recall how much history, not to mention intellectual energy, has been devoted in this century to the investigation, technology, and elucidation of death.

It is true that the atomic and nuclear bombs, with their related dangers, and AIDS were not factors to be contended with early in the century, but the affinities linking early twentieth-century physics to modern and postmodern art have been widely noted. AIDS may be regarded as a tragic physiological illustration of the Freudian thermodynamics of *Beyond the Pleasure Principle.* (*SE,* 18:10–11, 12–14, 21–22, 26–29). There, psychic life is structured by the dynamic tension between two energy fields: that required for the reception of stimuli, but also a no less vital one necessary to defend the organism (and mind) against the shocks that might destroy its equilibrium. The idea of disease not as the invasion of the body but as a letdown of the internal defenses against something already there is thus deeply ensconced in twentieth-century thought.

Writers traffic in the death of systems, not of people or of fictive surrogates. When the hero of Franz Kafka's novels, who, for the purposes of discussion, may be abbreviated as K., unearths the anomalies of the legal system, or pits himself against the bureaucratic morass of the Castle, or is bewildered by the telecommunications system of the Hotel Occidental or an American political rally, he is exploring the configurations and limits of language and concept systems.[4] These may be inherited, as in the case of the Law or the Castle bureaucracy, in which K. becomes witness or even agent of the disintegration of arcane, corrupt, and arbitrary mechanisms. Or K. may stumble upon the future. He then becomes the readership's surrogate in confronting for the first time technologies of proliferating complexity. The K. who assists at the dismantling of the paternal order luxuriates in—and transfers onto the reader—a certain Oedipal smugness. The other K. betrays some uncertainty about the crowning achievements of science-fictive innovation and is therefore more subdued. Jubilation is not the only emotional accompaniment to systematic dismemberment in Kafka's fiction.

Twentieth-century physics found the same two approaches to systematic death when it penetrated and opened the energy field of the atom. An almost infinite energy was released when an exceptionally compact and powerful economy of forces and particles in the nucleus was opened up, disintegrated, through fission. But scarcely less energy remained untapped by the fusion of the most spare, fundamental, and even austere atomic particles.

In assessing Kafka's relation to twentieth-century philosophy, it is difficult to avoid the fact that at least two major paths of development, generally regarded as inimical and antithetical, are implicated by his work. There is of course the release of the textual and interpretative possibilities held in reserve within such systems as the procedures of the Law and the Castle. Arbitrariness and fixity become deranged and overwhelmed by the hermeneutic potentials contained by the text, which also functions as a code of order. We have pursued this path before. It leads from Kafka's writing to the installation of poetic—that is, linguistic—attributes into the ontological ground of Being in the philosophy of Martin Heidegger; and on to the poetics of space, *ouverture,* and dissemination articulated by Jacques Derrida, which is made possible in part by his isolation and critique of certain residues of presence in Heidegger's work. As one of its advantages, such an approach is capable of undoing certain of the fixities that have crept into the secondary literature on Kafka: the focus on Kafka's representational and fictive experiments redirects thematic approaches to his work toward a crucial theoretical issue common both to his major writings and to those of his contemporaries.

But Kafka's work communicates no less intimately with another great project of twentieth-century philosophy, the attempt to transform philosophy into a language of measured but dependable rigor and exactness, partially by bridging the gap between discursive and mathematical languages. And if this path makes incursions into an exceptionally large segment of Anglo-American philosophical investigations, it does so by way of Kafka's fellow scion of the Hapsburg

Empire, Ludwig Wittgenstein. Given the degree to which the linguistic hovering accepted and explored by Heidegger and Derrida confirms so much of our current personal as well as literary experience—and I think there of such a phenomenon as cybernetics—it would be a simple and even attractive matter to dismiss Kafka's affinity to Wittgenstein and to the approaches of philosophy and language that he legitimized.

And yet, as I suggest above, a severe curtailment in the alternatives for death takes place in the twentieth century, even if the quantity of death is staggering. Kafka holds out two forms of available systematic death for his hero to explore, by explosion and by contraction. If one insists on an intimate exchange between Kafka and the set of possibilities known as "Wittgenstein," it is partially to account for the particular configuration of death in the twentieth century. And it may even emerge, in affirmation of the confluence of divergent paths charted by Proust early in the century, that the inquiries of logical analysis and deconstruction are not as remote from each other as might otherwise seem to be the case.

TWO VOICES OF OEDIPUS

The following demonstration hinges upon a close reading of certain passages, which have in turn been selected more as exemplary instances of style and tone than as unique statements by their authors:

> It is therefore as if what we call language could have been in its origin and in its end only a moment, an essential but determined mode, a phenomenon, an aspect, a species of writing. And as if it had succeeded in making us forget this, and *in willfully misleading us,* only in the course of an adventure: as that adventure itself. . . . And it now seems to be approaching what is really its own exhaustion; under the circumstances—and this is not more than one example among others—of this death of the civilization of the book, of which so much is said and which manifests itself particularly through a convulsive proliferation of libraries. All appearances to the contrary, this death of the book undoubtedly announces (and in a certain sense always has announced) nothing but a death of speech (of a *so-called* full speech) and a new mutation in the history of writing, in history as writing. Announces it at a distance of a few centuries.

> We already have a foreboding that phonocentrism merges with the historical determination of the meaning of being in general as *presence,* with all subdeterminations which depend on this general

form and which organize it in their system and their historical sequence (presence of the thing to the sight as *eidos*, presence as substance/essence/existence[*ousia*], temporal presence as point [*stigmè*] of the now or of the moment [*nun*], the self-presence of the cogito, consciousness, subjectivity, the co-presence of the other and of the self, intersubjectivity as the intentional phenomenon of the ego, and so forth.) Logocentrism would thus support the determination of the being of the entity as presence. To the extent that such a logocentrism is not totally absent from Heidegger's thought, perhaps it still holds that thought within the epoch of onto-theology, within the philosophy of presence, that is to say within philosophy *itself.*[5]

These passage are from the first pages in the body proper of Jacques Derrida's *Of Grammatology*. A great weight is attached to them. They not only begin a book in which Derrida establishes the tradition of Western phonocentrism as it extends at least from Rousseau through Saussure, Heidegger, and Lévi-Strauss, delineates the limits of this tradition, and articulates its ongoing counterpoint in the form of textual postures (for example, deconstruction) and tropes (for example, différance). They announce the end of an epoch of thinking and a critical engagement with certain works that consummate the logocentric tradition while ostensibly revolutionizing it. Derrida has opened fire and is under fire.

And yet these passages, in spite of their momentousness, or better, in justice to it, are literally overflowing with parenthetical interjections, asides, and qualifications. I am referring to the style of discourse necessary to announce the theoretical moment. There is a parenthetical interjection in the first sentence of the second passage consisting of no less than ten terms in apposition. In that passage there are no more than three independent clause elements, accounting for perhaps one-third of the language. The remainder of the passage consists of dependent clauses and modifiers applied thickly to the "moving parts" of the sentences. No less than seven dependent and qualifying elements are built into and around the last two sentences of the first passage cited above, including the fragment that appears as the final whole sentence. A dazzling simultaneity of propositions is one of the hallmarks of the Derridean style, a cacophony of statements exemplified by, among other passages, the introduction to "Plato's Pharmacy."[6]

The concepts that Derrida is articulating in these extracts are anything but simple, and the achievement that they consummate, the configuration of ongoing counterattitudes toward language in Western thought, has indeed radically modified if not transformed philosophical and literary studies throughout a large segment of European and U.S. universities. And yet the impact of the style fashioned for this crucial endeavor is often enigmatic. The effect of two phrases in the first passage above—"and this is no more than one example among others" and "(and in a certain sense always has announced)"—is to retract the thrust of their respective sentences and to reverse the force of assertion. Partially in justice to the complexity of the thought, but nonetheless paradoxically, Derrida's rhetoric of the moment and its momentousness coincides with a curiously evasive and florid style.

Of Grammatology is a work that must be admired not only for the originality and power of its conception but also for the quality of its innovation. The writers whose work it extends and with whom it sometimes takes issue are themselves difficult and vital to twentieth-century thought. Three of the more immediate forebears that Derrida addresses in this volume, Ferdinand de Saussure, Martin Heidegger, and Claude Lévi-Strauss, are all noteworthy, in different ways, for their considerable contributions to the deconcealment of the decisiveness of language to the structuring of thought and knowledge that may come to be regarded as one of our century's major achievements. If Derrida wishes to trace a certain nostalgia for presence and parallel contempt for the qualities of writing in Western thought, he is not content to do so with respect to the hatchet men of the tradition. His foils, in *Of Grammatology*, are men who have done much to disclose and celebrate the complexity of language and, as such, are men very much like himself. Saussure has demonstrated the differential genesis and nature of signifiers in language; Heidegger has endowed the existential fundament of philosophy, Being, with the qualities of densely written poetry and has installed the play of language within philosophical argumentation; and Lévi-Strauss has transformed anthropological data emanating from a variety of sources—including myths, social structures, and behaviors—and artistic decorations into the elements of the language characteristic of what he calls *la pensée sauvage.* For these writers to be Derrida's points of departure in *Of Grammatology* places him in a certain tension with his most immediate compères, from whom he has, by his own admission, gained a great deal.

In a way reminiscent of passages cited above, Heidegger has written:

Inasmuch as Being becomes present as the Being of beings, as the difference, as perduration, the separateness and mutual relatedness of grounding and beings, as what *is* most of all, account for Being. One comes over the other, one arrives in the other. Overwhelming and arrival appear in each other in a reciprocal reflection. Speaking in terms of the difference, this means: perdurance is a circling, the circling of Being and beings around each other.

[Insofern Sein als Sein des Seienden, als die Differenz, als der Austrag west, währt das Aus- und Zueinander von Gründen und Begründen, gründet Sein das Seiende, begründet das Seiende als das Seiendste das Sein. Eines überkommt das Andere, Eines kommt im Anderen an. Überkommnis und Ankunft erscheinen wechselweise ineinander im Widerschein. Von der Differenz her gesprochen, heisst dies: Der Austrag ist ein Kreisen, das Umeinanderkreisen von Sein und Seiendem.][7]

This passage takes up the difficult question of the relation between Being and beings, and like the movement it describes, it circles around a set of syntactical elements primarily consisting of verbs and prepositions, which it combines and recombines in kaleidoscopic variations. Although the recombinants, in the above passage, may well include *Sein, gründen, kommen, tragen, einander, in, aus,* and *über,* Heidegger's combinatorial technique of composition continues independently of any particular set of concepts or substantives. His stylistic performance, emblematic of his esthetics, is thus concurrent with his critique of a scientifically verifiable phenomenology.

Heidegger reveals a wavering and almost compulsive proliferation of meaning beneath the surface of language and therefore beneath the institutions that legitimate themselves linguistically. He exposes what, for unconscious as well as explicit reasons, has been suppressed. Derrida, likewise, exposes something that has been ignored by the likes of Saussure and Lévi-Strauss, and even by Heidegger: a nostalgia for plenitude and presence in language and a suspicion toward certain qualities associated with writing.

Heidegger and Derrida point up their predecessors; in relation to their forbears they exercise or act out a freedom analogous to the previously ignored linguistic play to which they are giving vent. The stylistic correlative to this movement is a discourse of prolixity, expansion, and apparent indirection, open to considerable qualification. In addressing and engaging authority, whether as exercised by disciplines or by specific writers, their language becomes tentative and impractically overweight. Obesity is a disadvantageous condition from which to wage Oedipal battle. And yet one of the crucial qualities of the flabby discourse by means of which they address their fathers is its repudiation of simplicity and directness in intention and action. By means of an instrument no more ponderous than prose style, Heidegger and Derrida resist the desire common to fathers, gamblers, and soccer fans that the ball penetrate the goal, that the object overcome the physical obstacles to the wish, that the intention be enacted. Given Heidegger and Derrida's shared commitment to the discernment of linguistic indeterminacy and the extrapolation of its conceptual and ideological implications, it is not accidental that in their writing a certain stylistic tremolo should escape in the upper register of assertion.

While one son may try to outweigh his father, however, through competitive eating and a language that expresses the possibilities to which the father will give no heed, another may refuse to partake of the meal and may parcel out his words sparingly, in the effort to crystallize a minimalist discourse. In the imaginary that produced the major works of twentieth-century literature and philosophy, there are only two corporeal possibilities: obesity and anorexia.[8] In the sphere of discursive style in the twentieth century, as it opens a window on the imaginary, there is no middle ground or middle weight or "Weight Watchers."

Not a happy eater, Franz Kafka experienced more revulsion at paternal assertiveness and energy than most; the isolation of his fictive surrogates from the satisfaction of others is unusual, whether this satisfaction be culinary, sexual, or economic. Common sense might tell us to regard the moments of floating in his work as images of exuberant apotheosis. The fact that this floating is made possible by the discarding of ballast, a loss of weight, or self-consumption suggests otherwise.

"Behind me is the pitiless stove, before me the pitiless sky," complains Kafka's Bucket Rider, "so I must ride out between them and on my journey seek aid from the coaldealer. But he has already grown deaf to ordinary appeals; I must prove irrefutably to him that I have not a single grain of coal left" (CS, 412). It is hard to tell there whether the bleak sky, emptied of metaphysical hope, or the inaccessible and unsympathetic proprietor is colder, but in relation to the coal dealer, the narrator is reduced almost to nothing, to the unspecified dimensions of a floating speck, to an entity whose greatest claim is to the point of space it occupies. "'Well, what does he want?' shouts the dealer," when he presses this claim. "'Nothing,' his wife shouts back, 'there's nothing here; I see nothing, I hear nothing; only six striking, and now we must shut up the shop. The cold is terrible'" (414). The narrator is a frail creature, vulnerable and in need. Up against the management of the coal store, which doubles as a family, he is as close to nothing as something can become. The narrator thinks of exotic and undoubtedly warmer camels as he floats in his bucket through the streets of cold realism, but in the end, "I ascend into the regions of the ice mountains and am lost forever" (414). The most sustained instance of anorexia in Kafka's fiction is, of course, the Hunger Artist, who may voluntarily renounce his nourishment, but who also loses his metaphoric sustenance in the course of the story, the attention of his audience. When he is eventually located at the remote fringes of the side show, he is almost indistinguishable from the "straw and sticks" of his pallet. Weaned with some violence from both forms of his sustenance, he speaks a language as measured, aphoristic, and spare as we can only imagine his physique to be. "I have to fast," he whispers at the end in explanation of his alimentary habits, "because I couldn't find the food I liked. If I had found it, believe me, I should have made no fuss and stuffed myself like you or anyone else" (277). One is reminded, by both the Hunger Artist's body and his style, of the final image of Gregor Samsa's body (or carapace), "completely flat and dry" (137), sharing the density of the charcoal ash with which it is discarded.

Intimately related to these particular details from Kafka's writing, however remote it may seem, is the documented fact that Ludwig Wittgenstein often could not countenance high table at Cambridge, so that a card table had to be laid for him at ground level.[9] This is the gesture of the prodigal academic son, whose repudiation of institutional conventions demonstrates both superiority and humility. Although in a different genre of writing, are not the following propositions, from the 1921 *Tractatus Logico-Philosophicus*, indicative of a wish that might well be at home in the sideshows of bucket riding and hunger artistry?

2.024 Substance is what subsists independently of what is the case [*was der Fall ist*].

2.025 It is form and content [*Inhalt*].

2.0251 Space, time, and colour (being coloured) are forms of objects.

2.026 There must be objects, if the world is to have an unalterable form. . . .

2.03 In a state of affairs [*im Sachverhalt*] objects fit into one another like the links of a chain.

2.031 In a state of affairs objects stand in a determinate relation to one another.

2.032 The determinate way in which objects are connected in a state of affairs is the structure of the state of affairs.

2.033 Form is the possibility of structure.

2.034 The structure of a fact [*Tatsache*] consists of the structures of states of affairs.

2.04 The totality of existing states of affairs is the world.

2.05 The totality of existing states of affairs also determines which states of affairs do not exist.

2.06 The existence and non-existence of states of affairs is reality. (We also call the existence of states of affairs a positive fact, and their non-existence a negative fact.)

2.061 States of affairs are independent of one another [*von einander unabhängig*].

2.062 From the existence or non-existence [*Bestehen oder nicht Bestehen*] of one state of affairs it is impossible to infer the existence or non-existence of another.

This is a highly distinctive script, and before addressing the textual interplay between the concepts deployed in the passage and the writing instrument, I would like to pause at certain gross features of the discourse itself. Readers accustomed as I am to the difficulty in ascertaining where the operative units or sections of narratives and philosophical arguments begin and end must be struck, and almost relieved, by the closure furnished by the system of numeration.

The numerical notation that Wittgenstein fashions for the *Tractatus Logico-Philosophicus* functions as a text in its own right, a continuous diacritical commentary with its autonomous internal presuppositions of magnitude, priority, causality, sequence, result, and therefore teleology. In general, the magnitude of the numbers is in inverse proportion to the priority of the concept introduced. Proposition 1, "The world is all that is the case," is of a more basic and inclusive nature than proposition 6, which enumerates "the general form of a proposition." Presumably, propositions 1–5, with all their derivatives and subderivatives, have contributed to the comprehensibility of proposition 6. Wittgenstein affirms this overall evolution of propositions in sequence when he writes, "5.124 A proposition [*Satz*] affirms every proposition that follows from it."

Added to this overall sequence and ordering of the different pictures of the world that propositions provide is a system of super- and subnumeration that represents units and orders of derivation. "The decimal numbers assigned to the individual propositions indicate the logical importance [*Gewicht*] of the propositions, the stress [*Nachdruck*] laid on them in my exposition. The propositions $n.1$, $n.2$, $n.3$, etc. are comments on proposition no. n; the propositions $n.m1$, $n.m2$, etc. are comments on proposition no. $n.m$; and so on."[10]

The succession of the numbers is indicative of the priority and the sequence of the concepts; the super- and subordination of the numbers illustrates relations of logical inference between concepts but introduces family or class affiliations into the system. All the derivatives of proposition 5 (for example, 5.01–5.641) belong to or illustrate it. Propositions 5.631, 5.632, 5.6333, and 5.6331 are subordinate to and derivative of proposition 5.63, "I am my world. (The microcosm.)"

Thus, the numerical notation that Wittgenstein devises for his prose, his twentieth-century version of medieval text illumination, allows his argument to develop in two ways at the same time. As the numbers increase in numerical value, the propositions supplant, succeed, and supplement one another. As they grow in their physical dimensions—that is, extend into further decimal places—they suggest an increasingly complex and indirect ramification. There is an inverse relation between the scale of a number—that is, the number of decimal places it encompasses, and its logical priority.

The numerological system that articulates the *Tractatus Logico-Philosophicus* is thus a highly intricate and precise machine whose wish, if not whose ultimate effect, is to fix every formulation that emerges in the discussion to a point: a point of sequence, of ordination, and of value. Wittgenstein's design is not to fit all his greater and lesser angels on the head of a single pin, but to find exactly one pin and one pinpoint for each of them, which he affixes like butterfly specimens to the frame of his argument. Wittgenstein's super- and subpropositions achieve, to borrow from Milan Kundera, an "unbearable lightness of being" as they are reduced to the points charted by his numerical coordinates.[11] His propositions, like Kafka's Bucket Rider, become almost nothing, difficult to see or hear, susceptible to considerable displacement by the slightest wind. "I am my world. (The microcosm.)"

So minimal are the propositions of the *Tractatus Logico-Philosophicus*, constructed of such light materials are they, that they might fly off the page were it not for their numerical weight. The careful successiveness that prevails between propositions and subpropositions lends the *Tractatus* a calm, meditative air. The text is a Chinese garden of formulations, each spare addition changing the overall conceptual landscape. Even when Wittgenstein's project shifts from dramatizing and performing the conditions of a logically constituted world to analyzing language into language games, the succession between concepts, the evolution of complexity out of relative simplicity, will remain a prevalent esthetic specification of the enterprise. Let us assume that deconstruction encompasses a broad and variegated set of interpretative postures and moves. Even if one assumes, rightly I think, that the analytical enterprise includes a deconstructive facet, the successiveness upon which Wittgenstein insists and which Derrida cannot tolerate constitutes an ineradicable difference between the two philosophers.

The long fragment from the *Tractatus Logico-Philosophicus* cited above (propositions 2.024–2.062) is situated in a particularly momentous section of the text. In it, Wittgenstein illustrates the overall project of the *Tractatus:* to construct the model of a world constituted and governed by logical relations. Note that a logical model is itself a representation. Wittgenstein would pretend neither that the logical model of the *Tractatus* could change or reorient the world; nor that it could exhaustively account for phenomena or what he calls facts. The elements of Wittgenstein's logically constituted world hang together querulously, touchily. They subscribe to a rigid division of labor. Propositions are radically different from the atomic facts. The project is hypothetical and thus joins that body of twentieth-century literature, including works by Musil and Borges as well as Kafka, that devotes itself to an exploration of the premise of the *als ob*, the "what if." What if, ponders Wittgenstein in the *Tractatus*, the world could be constructed according to logical principles and operations. What would it be like? Such a world would encompass some but not all discursive possibilities. Wittgenstein does not grieve too piteously for what would not fall within the purview of such a model.

From the outset of his work, Wittgenstein is rigorously aware that the medium for all models, postulations, and assertions is language. He would install within his model of a logically constituted world the variables and other influences emanating from its inherently linguistic nature. Wittgenstein is aware, however, of those linguistic qualities that can wreak conceptual havoc. He makes explicit mention in the *Tractatus* of synonymy and homonymy, for example. At certain key moments in the *Tractatus*, then, the linguistic medium that is so crucial to the logical enterprise peels away from the superstructure like a warped photograph or image. At the moment of the *Tractatus*, Wittgenstein is blocked at the stage of experiencing the intractable qualities of language as an ambivalence. He manifests some revulsion toward the slipperiness of language. One of the major enterprises of the language games developed in *The Blue and Brown Books* and subsequent works will be a more productive relation to those qualities of the linguistic medium that elude the model of a logically constituted world.

In the passage cited above, Wittgenstein asserts that the world, like his discourse, can be held together in a coherent system of determinate relations. Because objects and their interrelation can be determined, it is possible to observe and formulate the totality of the world. Wittgenstein has introduced the volume by defining the world as the case in a logical argument. "1 The world is all that is the case [*was der Fall ist*]." But "1.2 The world divides into facts [*zerfällt in Tatsachen*]," and "2 What is the case—a fact—is the existence of states of affairs [*Sachverhalten*]." The translation, by someone as aware of English and German as Wittgenstein, of *Sachverhalten* as "states of affairs" is indicative of how alternative agendas, in this case sexual, metaphorically slip into his work. I shall take up this form of suggestion in fuller detail below.

I pause over the passage in question because it condenses many of the issues that Wittgenstein has pursued since the beginning of the *Tractatus Logico-Philosophicus*. It inquires how it is possible to gain an overview, itself requiring stability and abstraction, of a logically constructed world whose objects are successive, "like the links of a chain" (2.03). States of affairs in the world are the result of a changing and unstable configuration of objects (*Wechselnde, Unbeständige*, 2.0271), but the object must be unalterable (*das Feste*), "if the world is to have an unalterable form" (*eine feste Form der Welt*," 2.026). The uneasy alliance between the stable and unstable elements necessary for a logical overview of the world is analogous to the classical distinction between substance or content and form (2.024, 2.025, 2.026, 2.033). States of affairs derive from the configurations assumed by objects in relation to one another, not from their substance. They are thus the forms of the relations between objects. In this passage, Wittgenstein demonstrates a keen premonition of the observational difficulties that will be noted by Heisenberg in relation to physics: how can the overview necessary for the construction of a logical world avoid disrupting successively emerging states of affairs?[12]

At least three separate lines of argumentation are condensed into the passage, which becomes a "configuration" of propositions if not of objects (2.0272). The classical form/content dichotomy is introduced in order to provide a form for the impossible impositions of fixity upon a succession of states. The notion of the world as "the totality of existing states of affairs" is the crux of the passage and opens up a horizon in which objects, states of affairs, and propositions, by virtue of their finitude, can be autonomous of and indifferent to each other. "2.061 States of affairs are independent of one another [*sind von einander unabhängig*]." By the same token, reality (*Wirklichkeit*), encompasses the states of affairs that do not exist. This last provision enables Wittgenstein to investigate hybrid creations of the sort peopling classical mythology and Kafka's fiction.

As is evident in propositions 2.024–2.062, cited earlier, in the logically constituted realm predicated by the *Tractatus*, individual propositions are governed by a strict division of labor. They stay off one another's backs like the crankiest of people. The enterprise of the *Tractatus* would set "limits to the much disputed sphere of natural science. It must set limits to what can be thought; and, in doing so, to what cannot be thought. It must set limits to what cannot be thought by working outwards through what can be thought" (propositions 4.113–4.114).

Even in the midst of this muscular and energetic limit setting, Wittgenstein recognizes the intractability of his linguistic medium. It is in proposition 3 of the *Tractatus* that he first addresses and then puts aside this slipperiness.

> 3.322 Our use of the same sign to signify two different objects can never indicate a common characteristic of the two, if we use it with two different *modes of signification*. For the sign, of course, is arbitrary. . . .
>
> 3.323 In everyday language it very frequently happens that the same word has different modes of signification — and so belongs to different symbols — or that two words that have different modes of signification are employed in propositions in what is superficially the same way.

At the stage of the *Tractatus*, this linguistic coyness emerges as an indiscretion at best. It will steadily move in subsequent work, however, toward the center of concern, toward the node of pain. In the *Tractatus*, Wittgenstein both acknowledges and squelches the metonymic slippage of language, making possible the following tentative mini-Tractatus of the *Tractatus*:

1. Logic is a model of the world related to it by representation.
2. Logic can clarify some situations (states of affairs), but does not account exhaustively for phenomena of language.
3. Logic does not impact concretely on the world, but neither can chance occurrences destroy the relations established through logic.
4. To interpret or paraphrase situations in accordance with logical principles adds a degree of clarity or rigor that would be lacking because of such factors as contingency or the customary slippage of language.

5. The form of logic may owe much to the dynamics of language, but there are cases in which rigor demands the suppression of some dimensions of linguistic play.

6. There is thus within the domain of language a divide between a "hard" substratum or usage, the values of which can be fixed and dependable, and an indeterminate usage that may be interesting, beautiful, or in other ways edifying but renders little service to logic.

7. Logic configures a rigorous language that more aptly describes certain situations than has hitherto been the case. Logic, or the logical use of language, can thus be productively "applied" to a number of other fields, including mechanics, ethics, psychology, and even theology. The formulations of these disciplines, when in conformity with logic, may appear or "sound" markedly different from the "classical" postulates.

8. There is no necessity for logic to encompass or incorporate all facts, phenomena, or statements. Logic can clarify or illuminate, but it need not determine. Logic thus demarcates a realm beyond itself perhaps best consigned to silence.

Wittgenstein's *Tractatus* describes the conditions for its own possibility at the same time that it formulates the conditions and operations of a logically determined world. It arrives at a definition of the world as a totality, but only after establishing the indifferent coexistence of incongruous elements and even reaching over into nonexistence. This world sets into relief its own construction out of consecutive but unsympathetic argumentative strands. A vital correlative to the condensation of language is the diffusion and coexistence of the often incompatible points. The separate formulas, whose autonomy has been guaranteed on the thematic level, are precisely that: threads. Some of these threads may be spun together through their affinity for each other, but nothing assures the cohesion of the tatters thus formed. Both the rag carpet and the rags may be unspun at any time to reveal the separate and nearly weightless threads. Like Eddington's unstable physical universe, the texture of the *Tractatus Logico-Philosophicus* has more in the way of empty space than solid matter.[13] There is a level, then, at which Wittgenstein's pretensions to exactitude and totalization are avowedly ironic.

The discourse of the *Tractatus Logico-Philosophicus* and the exemplary passages from Derrida and Heidegger above afford one an audition of two voices of Oedipus in the twentieth century, a florid language of expansion with a built-in capability for stuttering, and a language reduced to its molecular if not atomic level, which cannot account for the full scattering of its particles. Both discourses arise in the context of carefully designed philosophical and linguistic projects. In their exemplary moments, which are not consistently sustained, both the obese and anorexic discourses that evolve out of the necessity to engage the past critically are willing to reside at extremes of logic and to entertain anomalies possibly appearing absurd. Not only the family but also the academy makes for discontented sons. To some extent, Derrida buries his interlocutors under the weight of his asides. The discourse of the *Tractatus Logico-Philosophicus* enacts a certain withdrawal and self-denial.

A CONFRONTATION OF STYLES: KAFKA'S "DESCRIPTION OF A STRUGGLE"

The discursive and stylistic possibilities for twentieth-century fiction and philosophy do indeed follow the doubled but uncannily converging paths exhaustively mapped by Proust. The fact that in his early fiction Kafka discerned the necessity, characteristics, and interplay of these two models as means of articulating and dismantling authority may be not merely of historical interest.

Kafka rehearsed the careful scenographic construction of *Amerika* through the succession of scenes and characters in "Description of a Struggle" (*CS*, 9–51). In that early text, from 1905, a confrontation between adversaries, one of whom is the narrator, displaces itself from Prague on a wintry evening through a number of increasingly exotic settings and then travels back in reverse order through the same settings to Prague. Kafka's title for the story is fitting in its emphasis on conflict. While the scenes and characters change rather often, the structure of a rivalry, initially sexual in nature but whose most prominent feature is its displacement, its transferability to different themes and settings, remains constant. As a persistent structure, Kafkan conflict is not reducible to its motives, genesis, evolution, or effects. It is already there; it is free to assume the most whimsical forms and migrate to the most fanciful places. What lends itself most to the purposes of the present discussion is that Kafka dramatizes the generic, iterable, and nearly unmotivated conflict of the story as the dissonance between two countervoices. It is no less telling that the two voices styled by Kafka correspond to two of the major paths pursued by twentieth-century philosophical discourse. Let us briefly review this story.

At the center of the story, the earliest work displaying Kafka's full fictive potential, written in 1904–5,, stands the memorable line, "A tiny sea gull [mistranslated mosquito] with stretched wings flew straight through his belly without losing its speed" (CS, 29). The path of the sea gull describes a beeline through what remains Kafka's most fanciful and prophetic work of fiction, characterized by wild leaps of wit and association. The possessor of the belly penetrated by the bird is the Fat Man, whose "folds of fat were so carefully spread out that although they covered the whole litter and even hung down its side like the hem of a yellowish carpet, they did not hamper him" (25). The man whose folds of fat are linked by metaphor to the ornamental calligraphy of an oriental rug is a figure of the same expansion undergone by the story that begins as the encounter of two acquaintances at a party and builds upon itself through a dizzying sequence of shifts in scene, location, and characterization. The directness of the sea gull's flight is in ironic contrast to the story's displacements, substitutions, and nonsequential developments.

At the same time that this work is a unique exercise in stylistic and fictive metamorphosis, it is a love story, written when Kafka was twenty-one. Although thematically the story focuses a shared love for and competition over a woman, it is dominated by the characteristic Kafkan vacillation between heterosexual and homosexual yearnings. For all the devoted attention that Wittgenstein's work received during and after his life, his sexuality remains enshrouded in a similar uncertainty. Even this sexual vacillation has a place within the story's economy of absences and substitutions. At all times the story involves two interlocutors. In the first scene, which provides the basic information and sets into play the movements that will characterize all subsequent situations, the difference between the adversaries is that one enjoys relations with women and the other does not. Although Kafka later does everything possible to confuse and efface this difference, it is the basis of a thematic of jealousy most fully developed in "The Judgment," a jealousy justifying the "struggle" in the story's title.

The initial combatant, the narrator, is repeatedly described as a stick figure wearing ill-fitting clothes. The thin legs of the table at which he sits alone as a Prague party dissolves are metaphoric for his own. He has been unable to finish his cake. A young woman with whom he has uncomfortably spoken will later describe him as "cut out of tissue paper, yellow tissue paper, like a silhouette, and when you walk one ought to hear you rustle" (CS, 37). This character is obviously at home with the Bucket Rider and the Hunger Artist. One cannot avoid the resemblance between the narrator and Kafka's own physical person. They share the exaggerated elongation of the sketches Kafka left behind.

The narrator's language is spare, aphoristic, one might even say analytical. Like the other characters situated at the anorexic end of the Kafkan conflict, he, and his successor in the story's economy of characterological exchange, the Supplicant, speak in a voice of detached resignation. These characters participate vicariously in the world, from the perspective of the solitary voyeur. This voice places the entire world in a position of otherness. It comprises a discourse of detached generalization, characterizing the overall behavior of the society from which the speaker has been distanced by either judgment or choice. It is in this muted, distant style that the story's epigraph is couched:

> And the people in their Sunday best
> Stroll about, swaying over the gravel
> Under this enormous sky
> Which, from hills in the distance
> Stretches to distant hills.   (CS, 9)

This verse is written from the perspective of the sky encompassing and circumscribing the world of civil manners ("Sunday best") below, a world that in comparison to the heavens of logic, is reduced to the stature of gravel. Parties epitomize the conventionality of civil behavior ("ordinary language"), and this stylistic mode is a controlled lyrical retaliation for the suffering that such situations inflict.

Such anorexic characters as the narrator and the Supplicant of "Description of a Struggle" speak, as I have said, in a voice of detachment. They utter chains of fragmentary, minimalist sentences. In the midst of the story, the Supplicant resorts to the same logical enigmas and aphorisms that Kafka published as fragments under his own name in the 1913 *Betrachtung* (*Meditation*): "For [*Denn*] we are like tree trunks in the snow. They lie there apparently flat on the ground and it looks as though one could push them away with a slight kick. But no, one can't, for they are firmly stuck to the ground. So you see [*Aber sieh*] even this is only apparent [*nur scheinbar*]" (CS, 45).

Kafka did indeed publish this observation by the Supplicant separately, under the title "The Trees." In it and other fragments he fashions a discourse that is the fictive equivalent of logical analysis. "The Trees" is barely long enough to describe a winter setting, yet in its miniature scale, it twice reverses its logic and incorporates two major oppositions, between mobility and permanence and between being and seeming. The text begins as the conclusion of a logical inference, "Denn." It initially belies the apparent mobility of the tree trunks. But in fully acknowledging its own appearance, the text disengages everything it has said. By virtue of its own reduced scale, this fragment releases itself from its own conditions and thus achieves the same "lightness of being" that Gregor Samsa and the Bucket Rider ultimately achieve through their agony. It is not accidental that this minitext appears in the *Betrachtung* next to the most progressive and poignant image of flight in Kafka's fiction, "The Wish to Be a Red Indian." Other of Kafka's fragments, including "The Bridge," "The Silence of the Sirens," and "Prometheus" owe much of their distinction to Kafka's ability to distill complex logical problems in the briefest snatches of writing. By virtue of its compression, Kafka's aphoristic discourse earns its right to break the field of gravity, to escape the ground in which the trees are rooted.

"Description of a Struggle" also provides, however, for an esthetic of prodigious consumption, self-indulgence, and hyperbole. The voice of analytical spareness in the story will be opposed by a second, whose most memorable appearance is in the Fat Man's apostrophe to the landscape. This second voice is that of excessive naturalism, lyricism, the voice of bad romanticism. The Fat Man from whom it issues is the physical antithesis of the narrator, a successor to the initial womanizing adversary.

Of course the Fat Man experiences no problems with his eating. Kafka expresses, in the "Letter to My Father" and the *Diaries*, a mixture of admiration, loathing, and envy for his father's vigor, easy appetites, and healthy scale.[14] Hermann Kafka appears in these texts as a man whose business and personal conquests have been realized by an openness and directness of will similar to the appetite of the panther that supplants the Hunger Artist as a main attraction. The Fat Man of the "Description" is of course larger than the dimensions suggested by the photographic remains of Hermann Kafka—and emptier too, if the sea gull's flight is any indication. And the discourse that Kafka composes for this character is similarly broad and vacuous: "You green mountain by the river, with your rocks rolling against the water, you are beautiful" (*CS*, 26). Nothing could be more alien to this discourse than the careful release of fixity performed at times indirectly by Jacques Derrida. Yet even the mindless Fat Man knows that expansion and a certain expansiveness frustrate one form of power in asserting another. Twentieth-century philosophy, where it recoils at the enterprise of compression and minimalist precision, will undermine as it expands, crushing under its own weight the closed structures that it encounters.

Kafka's early story not only stages the interaction between two comically different prose styles and body types: it also predicts the major trends and conflicts encountered by literary and philosophical discourse in the twentieth century. Both discursive modes hang suspended between a nearly unthinkable compression and an equally monstrous expansiveness or prolixity. The geometry of the cone incorporates both of these movements. In twentieth-century literature, philosophy, music, and art, the drives toward minimalism and open-ended expansion are not antithetical or held in opposition: both movements transpire independently in their own right. The plastic arts, for example, explore both a minimalism in which a single wooden block can transform an entire room, and the vast reaches of landscape art and building wrapping.[15] The music of the same period experiments both with the fewest possible tones and articulations and with achieving ever more monumental cacophonies.[16] What is important about the vast fluctuation between minimalism and prolixity in the twentieth century is not the determination of any final winner but rather the shift of artistic and discursive activity toward the margins of extremity. The margin, as I shall have occasion to observe in relation to a Borges story, becomes the locus of articulate activity.[17] The mainstream has withered away, through supersaturation, disuse, or boredom.

Kafka's story may be regarded as a structuralist classic. Perhaps no other relatively brief work of fiction ever written offers so elaborate and complex a structural framework. There is an elaborate mechanism by which characters are eliminated and supplanted as the story moves from scene to scene. The opposition of adversaries remains a constant structure, so that new characters seemingly encountered by chance always occupy one of the two positions originally defined by the spare narrator and the womanizing adversary. When the autobiographical story of the Fat Man subsumes the line of the narrative, the narrative is taken over by the narrator's interlocutor, the Supplicant. In the story that the Supplicant proceeds to narrate on his own, his interlocutor becomes a drunk who, in a line of succession now difficult to retain, is a distant descendant of the adversary by way of the Fat Man. As the story builds toward the extreme (or core) of its geographical and characterological displacement (or fetishism), the double track of characters is both advanced and retracted.

A similar structural symmetry characterizes the scenic construction. The story's fidelity to a modest core of basic situations is as astonishing as the links and reversals it maintains between its characters. The story's constants are minimal: conflict over women, playful gestures of friendship and hostility, parties, climbing slopes. Yet on the basis of these givens, the shifts of setting and mood undergone by the story are nothing less than vertiginous. The story's most dramatic transformation may be the encounter with the Fat Man near the banks of a tropical river whose position is analogous in the story to that of the Moldau. Yet the story is characterized by a prodigious structural combination by which the main part of its data, minor as well as major details, are eventually repeated in strange settings, recycled, rehabilitated. The scenographic structure of the story first builds toward increasing remoteness and uncanniness and then retracts, or dismantles, its own constructions. After wandering, through the sheer momentum of *Einbildungskraft*, to increasingly remote settings, the story methodically returns to its point of origin, Prague on a winter evening.

In its structural fabulation and deconstruction, "Description of a Struggle" anticipates the fate of structuralism in twentieth-century philosophy and criticism. On multiple levels, of theme, setting, characterization, and internal organization, the story bears witness to its own fascination with structure. (Its thematic interests in links — bodily and narrative, and slopes of ascent — are cases in point.) But the story also gleefully deranges and obliterates the structural frameworks to which it has devoted so many resources. In the end, it is not clear whether the initial narrator or the "adversary" was the "woman killer." The story's structuralist invention expands toward an extreme (or core) of uncanniness and then dismantles the structural ladder that brought it there. In its deliberate construction the story corresponds to the modernist isolation and superimposition of structures discerned by Benjamin and practiced by the Pound of the *Cantos* and the Joyce of *Ulysses*. Yet Kafka's story also anticipates a bankruptcy, a disqualification of structure that is one of the earmarks of postmodernity. Authors of true originality, such as those just named, also incorporated the decline of structures into their work, anticipating the countermovement to modernism. "Description of a Struggle" thus not only marks a spot at which the discourses of logical analysis and deconstruction enter a productive dialogue: it also is an early yet decisive crossroads of twentieth-century theory and art, an important gateway into the discursive constellation of postmodernity.

If there is merit to the observations above, it is clear that the major projects of twentieth-century philosophy have placed enormous weight on the potentials implicit in literary style. Style becomes not merely an esthetic accompaniment of convenience, akin to the interior design of an office. It embodies and expresses the theoretical possibility of the discourse whose traits it provides.

In deconstruction and logical analysis, we find two philosophical approaches vividly aware of what they do and do not wish to accomplish and how they may and may not achieve some consistency between their conceptual, polemical, and stylistic programs. The philosophical discourse itself, through its design, becomes the medium, advocate, and generator of concepts. The design of philosophical discourse in the twentieth century becomes an art object in its own right; hence the affinities between philosophy and the pictorial, architectural, and planning arts may well be more crucial than in prior periods.

The design of a style is a highly selective process, depending as much on the alternate styles eschewed as on the traits ultimately selected. In "Description of a Struggle," despite its earliness both in Kafka's career and in the century, Kafka demonstrates a remarkable perspicacity regarding the interdependency of contrary styles. It is for this reason that so many resources are dedicated to dismantling the story's carefully constructed schemes. Hence the woman in contention changes hands between the narrator and his supposed adversary. The story obscures, as well as posits, its two opposing lines of characterological descent. Kafka is too aware of textual process to allow the design of this story to devolve into a static opposition between spareness and excess, appetite and renunciation, and "fat" and "thin" languages.

It should be recalled that the confrontation between excessive and spare discourses that we find in Kafka's story has been rehearsed for Wittgenstein within the bounds of philosophy proper. Wittgenstein's esthetics and stylistics are thus part of an ongoing conversation. I think particularly of the mathematical rigor that Gottlob Frege brought to the analysis of "On Sense and Reference,"[18] and to the curious combination of control and dottiness that Wittgenstein discerned in the work of his predecessor and mentor, Bertrand Russell. Though capable of enormous sophistication—for example, when he characterizes the ambiguities of language as a saving grace of social existence—Russell at other moments enters the persona of a philosophical Lewis Carroll. In the crucial "Philosophy of Logical Atomism," for example, where he justifies an atomic analysis of the world in part as an escape from Hegelian subjectivity, and where he defines the relation between propositions and facts, Russell is nonetheless capable of writing:

> Take, for example, the word "Piccadilly." We, who are acquainted with Piccadilly, attach quite a different meaning to that word from any which could be attached to it by a person who had never been to London: and, supposing that you travel in foreign parts and expatiate on Piccadilly, you will convey to your hearers entirely different propositions from those in your mind. They will know Piccadilly as an important street in London; they may know a lot about it, but they will not know just the thing one knows when one is walking along it. If you were to insist upon language which was unambiguous, you would be unable to tell people at home what you had seen in foreign parts.[19]

While accepting the premises of a philosophical discourse that avoids certain subjective and developmental delusions, Wittgenstein cannot tolerate the playful, hypothetical excess to which Russell occasionally gives in. He finds a preferable stylistic if not conceptual model for his own work in Frege, who isolates in the syntax of the sentence both the model and pitfalls of logic.[20] The sense of a proper name stands between what is now called its referent and its cognitive or subjective experience. "A logically perfect language," specifies Frege, "should satisfy the conditions that every expression grammatically well constructed as a proper name out of signs already introduced shall in fact designate an object, and that no new sign shall be introduced as a proper name without being secured a reference. The logic books contain warnings against logical mistakes arising from the ambiguity of expression."[21] Much of Wittgenstein's work on truth tables in the *Tractatus* arises out of Frege's explorations into the truth values of replaceable subordinate clauses in the sentence.

Whereas the fat man and the thin man may coexist in Russell's philosophizing, Wittgenstein, in choosing the path of rigor, allies himself with his intellectual grandfather, Frege. The propositions of the *Tractatus* would indeed purport to relate to one another as logical atoms. Yet Wittgenstein has sharpened Russell's approach, tempered his language, and endowed his entire project with a consistent modesty and asceticism extending to several dimensions of the discourse.

By the same token, it would be reductive to claim any ultimate separation between the minimalist and expansive projects of twentieth-century philosophy. These enterprises, in their widest dimensions, act quite differently on their antecedents and perform and seek two quite different forms of death, but one must marvel at the precision that Heidegger and Derrida bring to their respective deconcealings and at the bravery with which Wittgenstein, in his subsequent work, explores the self-imposed limits of the *Tractatus Logico-Philosophicus*. One need hardly assert the extraordinary rigor, as fine as any precision Wittgenstein could hope to achieve with the writing instrument of the *Tractatus*, with which Derrida pieces together the Socratic metaphysics from widely divergent sources or pursues certain key Mallarméan motifs at the syllabic level or discerns the slightest traces of presence in Heidegger, whose writing he has so carefully weighed. If Derrida deviates from the logical and instrumental aspirations of the analytical enterprise, he does so in full cognizance of its demand for precision. Wittgenstein departs from academia for nine years beginning in 1919. Upon his return he undertakes radical—and astonishing—adjustments to his project. The opening up of a metaphoric dimension in *The Blue Book* is not only a pivotal event in modern philosophy; it is also one of the most dramatic and poignant moments in twentieth-century literature.[22] The remainder of this essay will focus on the acceptance of metaphoric language in Wittgenstein's work after the *Tractatus*. No less than Derrida does Wittgenstein allow himself to be influenced by the ostensible Other of his discourse.

The full title of *The Blue and Brown Books* describes them as *Preliminary Studies for the "Philosophical Investigations"* and marks a transitional moment in Wittgenstein's work. Though the language games formulated in *The Brown Book* do strive to account for the usage and logical implications of language, the aspiration to generality that is so characteristic of the *Tractatus Logico-Philosophicus*—both in enunciating the conditions for all propositions and in accounting for all relations of derivation and ordination—has been considerably tempered. The language games do progressively increase in the complexity of the models that they hypothesize. But Wittgenstein devotes less energy than he does in the *Tractatus* to ascertaining the relation between one language game and the next and between the constitutive elements of a single language game. The relation of subsequent to prior games is expansive; the *Tractatus*, on the other hand, would purport to determine each subsequent or subordinate proposition.

Whereas in its program *The Brown Book* functions as a generative recapitulation of the *Tractatus Logico-Philosophicus*, *The Blue Book* is both compositional and conceptual *ouverture* to Wittgenstein's subsequent work. And if *The Blue Book* constitutes the future for Wittgenstein's writing, it does so by marking the point of expansion where logic incorporates the metaphor, where the language of logic turns from its instrumental function and addresses its multiple semantic possibilities. The design of a logic machine has exhausted a large share of the linguistic resources of the *Tractatus Logico-Philosophicus* (although an exploration into the metaphoric functions operating in this text would indeed warrant the effort).

Wittgenstein surely maintains his commitments to spareness and rigor in concept and formulation throughout *The Blue Book*. He writes there: "The difficulty in philosophy is to say no more than we know" (*BBB*, 45). But at the same time the examples that he evokes to illustrate various observations regarding the contexts and usages of language give sway to a metaphoric dimension whose limitation and careful control was one of the basic experiments of the *Tractatus*. The examples and hypothetical cases of *The Blue Book* are revealing not only of the choices made in their composition but also of their author's frustrations and even pains. One major effect achieved by this text is, then, a major shift in focus. The metaphoric play that was, in the *Tractatus*, all but subordinated out of the system, has now attained at least the wings, if not the center, of the stage. This redirection may occur intentionally, unintentionally, ironically, or in any combination, but whatever the case, *The Blue Book* achieves a remarkable result: the identification and detachment of the metaphoric element out of the instrumental function. Heidegger would describe this event as a retreat or delving that proceeds from the machine into the linguistic earth out of which it was fashioned. A slippage of the logical into the metaphoric achieves unprecedented prominence in *The Blue Book*. Once enlarged, the metaphoric dimension releases semantic potentials hitherto overlooked; it also absorbs and frames the logical project.

Pain, shadow, the color red, fire, and the eye are unlikely candidates to be the most prominent motifs in a text furnishing an exhaustive mathematical account of language, if that is *The Blue Book*'s purpose. But indeed, these are the recurrent metaphors that Wittgenstein admits into his text. Another curious motif that recurs as an instance of problems associated with representation is interlinguistic translation. And the model of translation, as Wittgenstein invokes it, is invariably associated with a certain pain, the pain of the non-native speaker of English, the pain of the linguistic outsider.[23] "Supposing I had a habit of accompanying every English sentence which I said aloud by a German sentence spoken to myself inwardly" (*BBB*, 34). The silent consecutive translation that the outsider renders is like the pain expressed only when the representational problems of logical language are opened.

The metaphors (for example, pain, red), models (for example, chess, music, color in general), and activities (for example, translation, interpretation) that Wittgenstein incorporates into *The Blue and Brown Books* all exemplify, explicitly or obliquely, the potentials and problems set into play by representation. I am arguing that the most prominent metaphors of *The Blue Book* operate equally well as logical terms and as figures of speech revealing the textual qualities of the discourse. They are thus shifters between the logical and literary domains and constitute an unbounded game that suspends the determinate rules of the *Tractatus Logico-Philosophicus*. (Wittgenstein formulates the distinction between bounded and unbounded games in game 22 of *The Brown Book*.) Some of these key metaphors give rise to homonymic slippage: as I shall show, there is some ambiguity between the eye and the *I* identified as "L.W."; between the color red and the *read* that is the past participle of *to read*. The metaphors, pain, red, fire, and eye, develop and ramify alongside and through one another. It is their mutual extension and elaboration of one another that constitute the textual composition of *The Blue Book*, drastically expanding this dimension within Wittgenstein's discourse.

No passage may be more indicative of this metaphoric density than the following one:

> "How can one think what is not the case? If I think that King's College is on fire when it is not on fire, the fact of its being on fire does not exist. Then how can I think it? How can we hang a thief who doesn't exist? Our answer could be put in this form: "I can't hang him when he doesn't exist; but I can look for him when he doesn't exist."
>
> We are here misled by the substantives "objects of thought" and "fact," and by the different meanings of the word "exist."
>
> Talking of the fact as a "complex of ideas" springs from this confusion (cf. *Tractatus Logico-Philosophicus*). Supposing we asked: "How can one *imagine* what does not exist?" The answer seems to be: "If we do, we imagine non-existent combinations of existing elements." A centaur doesn't exist, but a man's head and torso and arms and a horse's legs do exist. . . .
>
> But what do you mean by "redness exists"? My watch exists, if it hasn't been pulled to pieces, if it hasn't been *destroyed*. What would we call "destroying redness"? We might of course mean destroying all red objects; but would this make it impossible to imagine a red

object? Supposing to this one answered: "But surely, red objects must have existed and you must have seen them if you are able to imagine them"?—But how do you know that this is so? Supposing I said "Exerting a pressure on your eye-ball produces a red image." Couldn't the way by which you first became acquainted with red have been this? And why shouldn't it have been just imagining a red patch? (*BBB,* 31)

Perhaps no question is more pervasive throughout *The Blue and Brown Books* than that regarding the iterability or transferability of private experience.[24] If the paths of Wittgenstein's investigations literally all lead to language, this is because language embodies the only available means for the transference and objectification of personal sensation and impressions. Although Wittgenstein discerns a shadow "between the expression of our thought and the reality with which our thought is concerned" (*BBB,* 36, 41), he resists ascribing the indeterminacy of language to an unconscious or its metaphysics. The challenge he assumes may be partially described as an attempt through clarity and precision in language to head off recourse to an unconscious as a necessary explanation for incongruous thoughts and situations.

The passage above asks us, without positing some cosmological construct such as a collective or individual unconscious, how the mind can picture and describe both events that have not taken place and objects that do not exist. The examples for this situation are significant, and to some extent encompass the development of the entire *Blue Book:* thinking that King's College is on fire; hanging a fictive thief; a centaur; and "destroying redness."

Wittgenstein's inclusion of the centaur as an instance of language's reaching over into the nonexistent marks the growing decisiveness of a theory of metaphor to his work. It may well represent the point in his discourse closest to the fictive universe of Franz Kafka. "A centaur doesn't exist, but a man's head and torso and arms and a horse's legs do exist." Language annexes the nonexistent by functioning as a combinatorial matrix of the incompatible. Metaphor condenses, to use Freud's term, the implausible elements of the real. The combinatorial function of language, released from its service to verisimilitude, is free to commandeer the real, to posit hybrid, metaphorical objects and nonexistent events. Wittgenstein's centaur is thus close kin to Kafka's kitten-lamb, Odradek, and the human discourse that seems to emanate from an insect's frame.[25]

It must surely be distressing for Wittgenstein to admit such rampant distortion into the orderly utopia of his discourse, as distressing as the thought of King's College in flames must be to one of its students or instructors. Apart from the centaur, all of Wittgenstein's examples of the nonexistent that nevertheless exists in language are distressful: the King' College fire, hanging a thief, "destroying redness." Wittgenstein invokes yet another metaphor to reconcile himself to the violence in language: "the shadow of the fact; as it were, the next thing to the fact" (BBB, 36). "The shadow, as we think of it, is some sort of a picture; in fact, something very much like an image which comes before our mind's eye; and this again is something not unlike a painted representation in the ordinary sense (BBB, 36). For Walter Benjamin, in "On Some Motifs in Baudelaire," the spontaneous afterimage succeeding the visual stimulus exemplifies the sensory overload of shock.[26] The shadow of the fact introduces an analogous element of cognitive dissonance into an otherwise systematic enterprise. A shadow is a shade. It opens up a language of death and underworldly creatures that one would not expect to find in a logical tract. The shadow of the fact also makes Wittgenstein an interloper at Plato's cave, where it is the only evidence of reality evident to men. This shadow is inextricably grafted on the world, which is "all that is the case" as its margin for metaphoric distortion.[27] In the word painting that Wittgenstein is introducing into his text here, the King's College fire, possibly a glowing red, issues forth in a shadowy margin. But the "shadow of the fact," a name applied to an unsettling phenomenon in an effort to dispel a ghost, is already implicit in the figure of the centaur and in any metaphoric condensation.

The lengthy passage cited, displaying ample condensation in its own right, pursues two strands of images emanating from the hypothetical King's College fire: redness and pain. These dual complexes of images not only encompass the entire trajectory of Wittgenstein's meditation on the relation between language and experience; they also furnish a legend for the insinuation of the metaphoric and the indeterminate into Wittgenstein's discourse.

Though it requires no strenuous suspension of disbelief to observe the centaur emerge from the combination of its existent elements, the case of redness, a generalization induced from a specific sensory experience, adds new complexity to the problem of language and its relation to experience. "But what do you mean by 'redness exists'? . . . What would we call 'destroying redness'?" Wittgenstein suggests three possible ways by which the concept of redness may be constituted: first, as the compendium of all red objects; second, as a subjective experience that could be produced, hypothetically, in a uniform way; and third, simply as an individual personal experience. The impossibility of destroying all red objects dispenses with redness's possible existence as a compendium, as the sum of its parts or the totality of its variants. Wittgenstein's choice of a model for the conception of redness as a subjective experience somehow experienced uniformly is a significant one: "Suppose I said 'Exerting a pressure on your eye-ball produces a red image.' Couldn't the way by which you first became acquainted with red have been this?"[28]

The effect of Wittgenstein's investigations into the term *redness* is to demonstrate that the concept has no existence other than as a signifier. Yet the model that he produces as an instance of uniform subjective redness is at the core of his enterprise. If redness is "out there," the eye is presumably the mediator between the external world and the mind, and yet this hypothetical model involves an internal production of the experience of red through the application of pressure from outside, in all likelihood by a finger (This seemingly gratuitous assumption on my part will be corroborated by the examination below of subsequent passages from Wittgenstein's text.) Not merely a digit and a manipulative member, the finger is the corporeal instrument of indication, in *The Brown Book* the most fundamental act of language. The eye is a highly sensitive organ, so that an application of pressure to it to the point of mentally seeing redness approaches the threshold of pain, a self-inflicted pain produced by one's own finger. It cannot be insignificant that the example of internally produced redness involves the closing of the eye, a shutting off of the organ most intimately associated with sensory reception.

Wittgenstein's model for a subjectively constituted abstraction, even though it undergoes disqualification, thus involves and restructures many of his fundamental concepts of language. The gesture of pointing to an external and presumably autonomous object has been internalized toward the eye. The eye produces rather than receives sensation. The eye is closed rather than open. The eye gives rise to pain, and pain is associated with the color red through the painful thought that King's College might be on fire. The gesture of pointing is thus more complex than appears to be the case. At times it is the only instrument for the transference of otherwise noniterable experiences. Pointing to pain is Wittgenstein's primary example of the instrumental representation of the noniterable. Yet the corporeal pointer, the finger on the hand, is itself a sensory organ capable of receiving and inflicting pain. It is for this reason that Wittgenstein writes: "This act of pointing, by the way, is not to be confused with that of finding the painful spot by probing. In fact the two may lead to different results" (*BBB*, 50)

Pointing to pain is not merely Wittgenstein's paradigm for the manner in which language addresses the noniterability of personal experience; it is also his key model for the relation between language and subjectivity. In a sequence of passages that I shall follow, pointing to one's own pain as a means for conveying experience expands into a model of the progress by which the subject communicates with itself. The eye of observation, pain, and inner experience enters into an intimate relationship with the *I* of the author of Wittgenstein's text, and the finger of pointing becomes the instrument of language whose mediation is the subject's only means of constituting, knowing, and experiencing itself.

> The reason for this particularity of our language is of course the regular coincidence of certain sense experiences. Thus when I feel my arm moving I mostly can also see it moving. And if I touch it with my hand, also that hand feels the motion, etc. (The man whose foot has been amputated will describe a particular pain as pain in his foot.) We feel in such cases a strong need for such an expression as: "a sensation travels from my tactual cheek to my tactual eye." . . . Thus we can imagine a person having the sensation of toothache plus those tactual and kinaesthetic experiences which are normally bound up with seeing his hand travelling from his tooth to his nose, to his eyes, etc., but correlated to the visual experience of his hand moving to those places in another person's face. Or again, we can imagine a person having the kinaesthetic sensation of moving his hand, and the tactual sensation, in his fingers and face, of his fingers moving over his face, whereas his kinaesthetic and visual sensations should have to be described as those of his fingers moving over his knee. (*BBB*, 52)

In this passage the problems regarding communication and the noniterability of experience that Wittgenstein has raised on an interpersonal level extend to within the subject itself. The communication of pain is again the central model for language. As instances of pain, Wittgenstein selects two very different examples. The amputation of a foot is a very intense disfiguration arising mostly out of extraordinary or abnormal circumstances such as an industrial or military accident. Toothache is, on the other hand, while possibly intense, one of the most everyday aches and pains. The successful communication of all the pains along this rather wide range of suffering involves an analogy that must be apprehended and correctly interpreted at both ends of the communicative act. There must be a correlation between the pain and the gestic representation of its location, direction, and intensity; and the analogy must be successfully transmitted and received, whether by an Other or by the subject of the pain. In the course of this passage, Wittgenstein explores a number of things that can go wrong with the analogy or with its transmission or reception. These difficulties furnish a gloss on the noniterability of personal experience.

Wittgenstein grounds his account of language in the most intense and immediate human experience possible: pain. Yet no sooner does the analogy as the medium of experience enter the picture than the process goes completely awry. For one, pain, while perhaps a direct experience, involves a remarkably large number of elements. There is the pain itself and its location, the member pointing out the pain and its movement, and the subject's sensation of that indicative act. Wittgenstein's chief figure for the perspectivism necessarily surrounding an act, the multiple perspectives from which it may be experienced, is synesthesia, the coincidence of different senses.[29] Wittgenstein is quite aware that even the simplest gesture of indication is both felt (the "tactual experience") and seen (the "visual experience"). Added to these elements of Wittgenstein's analysis of the indicative gesture is the "kinaesthetic experience," an intuitive supplement or body English enabling the gesture to be represented in the mind of the subject. The kinaesthetic experience supplies the information regarding the location, intensity, and direction of the pain that places the subject in a position to represent it, although, as Wittgenstein points out, the *Gestalt* that the pain assumes may be very misleading.

Not only does the experience and communication of the pain involve a vast array of not-so-simple elements. The analogy between it and the subject's gesture has every opportunity to break down. The example of the amputee suggests that the gestic analogy can continue even when its physical source, say a foot, disappears. In addition, the analogy may be correlated not to the subject's "tactual and kinaesthetic experiences" but "to the visual experience of his hand moving to those places in another person's face." Wittgenstein's analogy, in other words, depends on projection, displacement, and the absence of an Other. In his description of the correlation of one's own toothache with another's face, Wittgenstein is close to Derrida's account of auto-affection and its basis in absence in *Speech and Phenomena*.[30] Finally, like any machine, the analogy can break down; the tactual, visual, and kinaesthetic elements of an experience can go "out of sync." Wittgenstein's example involves an individual some of whose members and receptors reenact a movement of the fingers over the face while others experience moving the fingers over the knee.

The analogy as the facilitator of the most basic language act is thus fraught with difficulties and possible inaccuracies. Yet it cannot be circumvented; it and its derivatives are, to some extent, "the only games in town." The subject is, by the same token, hardly the most efficient organizer of experience and user of language. Yet it too is a construct upon which Wittgenstein's investigations rely, and it is constituted by the language games it plays, however unpredictable the outcome. As a correlative of the inability of knowing what another man sees, Wittgenstein writes, "'what he looks at' . . . is *before his mind's eye"* (*BBB*, 61). He then proceeds to a lengthy exposition in which the cognitive mechanics of indication unfolds itself to the mind's eye, and in so doing he implicates the *I*. This passage illustrates the irrevocable damage wreaked by linguistic play upon the enterprise of logic.

If a man tries to obey the order "Point to your eye," he may do many different things, and there are many different criteria which he will accept for having pointed to his eye. If these criteria, as they usually do, coincide, I may use them alternately and in different combinations to show me that I have touched my eye. If they don't coincide, I shall have to distinguish between different senses of the phrase "I touch my eye" or "I move my fingers towards my eye." If, e.g., my eyes are shut, I can still have the characteristic kinaesthetic experience in my arm which I should call the kinaesthetic experience of raising my hand to my eye. (*BBB*, 63)

As to visual criteria, there are two I can adopt. There is the ordinary experience of seeing my hand rise and come towards my eye, and this experience, of course, is different from seeing two things meet, say, two finger tips. On the other hand, I can use as a criterion for my finger moving towards my eye, what I see when I look into a mirror and see my finger nearing my eye. (*BBB*, 64)

And here I am tempted to say: "Although by the word 'I' I don't mean L.W., it will do if the others understand 'I' to mean L.W., if just now I am in fact L.W." I could also express my claim by saying: "I am the vessel of life"; but mark, it is essential that everyone to whom I say this should be unable to understand me. It is essential that the other should not be able to understand "what I really *mean*," though in practice he might do what I wish by conceding to me an exceptional position in his notation. But I wish it to be *logically* impossible that he should understand me, that is to say, it should be meaningless, not false, to say that he understands me. (*BBB*, 64–65)

And therefore, if I utter the sentence "Only I really see," it is conceivable that my fellow creatures thereupon will arrange their notation so as to fall in with me by saying "so-and-so is really seen" instead of "L.W. sees so-and-so," etc., etc. What, however, is wrong, is to think that I can *justify* this choice of notation. When I said, from my heart, that only I see, I was also inclined to say that by "I" I didn't really mean L.W., although for the benefit of my fellow men I might say "It is now L.W. who really sees" though this is not what I really mean. (*BBB*, 66)

The word "I" does not mean the same as "L.W." even if I am L.W. (*BBB*, 67)

In the first two extracts, Wittgenstein's model for language has evolved from pointing to a pain to pointing to the eye. Some of the constraints from earlier models still apply: the experience divides into tactual, visual, and kinaesthetic elements, which may become disengaged from one another, causing some misunderstanding. But when one points to a toothache or the site of an amputated foot, the object of scrutiny, while sentient, is blind. In pointing at the eye, one points at the paradigmatic receptor, the organ that "sees back." There is a mirroring effect already implicit in the exercise of seeing the organ of sight, so that Wittgenstein's distinction, in the second extract, between seeing two members meet in space and seeing the finger approach the eye in a mirror comes as no surprise. In the context of Wittgenstein's search for precision, the relocation of the paradigmatic act of language to the mirror of doubled perspective can only be regarded as a highly self-conscious gesture.

The mirror provides a criterion for "what I see when I look into a mirror and see my finger nearing my eye." When I look into a mirror, I also see my finger nearing my I. The figure of the mirror is the epitome of a certain self-reflexivity that coincides with the history of Western thought, a tradition that has been productively reviewed in recent work by Rodolphe Gasché.[31] The plane before the mirror also constitutes the decisive stage in the formation of subjectivity in Jacques Lacan's scenario for psychosexual development. For Lacan there is no individuated selfhood until the child has recognized its image in the mirror, and a variety of personality dysfunctions can emerge from the unsuccessful completion of this stage. Wittgenstein's phrase, "my finger nearing my eye," is ambiguous both syntactically and homonymically. The constitution and operation of subjectivity are implicated by the model of indicating in a mirror the object that is also the receptor of experience and the progenitor of subjectivity.

The model of the "seeing-eye mirror" represents a certain climax or consummation of language gamesmanship (and analysis) as well as of self-consciousness. Wittgenstein is as uncomfortable with this hypothetical moment of self-reflexive totalization as are philosophers with whom he is not usually associated, such as Heidegger and Derrida. No sooner does the sport of language games absorb subjectivity and assert a formative role in its structuring than Wittgenstein tests his discourse and distances it from these claims. The new model for the noniterability of experience becomes a subject that asserts, "I am the vessel of life" and "Only I really see." Does the full-blown model of indication, in which there is a reciprocal stand-off between the pointing and receiving functions of subjectivity, necessarily give rise to paranoia? The examples that Wittgenstein selects at the end of the passages quoted above would suggest this to be the case. And accompanying the claims of a subjectivity that has achieved self-consciousness on so many levels of its functioning is a rhetoric of humanitarian concern: "for the benefit of my fellow men."

Paranoia, then, is the fullest extension of the noniterability of personal experience, and it is aggravated, not diminished, by the specificity and precision of the language games applied and the analysis they furnish. Even if the paranoia that the reader confronts in these pages is hypothetical or calibrated to a specific language situation, it involves both an exaggerated concern for and suspicion toward the interlocutor: "It is essential that the other should not be able to understand 'what I really mean.'" Wittgenstein may logically insist that no other can understand a subject in exactly the same way as that subject understands him/her/itself, and the refinement and confirmation of this separation only increases the discomfort and pain that pervade *The Blue and Brown Books.*

It is not inconceivable that one should wish to escape the involution of successful analysis and its implicit paranoia. Wittgenstein accomplishes this rupture with his own reasonings through an act of dissociation: L.W. is no longer *I;* if L.W. perpetrates this fiction, it is "for the benefit of my fellow men"; by implication, the *I* as a vehicle for personal expression is always a fiction; the law of identity is problematical (*BBB,* 66). Much of Wittgenstein's incredulity at the proposition of identity runs along the same lines as Heidegger's in *Identity and Difference.* In the course of *The Blue Book,* then, the metaphor of the eye has traveled a truly circuitous path. Initially it serves as a model, then as a locus and instrument for the problems of communication. It closes the book transmogrified into the *I* of hyper-self-consciousness and exhaustive logical analysis, renounced by L.W. as a too demanding relative, relegated, like the Hunger Artist, to the side show.

The story of the eye in Wittgenstein is emblematic of the power and fate of the metaphor. In response to logical positivism, the later Wittgenstein first admits and then folds in the metaphor. The eye, which is examined open, closed, and under pressure, becomes the *I* of volition and authorship. The red of optics, fire, blood, and pain—is read. "The imagery of the wish surely shows us something less definite, something hazier, than the reality of the paper being red"—or, as the syntax allows, being read (*BBB*, 60). Wittgenstein wishes for an alternate term for *red*, two terms for every quality, "one for the case when something is said to have it, the other for the case when something is said not to have it. The negation of 'This paper is red' could then be, say, 'This paper is not rode.'" If red is not rode, why can't it be read?

Through the metaphoric by-play that Wittgenstein admits into his discourse in *The Blue and Brown Books*, he achieves what his early investigations deem impossible.[32] He iterates his most intense and private concerns by means of a rigorous instrument of language. His key metaphors—pain, red, the eye, shadow—all enter tentatively, as examples. Through a process of infolding that I have attempted to characterize, these metaphors rotate through hypothetical, thematic, and textual levels. Wittgenstein inveighs against identifying L.W. with *I*. Yet his metaphors are the only source that intimates his incongruous wishes. For so devoted a student as himself, the image of King's College on fire is almost of a suicidal nature. And although Wittgenstein's questioning of the biases and presuppositions underlying any notion of the unconscious is well taken, why is it that as his instance of color he focuses, almost obsessively, on the color red? Could this color represent the very trace of his own sexual yearning that he admits, through a back door, into his text? If the discourse of the *Tractatus Logico-Philosophicus* is indeed anorexic, as I suggest, then the later Wittgenstein does, in the end, find some food he can eat: the shadow of the metaphor, the residue of metaphoric infolding that accounts for the text's operation as a text. In order to do this, Wittgenstein must violate his diet and renounce his vows of spareness and severity. But his work, and twentieth-century philosophy, emerge all the richer.

This philosophy can articulate itself only in extremes: the hyperbolic and the anorexic. In the writings of Franz Kafka, both of its contrary undertakings find a common ground.

CHAPTER FOUR

The Circle of Exclusion:
The Dissolution of Structure
in Kafka's *Castle*

They cut us off from the community forever. —Olga

THE IMAGE OF THE CASTLE

The image of the Castle dominates Kafka's novel much as it governs the lives of the people in the village below it. Elevated, remote, inscrutable, it presents the novel with a talisman just as, in demarcating the horizon around the existence of the villagers, it establishes the starting point of their desire, the extent of their hope, and the objects of their derision. Hover as it may above the landscape, this structure is never grasped, by K. or the reader, as a transcendent symbol, a supratextual index to the novel's cohesions. The centrality of the image is ironically reduced by the cycle in which metaphysical naïveté and indifference supplant each other endlessly in the course of the novel and by numerous instances of the displacement and penetration of the borders defining the novel's categories of sameness and difference. The novel's center thus shifts to its periphery, for K., the villagers, and the reader come to experience the Castle (*Schloss*) only as an encompassing statute of limitations. It is in this sense that K. truly is a Land-Surveyor. At manifold points he collides with a shifting border in his attempt to penetrate the village under the aegis of the Castle. A centralized, sublime locus is ascribed by the villagers to the power source as K. confronts their prevailing metaphysics, but the image of the Castle functions only as a divider, itself divided.

This conflict is anticipated in the first glimpse that the reader is afforded of the Castle. Like the novel's thematics of the glimpse (*Blick*), in which the fundamental mode of interpersonal contact is joined to the indifferent gaze of repudiation, the image of the Castle always encompasses the doubled and self-negating perspective of paradox. The first segment of the description shares the clarity of definition that will characterize the world order assumed and defended by the landlady, the Mayor, and the teacher in their confrontations with K.

Now he could see the Castle above him, clearly defined [*deutlich umrissen*] in the glittering air, its outline made still more definite by the thin layer [*Schicht*] of snow covering everything. There seemed [*schien*] to be much less snow up there on the hill than down in the village, where K. found progress as laborious as on the main road the previous day. There the heavy snowdrifts reached right up to the cottage windows and began again on the low roofs, but up on the hill everything soared light and free into the air, or at least so it appeared [*schien es*] from below. (*C*, II)

The recurrence in this passage of the verb *scheinen*, to appear, both in the sense of manifestation and seeming, emphasizes that the Castle is above all an appearance, a transitory etching of the condition of clarity itself. Clearly defined (*deutlich umrissen*) by the clean air, the Castle is doubly clarified by the snow, an indifferent denominator assuming the function of a representational medium. This clarity extends to the neat stratification delineating the present, the here, from the form or image that is the Castle. The Castle seems to radiate an aura of lightness and freedom lacking in the present, which is rendered diminutive by the village's low roofs. The present buckles under the sense of burden figured in the heavier blanket of snow seeming to cover the village. The outline making the Castle a clear image thus implies an ontological stratification of realms. This is, however, merely a fleeting impression, immediately succeeded by a complementary, and for this reason, intimately related formulation.

On the whole this distant prospect of the Castle satisfied K.'s expectations. It was neither an old stronghold nor a new mansion, but a rambling pile consisting of innumerable small buildings closely packed together and of one or two stories; if K. had not known that it was a castle he might have taken it for a little town. There was only one tower as far as he could see; whether it belonged to a dwelling-house or a church he could not determine. Swarms of crows were circling round it. (*C*, II)

The second appearance of the Castle continues the suggestion of its imagistic character. The Castle corresponds to a prior image, K.'s expectations, a correspondence that will prove short-lived. The intermediary position of the Castle's era of origin, neither medieval nor modern, extends as well to its architectural style. The Castle is an extended arrangement. The height of its low buildings is uniform. Its structures extend only horizontally. In their closeness to one another, its buildings appear to interlock. Only one nondescript tower emerges from this image of leveling, and it is circumscribed by crows, which serve notice that not only the village is enclosed and subject to limit.

In its horizontal extension, in the impacted architecture preventing its forms from attaining eminence, the Castle, in its second appearance, undermines the structure and stratification so confidently asserted in the first. Whatever violence this undermining may involve, however, the juxtaposition of the two views makes their comparison inevitable. This is merely the first in a long series of analogies that will include the one between the farmers' tavern and that reserved for the Castle officials (C, 46), and the one between the reactions of Frieda and Amalia to the sexual propositions of Klamm and Sortini (253–54). It is, nonetheless, not by accident that, in the novel where Kafka most doggedly deploys a rhetoric of similarity and establishes ratios of interdependence, one finds some of the most striking instances of spatial incoherence and temporal discontinuity in his writing.

As opposed to the metaphysics of clear differentiation in the background of the first glimpse of the Castle, the containment within a single plane that the Castle also images is presupposed by a certain hierarchy-leveling indifference. The Castle is in fact indistinguishable from the village and from K.'s hometown.[1] The indistinct separation of the Castle from the village is suggested by Schwarzer, the Castellan's son, who interrupts K. as he sleeps in the tavern "Zur Brücke upon his arrival in the village: "This village belongs to the Castle, and whoever lives here or passes the night does so, in a manner of speaking, in the Castle itself" (C, 4). Like Lacan's lavatories, the Castle is identified only through cultural usage.[2] Any distinction between the Castle and village is best described as stylistic, as a later contrast between the Castle officials and the farmers according to the cut of their jackets will indicate (228). If K's point of origin is "hardly inferior" (12) to his destination, his experience is circular, as is the main street of the village, which seems at first to lead to the Castle but suddenly veers off and closes its circuit (14–15). The sameness implied by these formulations is the context for the striking descriptions of the Castle's only visible tower, which may belong to the palace.

> The tower above him here—the only one visible—the tower of a house, as was now evident, perhaps of the main building, was uniformly round, part of it graciously mantled with ivy, pierced by small windows that glittered in the sun—with a somewhat mania-

cal glitter—and topped by what looked like an attic, with battlements that were irregular, broken, fumbling, as if designed by the trembling or careless hand of a child, clearly outlined against the blue. It was as if a melancholy-mad tenant who ought to have been kept locked in the topmost chamber of his house had burst through the roof and lifted himself up to the gaze of the world. (C, 12)

In the rhetorics of appearance, definition, and now madness surfacing in the series of analogies joining the village, the Castle, and K.'s point of origin, it becomes evident that their imaging is reciprocal, that they are mutually referential. The conclusion (Abschluss) reached by the tower is both architectural and rhetorical. From the viewpoint of its flattening indifference, the Castle's architectural assertion of eminence becomes an image of madness or infantile unreality. Madness thus arises as an effect of a metaphysical dispute, the opposition between hierarchical differentiation and indifference as possible primordial conditions.

Perhaps the most enigmatic paradox of *The Castle* is that the powers imputed to the Castle, making it a superior and exclusive realm, do not prevent the border separating it from the village from being penetrated almost at will, as the quite tangible intercourse between the officials and villagers most concretely attests. Conversely, the manifold penetrations of the border do not weaken the belief, on both sides, in its efficacy and the prevalence of the ontological and normative categories for which it serves as a point of reference. K.'s doubled *Blick* into the Castle encompasses the contradictory thrusts of this paradox and thus prefigures the overall movements of the novel.

The landlady is a character of surprising importance because she is the most vigorous and comprehensive exponent of the metaphysics of hierarchical differentiation in the novel. She contends that it is fruitless for K. to seek an unmediated confrontation with Klamm and that Klamm will never relinquish his hold on Frieda.[3] The most eloquent proof of the functioning of the ontological order that she implicitly propounds is the scene where K. lies in wait for Klamm in the *Herrenhof* courtyard (C, 132–39). K.'s presence here is literally the condition for Klamm's absence and vice versa. The world order represented most comprehensively by the landlady is indeed of great consequence throughout the novel. It provides the difference whose traversing is the motive for all yearning in the novel. This yearning assumes many forms: K.'s desire for acceptance, the anticipation of their womanhood by Barnabas's sisters, and the family's subsequent hope for reconciliation with the community.

The structures clearly defined by this metaphysics undergo, however, the same process of flattening, interlocking, impacting, and reversal prefigured in the second glimpse of the Castle. Initially impervious to the hierarchy assumed by the villagers, K. will submit himself to its pronouncements more fanatically than them all, once he is drawn into his own affairs. At first cast in the role of the victim of a bureaucratic indifference and inefficiency thwarting his desires, K. comes to learn that he has figured centrally in the aspirations of others and that he has failed them.

Like the buildings in the second description of the Castle, the fates of the central characters interlock. In amazement K. learns how the effort on the part of Barnabas's family to regain grace hinges upon his own striving for inclusion. Olga's recounting of the family's recent history is itself an extended digression inserted into the story of K.'s quest, a gloss upon his prior experience at the same time confusing its apparent direction. Such coincidences do not negate but rather set the stage for the temporal lags, misplacements, and forgettings recurring throughout the novel. K.'s initial calling results from a misplaced directive and a failure in the Castle bureaucracy's corrective apparatus, even though, as the Mayor explains, "There are only Control authorities" (C, 84). Such malfunctions are as necessary to the hierarchical orders operating in the novel as the decisions that they supposedly resolve.

The image of the Castle is the model for a doubled epistemology, whose mutually disqualifying moments serve each other as the limit of efficacy. Through the ongoing vacillation between innocence and desperation, in the clarity of definition belied by the novel's temporal and spatial disjunctions and by its ratios of interdependence, the reader is afforded not only a view of an image upon which a novel hinges but, far more, an insight into the dimensions of metaphor itself. Of its age and beyond it, the novel anticipates the vicissitudes of structuralism in twentieth-century theory and art. The image informed thoroughly by its own metaphoric conditions is no less intensely aware of its in-built potentials for dismantling. As richly structured as it is, then, *The Castle* and its talisman peer beyond themselves toward a radical indifference.

The image of the Castle is built between the extremities of an impossible yearning and a remorseless despair. The picture of Amalia in the first bloom of sexuality, resplendent in lace and borrowed jewelry, on the occasion of the dedication of a new fire pump, a prelapsarian festival where the village and Castle are for once joined (*C*, 244–49), may be the most poignant image of innocence in all of Kafka's fiction. There is no room for such a scenario in *The Trial*, nor for the pranks and bungling of the assistants, for that novel traces a remorseless trajectory, the discomposition of an everyday existence as it is penetrated and violated by the textuality of the legal code. Though *The Castle* emerges as perhaps a more uneven and fragmentary work, it is, nevertheless, more ambitious and rewarding, for in it Kafka reaches toward the moment of innocence that is as essential to the textual theater as violence. The innocence is at once a malfunction within the textual machinery and the basis for its continuity.

The naïveté of K.'s early declaration, "I like to be my own master [*ich will immer frei sein*]" (*C*, 9), is quickly forgotten in his first confrontation with the innkeeper's wife, Gardena, whose name itself suggests the primal purity of Eden. In these encounters K. appears as a demystifier, the leveler of a preestablished and unquestioned hierarchy. One of the novel's few reminiscences of K.'s prior life suggests that this role is not alien to him: "At home they called him 'the bitter herb' on account of his healing powers" (190). Having literally fallen upon Frieda, K. seeks to apply his medicinal power to her, to extricate her from her past by establishing contact with her prior lover, the Castle's chief administrator for the village, Klamm. It is indicative of K.'s initial role as a negator of imputed differences that the desire with which he confronts Gardena is not so much to converse with Klamm as to stand opposite him, to be physically on the same plane.

> Lots of things may come up in the course of talking, but still the most important thing for me is to be confronted with him [*dass ich ihm gegenüberstehe*]. You see I haven't yet spoken with a real official. That seems to be more difficult to manage than I had thought. But now I'm put under the obligation of speaking to him as a private person, and that, in my opinion, is much easier to bring about. (*C*, 112)

K.'s desire for immediate contact with Klamm is in direct conflict with Gardena's presupposition that Klamm's only links to the village are like language, representational and referential. Klamm can be reached only through an established ritual of protocols mediated by his representatives in the village. The act by which Amalia reverses her family's fortunes will be described as an insult to the messenger (*C*, 264), injury to Klamm through one of his delegates. Allied with one of these, the village secretary, Momus (whose name, after the Greek god of mockery, suggests both mimicry and superiority), Gardena attempts to persuade K. to help in the completion of an administrative questionnaire, but K., angered that the document will not necessarily reach Klamm's eyes, refuses. Gardena: "But consider that Klamm appointed him [Momus], that he acts in Klamm's name, that what he does, even if it never reaches Klamm, has yet Klamm's assent in advance. And how can anything have Klamm's assent that isn't filled by this spirit?" (150–51). K.'s refusal to acknowledge a difference between the Castle and the village involves his rejection of the mediations between them, which, as described in the passage above, operate according to principles of representation, substitution, and reference. K.'s initial iconoclasm consists in a rejection of the surrogate presented as an instrument of Klamm's spirit.

That an elaborate medium of communication between the Castle and village exists is attested by the Mayor's description of the Castle telephone system (*C*, 93–94). The term repeatedly applied to this communication is *Verkehr*, an apt nomenclature, connoting commerce in all its gradations from the skin trade to administrative business.[4] Though the communicative system joining the Castle to the village may be referential, it is not at all necessarily exact. According to the Mayor, what the villagers hear as a dial tone is actually the Castle's communications, speeded up to an incomprehensible velocity. Similarly, the number of intermediary operators with whom one must be connected in order to reach one's party makes it impossible to ascertain whether the desired connection has been made or to whom one is speaking. K.'s skepticism regarding this medium of communication is borne out by a letter from Klamm (154), in which he is lauded for his work as Land-Surveyor when he has been forced to accept a position as a school custodian. As K.'s experience in the village teaches him, however, the fallibility built into this network does not imply its dispensability.

Not incompatible with the necessary but imperfect communication between the Castle and village is Frieda's belief in a silent, unknowable, and remote Klamm.

A man like Klamm is to talk with you. It vexed me to hear that Frieda let you look through the peephole. . . . But just tell me, how did you have the face to look at Klamm? You needn't answer. . . .

You're not even capable of seeing Klamm as he really is. . . . Klamm is to talk to you, and yet Klamm doesn't talk even to people from the village, never yet has he spoken a word himself to anyone in the village. (*C*, 64)

The dogma of Klamm's inaccessibility is reinforced elsewhere in the novel (44, 88) by the curious belief implanted in the villagers that the extreme sensitivity of the Castle organization and officials makes direct contact with an outsider such as K. impossible.

As described in the passages above, Klamm's superiority consists in his ability to maintain silence, to abstain from the *Verkehr* of language that joins, however imperfectly, the Castle and village. Klamm is akin to the deity of Judaism not merely in his silence.[5] His name functions as a talisman that Frieda can invoke in herding the servants from the *Herrenhof* (*C*, 52) and that Gardena (paralleling the strictures of Jewish law with regard to the utterance of God's authentic name) will forbid K. from pronouncing (111). Even while protesting the excess of Klamm's influence in the village and upon Gardena's life, K. acknowledges that Klamm functions as an encompassing reference, a point of origin to which all her vicissitudes may be ascribed (109).

The awesome and unattainable power attributed by Gardena to Klamm did not, however, prevent her from serving as his mistress. It is indeed a measure of his power that he could penetrate the most intimate tissues of the villagers' existence while never breaking the silence that is a function of his remoteness. The maintenance of a distance that is not negated by entrance into the most familiar realms of everyday life has much in common with the exclusive but personal deity of Judaism. In the absence of any personal intercourse with Klamm, Gardena has preserved three icons of their relationship: a photograph, a wrap, and a nightcap. Because her memory of the relationship consists of things, Gardena can invest it with values that, like any personal intimacy, were lacking in the affair itself. Hence she speculates that her own liaison with Klamm, having produced three signs, was more meaningful than Frieda's even if briefer and twenty year in the past (*C*, 102). K. finds the preciousness with which Gardena endows these objects incomprehensible; this bewilderment is one of the novel's paradigmatic ironies and exemplifies the frequent play between interiority and exteriority.

From a different point of view, however, even at this stage K.'s demand for a direct confrontation with Klamm may not be as iconoclastic as it seems. It implies a belief in the possible immanence of a transcendent and therefore absent entity. However simple Gardena's faith may seem, she has managed to relinquish the hope of immediate contact with her master, of being in his presence. Her fidelity is modified and sophisticated by her separation in time and place. Her original contact with Klamm is so remote that it might have been imaginary. K.'s refusal to accept Klamm's absence is tantamount to repressing the necessity and problematical nature of language in communication.

As the novel develops, the simple configuration linking K. to the villagers, in which they are subservient to the hierarchical order while K. penetrates their myths, undergoes a telling revision. K.'s critical detachment from the world order subsuming the villagers degenerates into a subservience more pronounced than the orthodoxy of any insider. Gardena's mockery of K.'s ignorance ("never forget that you're the most ignorant person in the village" [C, 72]) and her accusation that he intentionally falsifies information in order to advance his schemes (148) at first appear gratuitous and spiteful, but these observations are revealed to contain some truth. That K. is not above fabrication to gain advantages is apparent from the beginning, where he claims to have nonexistent assistants (9), rebukes Arthur and Jeremias for forgetting nonexistent equipment (24), and pretends, over the Castle telephone, to be one of the "old assistants" (27–28). In the course of his encounter with Gardena, the Mayor, and the teacher, K. begins to lose the detachment and humor permitting such inventions. Shortly before the narrative interlude signaling the end of their relationship, Frieda complains that K. has begun to take his aspirations seriously, that his prior hopelessness was preferable to his present ambition (202–3). This confirmation of Gardena's point of view will be echoed by Jeremias, who, once a liberated man, declares that K.'s outstanding failure as a master was his inability to accept the assistants' playfulness good-naturedly (302–3). The full extent of K.'s devolution from critical detachment to naïveté is apparent in his lack of sympathy for Barnabas's quest for certification. By the time this exasperating experience is related by Olga, K. takes the utterly simple-minded view that any contact with the Castle is ground enough for hope (240).

A turning point in the reversal through which K.'s critical distance dissolves and Gardena's orthodoxy proves to be more penetrating than was at first apparent occurs at the moment when K. refuses to be interviewed by Momus.

The landlady's threats did not daunt K.; of the hopes with which she tried to catch him he was weary. Klamm was far away. Once the landlady had compared Klamm to an eagle, and that had seemed absurd in K.'s eyes, but it did not seem absurd now; he thought of Klamm's remoteness [*Ferne*], of his impregnable dwelling, of his silence [*Stummheit*], broken perhaps only by cries such as K. had never yet heard, of his downward-pressing gaze [*Blick*], which could never be proved or disproved, of his wheelings [*Kreisen*], which could never be disturbed by anything that K. did down below, which far above he followed at the behest of incomprehensible laws [*Gesetzen*] and which only for instants were visible — all these things Klamm and the eagle had in common. (*C*, 151)

This passage begins with a reference to a prior comparison made by Gardena (72) in which Klamm appears as the eagle rightfully prevailing over Frieda and K. appears as the snake in the grass who has stolen her away. Now K. begins to understand the logic behind the comparison, which, like that between the Castle's two appearances, forms an impenetrable divide between two realms at the same time that it unites them. Woven together in this passage are five of the novel's most important images for the limit that articulates difference and yet preconditions the contiguity effected by comparison: distance (*Ferne*), silence (here *Stummheit*, usually *Schweigen*), the gaze (*Blick*), the circle (*Kreise*), and the law (*Gesetze*). The concurrence of these images coincides with K.'s resignation to the impossibility of standing face-to-face with Klamm, with the abdication of his quest for contact with an ontological realm whose difference from his own he now begins to acknowledge. That the limit figured in five different ways in this passage occasions an abandonment of K.'s hopes suggests that he, not Gardena, is being shaken from a state of metaphysical innocence.

Like the image of the Castle itself, the five images of limit are paradoxical; they each sustain inclusive and exclusive movements. Remoteness and silence, as I have already suggested, do not negate the intimacy of the areas to which the power of Klamm and the Castle extends. The notion of *Blick*, while serving as the fundamental mode of contact, at the same time establishes superiority of position. The image of the circle is just as paradoxical, for it serves both as the sealed perimeter of (*societal*) exclusion and as the circuit of renewal underlying the novel's recurrences. The neighbors form a circle around Barnabas's father as they strip him of his diploma of service as a volunteer fireman, in an act bespeaking the pettiness of village anti-Semitism (*C*, 263–65).[6] As the Mayor explains, K.'s arrival in itself initiates the reopening of a controversy assumed many years before and with great relief to be finally terminated. The power struggle stemmed from the debate over the necessity of summoning a new Land-Surveyor. Like the final scrap of paper remaining in the hands of the *Herrenhof* mail distributors, K. is himself a remnant from a prior drama already played out, but he is also the impetus for the conflict at hand. "And now imagine to yourself, Land-Surveyor, my dismay when after the fortunate end of the whole business—and since then, too, a great deal of time had passed by—suddenly you appear and it begins to look as if the whole thing must begin all over again. You'll understand, of course, that I'm firmly resolved, so far as I'm concerned, not to let that happen in any case?" (90). In this sense the narrative is itself only the postponed reprisal of a history already ended, one further turn around a circle leading to the realization of already familiar limits. *Gesetze* join the catalogue of limits coinciding with K.'s resignation because a textual body of laws and customs stands behind Gardena and Momus's explanation of why K.'s wish to confront Klamm cannot be granted (62–66). These laws may not be consistent, as Olga's reference to the fickleness of official decisions suggests (227), but they do assert power.

These five images join at the moment when K.'s innocence is lost, just at the moment when it is first revealed. By now this innocence is hardly distinguishable from critical penetration. Thereafter, K. confirms the accusations by Gardena and Frieda of obsequiousness and opportunism.

The debate between K. and Gardena, whose part is later taken up by Frieda, serves as a model for the play between the naïve and critical versions of metaphysics negating each other in the course of the novel. This play is enriched by the fact that the conflicting positions not only supplant one another but reverse themselves.

The duplicity of the categories established by the confrontation between K. and Gardena extends to the novel's other outstanding moments of innocence and desperation as well. The father's face "as he gazed through the open window at the sky . . . [is] young and shining with hope" (*C*, 261) just before he hears of Amalia's destruction of Sortini's obscene letter, the beginning of the family's misfortune. Had the family been able to maintain the appearance that nothing had happened, the deviance comprised by Amalia's resistance might have been prevented. The pardon for which the father squanders the family's few resources and relinquishes his physical and emotional strength is absolution from a sin that cannot be exactly determined. Like the burden of original sin, the offense committed by Amalia does not have a direct bearing on the present. The father nevertheless begins a futile quest for absolution hardly alien to the personal trial of the soul in Judeo-Christian theology: "What was it that he wanted? What had been done to him? What did he want to be forgiven for? When and by whom has so much as a finger been raised against him in the Castle?" (274). The narrative verges on melodrama as it describes his winter vigil by a fence (*Gitter*, a universal figure for exclusion in Kafka's writing) on a road leading to the Castle.[7] Such efforts in the wake of a not even fully explicable exclusion are motivated by an anticipation that becomes, paradoxically, more rather than less naïve. Though Amalia functions at the level of a moral absolute and insists that there be no communication between the family and the Castle or village, the other family members cannot exist entirely in the absence of hope for redemption. The most peculiar aspect of this irresistible moment of hope is that the further it recedes, the more obstinate becomes the belief in it: "And Father, instead of growing skeptical, only became more and more credulous" (276).

In the end, the novel's scenario of metaphysical innocence being supplanted by critical penetration becomes an endless and demonic process. The detachment that seems to challenge subjection to preestablished hierarchies becomes hardly distinguishable from blindness, and acquiescence becomes hardly distinguishable from an honest acknowledgment of limit. The moment of innocence necessary for the staging of the drama has been produced by the hierarchical order as an inevitable lapse in its own precision. The innocence that has also placed the order fundamentally in question will be ravished by the next assertion of its power. Yearning, in *The Castle*, is perhaps the most poignant and pervasive form of innocence, but yearning has been created as a consumer demand by a hierarchy that sustains paradox at the same time that it wields its power. This is the context for the freedom that becomes as meaningless as K.'s battle to gain it has been desperate, the context for a waiting that yields a dubious invulnerability.

> It seemed to K. as if at last those people had broken off all relations with him, and as if now in reality he were freer than he had ever been, and at liberty to wait here in this place, usually forbidden to him, as long as he desired, and had won a freedom such as hardly anybody else had ever succeeded in winning, and as if nobody could dare to touch him or drive him away, or even speak to him; but—this conviction was at least equally strong—as if at the same time there was nothing more senseless, nothing more hopeless, than this freedom, this waiting, this inviolability. (*C*, 139)

If Kafka's conception of the novel as a narrative form were to parallel the intercourse linking the Castle and village, the novel would be a necessarily representational communication whose signifiers are, however, woefully inadequate. It would be a context whose intelligibility depends upon the arrangement of certain coincidences or similarities that are at the same time disjunctions and upon the establishment of certain distinctions that become, through accident and repetition, hopelessly confused. Indeed, the machinery that *The Castle* seems to analyze and question most penetratingly is its own. This is evidenced by the repeated application of categories of similarity and difference to the narrative and by the conspicuous instances of mislocation, confusion between near-identicals (for example, Sordini-Sortini), and the failure to apprehend coincidences.[8] As the official Bürgel explains to K. that in intruding upon the wrong official at the wrong time and in an area forbidden him, K. has stumbled upon just the strategy to further his cause best (*C*, 332–52), the novel furnishes itself with a simultaneous running commentary on its movements and dimensions that is as large as and hardly distinguishable from itself. Like K. listening to Bürgel, however, the reader is asleep, hence oblivious to this hidden double of the text, for it has taken all the reader's energy to keep up with the story. Of all the discrepancies unleashed within the novel by Kafka, simultaneity and identity are the most disruptive.

Like the Mayor's description of the Castle bureaucracy—"It's a working principle of the head bureau that the very possibility of error must be ruled out of account. This ground principle is justified by the consummate organization of the whole authority, and it is necessary if the maximum speed in transacting business is to be attained" (*C*, 84)—the text of the novel is a virtually flawless organization, touching off an unlimited set of sympathetic reverberations between its events and characters. The only mistake allowed by this machinery[9] ("your case would remain one of the slightest" [86]) is the very lapse that propels narration itself, the misplaced directive that, by bringing K. to the village, is the occasion for inscription. Characteristically, this mistake is a mistake in reference. The village's negative reply to the Castle's inquiry as to whether a new Land-Surveyor should be summoned finds its way to Department B instead of Department A. "Meanwhile Department A was waiting for our answer; they had of course, made a memorandum of the case, but as, excusably enough, often happens and is bound to happen even under the most efficient handling, our correspondent [*Referent*] trusted to the fact that we would answer him, after which he would either summon the Land-Surveyor or else, if need be, write us further about the matter. As a result he never thought of referring to his memorandum, and the whole thing fell into oblivion" [81]). It should not pass unnoticed that the mistake in the organization's referential function immediately occasions a lapse in more psychological terms, for forgetting is one of the predominant figures for the spatial and temporal disruption through which this "original" lapse is recalled throughout the narrative. These moments of disjunction, however, in no way derange the perfect system of reference that the novel also constitutes. At the same time, the novel cannot be read in obliviousness to the fact that it is, both in entirety and in innumerable specific instances, a mistake.

In serving as the medium for the discernment of the similarities and differences it puts into play, the novel comes closest to realizing the figurative potential of the Castle. Like the image of the Castle, figurative language undermines its assertions of reference and identity while presupposing the necessity of their possibility. I have already observed, on metaphysical and ontological levels, how the very images (such as remoteness and silence) by means of which the Castle asserts its superiority over the village are responsible for dissolving this assertion within a plane of indifference. In the same way that it is impossible to extract consistent metaphysical postures from the characters' attitudes, it is impossible to define the Castle's rhetorical function exclusively either in terms of establishing cohesions or of marking disjunctions. The image of the Castle remains enigmatic because, like figurative language, it occasions a wide variety of linguistic usages and misuses, so wide that the Castle participates in mutually negating rhetorical functions. Thus the image of the Castle resists characterization by any single trope or movement. Rather, at all levels of its rhetorical functioning, whether as the basis of analogies or as the agent of the admittedly more disjunctive operations of metonymy, synecdoche, and metalepsis, the image of the Castle encompasses the double action of inclusion and exclusion. As the surveyor of the Castle, K. finds himself unwittingly cast in the role of an apprentice in the science of rhetoric. The time and space he will discover to surround the Castle as a rhetorical figure will be infinitely more complex and enigmatic than the commonplace spatial and temporal preconceptions that he imports from the outside world, preconceptions marked by a Euclidean symmetry and consistency.

That the novel itself serves as the medium for the discernment of the analogies and disjunctions it puts into play is apparent from the beginning. K. himself enforces the novel's analogical function, declaring his assistants "as like as two snakes" (C, 24) and subjecting them to an absurd synecdochical reduction by referring to both as Arthur. This devaluation is itself analogous to K.'s treatment by the authorities and villagers. In the chain of command beginning with Count Westwest, passing through Klamm, Momus, the Mayor, and the teacher, and extending beyond K. to Barnabas and the assistants, relationships in the novel mirror one another. K.'s treatment of his assistants is always analogous to his harassment from above (particularly by his immediate superior, the teacher). The final picture of the assistants clinging to a railing near the school in freezing weather so as not to be uprooted from their place in the social order by K. is an image of K.'s own clinging to a closed society.

The novel's intricate system of ratios and correspondences finds its fullest measure in the novel-within-a-novel provided by Olga's extended narration of her family's recent history. This narrative, segmented into titled chapters, is indeed a counternovel that bears heavily on the text as a whole while being framed by it. Having completed its digressive course, the narrative explains how K. and Barnabas's family came to be cohorts in exteriority. The causes and nature of their exclusion, as well as their hopes and efforts to bring about reconciliation, are shown to be parallel in many respects. Long before the entire family has been introduced, this parallelism is prefigured by K.'s uncanny affinity for Barnabas. "His face was clear and frank, his eyes larger than ordinary. His smile was unusually joyous [aufmunternd]" (C, 29). "Barnabas was about the same height as K." (35).

As the Mayor explains (C, 77), there is no position for K. because there is no place for his evaluative or critical function as a Land-Surveyor within the purely practical economy of the village. The family, on the other hand, has been ostracized because Amalia denied the wish of a Castle official, an act reflecting the same hierarchy-leveling defiance manifested by K. to Gardena in his insistence on confronting Klamm. Barnabas's later struggle for acceptance into the Castle service strikingly confirms K.'s early experience with the bureaucracy. And Olga's descriptions of the seemingly endless waiting endured by Barnabas during his first two years of service (226–42) and of his ambiguous status as one of the unofficial Castle personnel (287–89) are hardly unfamiliar to K. Deliberations with such intermediaries as the Mayor and the teacher have effectively separated him from Klamm; his makeshift position as a school custodian, neither confirming nor denying his acceptance into the service, is only the shakiest of power bases from which to press his claim. In addition, the fundamental problem of locating and identifying Klamm is as exasperating for Barnabas as it has been for K. The most agonizing of the doubts tormenting Barnabas in the indefiniteness of his position is "whether it's really Klamm he speaks to or not" (231), an uncertainty rendered hopeless by the hodgepodge of conflicting reports making up Klamm's composite image. Not only is Klamm described differently according to varying reports, but he is rumored to appear differently in different situations.

Because of the ambiguities surrounding Klamm's appearance and identity, Barnabas's dealings in the Castle are exclusively with a class of mediators, the scribes; in similar fashion, K. has been distanced from Klamm by the telephone, Barnabas, the Mayor, the teacher, and Momus. These scribes switch places while the texts that they consult and write stay put; they write out the activity of the realm even when the dictation they take is inaudible, when it is impossible to determine if there exists an original voice behind the script (C, 233). The image of Klamm, absent in mind if not in physical presence, inert while the scribes order the business of the day, presents the reader with a solution to the enigma tormenting K. in his initial quest. Klamm cannot be met because he embodies the condition of absence itself. In the place of his nonpresence there is only writing: Barnabas reaches only the scribes and their script.

Just as K.'s critical detachment degenerates into simplemindedness and obsequiousness, Olga, Barnabas, and the father betray Amalia's demand for silence and launch a series of schemes to rectify their relation to the Castle and reintegrate themselves into the community. The family's improbable schemes become the wishful fantasies of the oppressed, tantamount to the superstitions and signs in which the defendants of The Trial claim to read their fates. The futile efforts of the Barnabas family parallel the inflated hopes that K. invests in his few, tenuous contacts, his association with Barnabas and a fancied alliance with the Brunswick family through Hans.

That Olga realizes her hope when the half-serious suggestion of one of her clients results in Barnabas gaining a foothold in the Castle is not a haphazard occurrence. A peculiar logic is written into the striving to which both K. and Barnabas's family subject themselves. The Castle and village, as images of each other, are joined by difference. The mutual referents may be free to exclude one another, but this does not give them the power of mutual obliteration. The hierarchy may yield no certainty, but neither does it definitively abolish.[10] This is the logic behind the Mayor's statement to K., "Nobody keeps you here, but that surely doesn't amount to throwing you out" (C, 96). The same principle is applied by K. when he establishes that he cannot be dismissed by the teacher because it was not the teacher who engaged his services (174). The indeterminacy confronted by both K. and Barnabas's family is thus consistent to the very end, an end withheld from any finality.

As Olga's narrative approaches the completion of its cycle, the analogies between K.'s experience in the village and the family's history appear to reach even into the future. K.'s arrival in the village and the assignment of Barnabas to relay his communications with the Castle signal the first certification of Barnabas's service, an articulation in the doubt that has disoriented the family since its excommunication, "the first signs of grace, questionable as they are, that our family has received for three years" (C, 296). An interlocking that began by K.'s hanging on the arms of Barnabas and Olga has run its course to the point where the family's fate is literally pending on K.'s own. K. has joined Barnabas as a figure for the untrained son who can forge ahead without stigma into the future. Having together completed the circle of exclusion described by Olga's narrative, the outcasts arrive at an equally inevitable moment of hope. It must not be forgotten, however, that the two letters serving as the foundation for the family's revived hope are also empty signs. Like the letter that a scribe writes in Klamm's name to praise K. for his surveying when he has never performed that function, these communications underline a malfunctioning in the system of reference between the realms.

Olga's entire narrative, in the parallels that it draws between the experience of K. and Barnabas's family, functions as an analogon to the text of the novel. However, in reenacting the novel's analogy-making function, this narrative cannot avoid also incorporating the tendencies toward disjunction and the effacement of structures that have formed K.'s experience in the village. Even at the beginning of the novel, the concern for establishing ratios of analogy and reciprocity is matched by an equally pervasive recording of differences. Beyond his initial shock of being in the village, K. begins to discern the differentiations, often minor ones, in what he sees. Approaching the *Herrenhof* with Olga for the first time, his logical point of contrast is *"Zur Brücke"*: "All the houses in the village resembled one another more or less, but still a few small differences were immediately apparent here; the front steps had a balustrade, and a fine lantern was fixed over the doorway" (C, 43). The discernment of discrepancies, thematically marked in these passages, will be repeated on a rhetorical level as the image of the Castle occasions metonymies and metalepses indicative of confusion within its spatial and temporal configurations.

In this sense, Olga's narrative also succeeds in differentiating itself from its context within the novel. For one, the retelling of the family's history furnishes the other side of the story implied, but never elaborated, in Gardena's and Frieda's pronounced displays of contempt whenever Barnabas and his sisters are mentioned (C, 70, 179). Olga's narrative also adds a dimension lacking in the preceding description of K.'s early encounters in the village and his quest for Klamm, namely the dimension of time. K.'s experience in the village is confined to one week (when Olga relates her history, he has been there closer to five days), hardly longer than an extended present. As a result of this temporal telescoping, the "differences in strength" that K. confronts are articulated primarily in spatial terms. In this sense the doubled view of the Castle at the beginning of the novel is paradigmatic of his experience. As opposed to this spatially constituted image, the narrative of the family's recent history, like the explanation of how K. came to be summoned, spans several years, long enough for its rises, falls, and reversals to be plotted on temporal coordinates. The story thus records the reversal of the sisters' status from slightly snobbish *Bürgermädchen* to objects of the entire village's contempt, the father's degeneration, in three years, from a fireman capable of carrying Galater from a smoking building (245) to an old man who cannot feed or clothe himself, and the rise of Brunswick from the father's employee to his employer (261). The historical element of Olga's narrative discloses the complementary matrix upon which the limits emerging from the novel's movements of inclusion and exclusion are to be charted.

Olga's history thus exists in a supplemental as well as an analogous relation to the remainder of the text. In its aftermath, there is an even greater disruption to the slowly retarding rhythm of events established prior to it in the novel. In the episodes describing K.'s visit with Bürgel and the distribution of mail in the *Herrenhof* hallway, an increasingly large and detailed body of narrative material is compressed into shorter and shorter units of time, unleashing a deluge of perceptions and observations that have the relentless continuity of K.'s sleeplessness. Coinciding with the blurring of temporal articulation in the course of the night, certain grammatical constraints within the narrative are lifted. The sentence abdicates its function as a grammatical unit, at times barely managing to end.

The Circle of Exclusion

Paragraph divisions become rarer and more haphazard. On the level of argumentation, Bürgel's discourse becomes increasingly permeated by parenthetical material.

The shock created by this final break in an already irregular rhythm of days and nights pacing the appropriation of events describes the breakdown of the novel's analogical framework. Spatially, this incoherence is effected by such movements as (1) the transformation of relations of remoteness into ones of contiguity; (2) the impacting or internalization of spatial boundaries; (3) the displacement, misplacement, and replacement of objects and characters; and (4) the failure to contain things to their customary spaces. The novel's temporal coordinates undergo derangement in the following ways: (1) confusions between the fictive past and the fictive future; (2) lags, forgettings, and anachronisms in the memories of the characters and in the operation of the Castle and village administrations; (3) the repetitions at the basis of the narrative's inscription and continuity; (4) the concurrence of simultaneous, but vastly differing, velocities of activity; and (5) the simultaneity with which the text comments on itself. These movements, registered upon the counterindexes of time and space, contribute to an essential context of disjunction that coincides with but does not negate or even compromise the highly efficacious system of reference pervading the novel.

I have already shown, on the basis of the paradigmatic description of the Castle at the beginning of the novel, how the Castle's remoteness does not negate its presence at hand, how the spatial zones it demarcates exist to be trespassed from both sides, and how the fundamentally spatial categories that it establishes are displaced when internalized by the villagers and applied to their own. In its capacity to transpose its boundaries, the space of the novel assumes the classical function of metaphors, the transporting of significance from one signifier to the next. Added to the confusion is the displacement that results from the novel's repeated instances of replacement. K. both supplants and is supplanted by three maids as the inhabitant of a shabby room in *"Zur Brücke."* Although the narrative focuses on K.'s relationship with Frieda, it develops that he is merely a way station between Klamm and Jeremias and that she will be succeeded as an object of interest by Amalia, Olga, and Pepi. Such supplantings eliminate any functional notion of spatial integrity in the novel. Significantly, the novel breaks off with the display of the *Herrenhof* landlady's countless interchangeable coverings (*C*, 411–12).

A certain irony is likewise effected whenever a perspective of temporal remoteness suddenly opens within the closed world comprised by the village and Castle, and we see the characters as mythological figures or biblical heroes. We see Frieda as the enchantress Circe herding Klamm's servants from the *Herrenhof* (*C*, 52) and Zeus's lightning crashing down from the tumbling columns of documents in Sordini's office (86). The trumpets blaring at the celebration where Sortini sets eyes on Amalia are the millennial horns of the archangel (247), and the stupefying "sweet Castle wine" dispensed at the festivities (248), like Klamm's cognac, is possessed of a power comparable to that of the god's nectar.

The instances of temporal reversal are closely related to this allusive function, as when past and future are inverted or juxtaposed (metalepsis). Such is the effect of the scene in which K. befriends and plots strategy with Hans Brunswick (*C*, 185–98), the son of the cobbler who originally clamored for the appointment of Land-Surveyor but now joins the general indifference toward K. Behind this scene lies the temporal paradox in K.'s alliance with a youngster who is in many respects his master. It cannot be coincidental that in the background of their meeting, forming a large portion of its subject, is the defection of Hans's mother from the Castle to the village and the sickliness that she suffers as a result of the village's poorer air. Although Hans initially consoles K. for the punishment he has received for not fulfilling his custodial duties, the subject of their conversation quickly shifts to how K. may rescue Hans's mother, by healing her, helping her flee the village, or merely by speaking with her, in the face of certain opposition by Brunswick. This Oedipal situation is an impacted version of K.'s robbing Klamm of Frieda. Significantly, then, in a scene in which K.'s machinations become intertwined with a patriarchy-toppling conspiracy—

> There was something imperious in his character, but it was so mingled with childish innocence that they submitted to it without resistance, half smilingly, half in earnest. . . . And now he had to tell about his mother; . . . it was clear now that he was only a child, out of whose mouth, it is true—especially in his questions—sometimes the voice of an energetic, far-seeing man seemed to speak; but then all at once, without transition, he was only a schoolboy again. (*C*, 186–87)

—Hans's foresight, mixed with his youthful ineptitudes, enables the future to be juxtaposed directly ("without transition") to the present.

Just as the narrative medium of the novel accommodates such shifts in time, Hans himself lives in his present and future at the same time. He is virtually an experimental model for the novel's metaleptic function. "And it was just this absurdly distant future and the glorious developments that were to lead up to it that attracted Hans; that was why he was willing to accept K. even in his present state. The peculiar childish-grown-up acuteness of this wish consisted in the fact that Hans looked on K. as on a younger brother whose future would reach farther than his own, the future of a very little boy" (C, 197). Hans is presented here as a prior version of K. That he can evaluate K.'s experiences before undergoing them demonstrates that his vision reaches further in time than K.'s immediate involvement permits. Prior and subsequent incarnations of K. thus stand side by side. This context of temporal paradox, in which the past and future exchange positions, and in which youth can therefore usurp the privilege of adulthood and vice versa, will be remarked in the premature aging brought upon Barnabas by taking responsibility for the family's sole remaining hope (293). Similarly, Amalia, the youngest of the siblings, assumes responsibility for the care of the parents, who have been in turn reduced to childishness by the traumas of ostracism and unanswered attempts at reconciliation. This is also the context for Jeremias's sudden maturation as a result of serving K.

Forgetting is another essential form of discontinuity confusing the novel's temporal coordinates. On one level, forgetting comprises a temporal counterpart to the instances of misplacement in the narrative. Something forgotten, like the misplaced document so integral to the occasion for the novel's inscription, has the capacity to crop up at an unexpected moment and divert the course of events. It is in this sense that the failure to receive a response from the village with regard to the hiring of a new Land-Surveyor causes the official in Department A handling the matter to forget it entirely. The delay of many years that this act occasions in the functioning of the Castle bureaucracy, the extraordinary slowness with which the machinery is capable of responding to its own malfunctioning, is yet another form of derangement infused into the novel's temporal framework.

A final form of temporal disjunction posed by the narrative in opposition to its internal network of similarities and correspondences is the staging of simultaneous activities occurring at such widely disparate velocities that they render each other absurd, if not unintelligible. A masterstroke of such disorientation is to be found in the middle of K.'s first visit to the Barnabas household, after it has taken all his energy to keep up with Barnabas's smart pace:

His [Barnabas's] surroundings not only corroborated all this, but even emphasized it, the old, gouty father who progressed more by

The Dissolution of Structure in Kafka's *Castle*

the help of his groping hands than by the slow movements of his stiff legs, and the mother with her hands folded on her bosom, who was equally incapable of any but the smallest steps because of her stoutness. Both of them, father and mother, had been advancing from their corner toward K. ever since he had come in, and were still a long way off. (*C*, 40–41)

Equally disconcerting is the discrepancy between Castle time and the time scheme of the outside world. As has already been noted, the hum on the Castle telephones is really the Castle's communications, accelerated to the necessary speed to accommodate their quantity. The days in the Castle's realm also pass with astounding speed, as K. notes during his first day there (23). They are the abbreviated days of the unvarying, almost year-long winter described by Pepi at the end of the novel (407–8). The novel thus does not merely shift randomly back and forth between the past and future of its events and modify the pace at which the narrative, in its forward thrust, is appropriated, but it also accommodates a synchrony of activities that differ jarringly in their respective paces.

Two episodes in particular indicate that the novel's temporal and spatial discrepancies merge into one another to form a context of disjunction coexisting with the novel's operation as a system of reference. In the first of these the Mayor's attempt to provide documentary proof of the mistake that resulted in K.'s calling (in the form of the initial ordinance permitting the village to hire a Land-Surveyor) is interspersed with his explanation of why K. cannot occupy his rightful position if he is to remain within the village (*C*, 76–91). Just as the Mayor's explanation hinges on the misplaced response of the village to the Castle's ordinance, he now cannot locate the original ordinance itself. The search on the part of the Mayor's wife, Mizzi— later disastrously joined by the assistants—for the original text, the first cause of K.'s move to the village, is a high point in the novel's comedy. This quest is at the same time almost certainly a parodic and critical rendering of the account in which Victor Eremita explains how the countertexts comprising *Either/Or* came into his possession. In Kierkegaard, the surrogate editor, Eremita, relents to an obsessive desire to purchase an expensive secretary, because of both its prohibitive value and its superficial beauty.[11] The secretary produces its secret contents, the texts of *Either/Or*, only when Eremita, driven to desperation by the need to find money immediately, smashes it open with an ax.

Kafka must find this allegory of textual production excessively neat, despite the violence involved in penetrating the secretary.[12] The attempt to find the Castle's original ordinance has also been hopelessly retarded, and the cabinet in which the Mayor directs his wife to seek the document also yields its contents in an unmistakable form. "The cabinet was crammed full of papers. When it was opened two large packages of papers rolled out, tied in round bundles, as one usually finds firewood; the woman sprang back in alarm" (*C*, 78). In Kierkegaard's allegory, the discovery by which the text is produced or released from the repository of memory, individual or cultural, occurs accidentally. The process is already resolved when the text is at hand. Thereafter, Eremita has merely to finish the documents for publication. Kafka's version describes not so much the production of an undesired text as the nature of an unanticipated production. The quest never produces the desired document, but what it does yield signals only the beginning of the trouble. The search for the unique ur-text that has been misplaced touches off an unending deluge of writing: "The woman obediently threw them all out of the cabinet so as to reach those at the bottom. The papers now covered half the floor" (78). Propelled by a force far greater than the initial desire to locate a piece of it, the writing overflows the coordinates of spatial cohesion.

In this deluge, the attempt to locate "a document with the word 'Land-Surveyor' underlined in blue pencil" (*C*, 80) is absurd. For Kafka, the problem is not so much producing the writing as endowing it, as a phenomenon whose existence is a foregone conclusion, with cohesion and returning it to its dresser.

> Mizzi and the assistants, left so long unnoticed, had clearly not found the paper they were looking for, and had then tried to shut everything up again in the cabinet, but on account of the confusion and superabundance of papers had not succeeded. Then the assistants had hit upon the idea that they were carrying out now. They had laid the cabinet on its back on the floor, crammed all the documents in, then along with Mizzi had knelt on the cabinet door and were trying now in this way to get it shut.
>
> "So the paper hasn't been found," said the Mayor. "A pity, but you know the story [*Geschichte*] already; really we don't need the paper now." (*C*, 91)

A misplaced document has served as the occasion for the recounting of the history leading up to K.'s arrival in the village. K.'s arrival has in turn occasioned the reopening of a controversy long considered resolved. The novel, which records this cycle, begins as the repetition of a repetition. The misplaced document thus serves both as a mark of spatial incoherence and as the occasion for an anachronism. United by this sign, time and space merge into each other, forming a common context of disjunction. As the *Geschichte* substituting for the lost origin, the novel joins the deluge of writing that has taken the place of the first paper. The text-producing repository, like Kierkegaard's allegory, has been turned on its side, where its perhaps structurally weaker and less attractive parts show. The paper sought in this scene documents the metaphysical past of K.'s presence.

Near the end of the novel, the scene in which K. observes the *Herrenhof* mail distributors (*C*, 356–64) suggests what the metaphysical future of this original paper may be. These functionaries do not merely serve the Castle but are also readers of the text. Each room with which they effect an exchange of paper, collecting documents and leaving others in their place, is a different episode strung along a narrative figured as a corridor. The *Gang* or corridor that is the scene of this exchange also signifies process, a process both literally and metaphorically textual. Equal to their task, the distributors wend a fitful and discontinuous path through the too narrow hall, knowing at each juncture what strategy they must employ — cajoling, intimidation, or ruse — to effect this exchange. Perfectly coordinated, they orchestrate their individual efforts to the maximal speed and efficiency of their common task. Like the novel's own network of correspondences, or like the hypothetical critic who effects a perfect exchange with the text, meeting each one of its details with an apt explanation and compiling these explanations into a coordinated body, the distributors have incorporated a closed economy into their reading. But there remains the final, ineradicable scrap. It may even be the answer to all K.'s hopes and yearnings.

> Meanwhile the servant had finished his work; only one single file, actually only a little piece of paper, a leaf from a note-pad, was left in the little cart, through his helper's fault, and now they did not know whom to allot it to. "That might very well be my file," it flashed through K.'s mind. The Mayor had, after all, constantly spoken of this smallest of small cases. . . . And though here in the passage he would probably have delighted any occupant of a room by allotting this piece of paper to him, he decided otherwise, he was now sick and tired of distributing things; with his forefinger [*Zeigefinger*] on his lips he gave his companion a sign [*Zeichen*] to be silent, tore — K. was still far from having reached his side — the piece of paper into shreds and put the pieces into his pocket. It was probably the first irregularity that K. had seen in the working of the

administration here; admittedly it was possible that he had mis-
understood this too. And even if it was an irregularity, it was pardon-
able. (C, 362–63)

The irregularity, the single scrap that will not submit to the instrument of appropriation, is nonetheless dispatched by means of the
same referential system (*Zeigefinger* . . . *Zeichen*) according to
which the other documents are distributed and the novel functions.
The document (it is really a notation) now defies situation, not location. It may contain a projection of K.'s fate, not a documentation of
his origin. Though it stands at the other pole of K.'s metaphysical
horizon, however, the scrap remains the trace of a fundamental spatial incoherence. If not destroyed, it may well set the script once
again in motion, swept up in its temporality of delayed repetition.
The relentless recurrence resulting from the fundamental mark of
spatial incoherence, the scrap, is thus terminated only by an act that
shares the arbitrariness and finality of the misplacement that was at
its origin. As the potentiality of recurrence, the discomposing remnant is the sole moment of metaphysical innocence retained within
a self-negating textuality. Whether the remnant is obliterated or not
must remain a rhetorical question. Once again, the disorganization
of space merges into the disordering of time, for the impossibility of
placing the scrap and the compulsive ongoingness of the narrative
describe the same condition.

As allegories of textual production and appropriation, these two
episodes draw us back to what may be the novel's most subtle yet
devastating undercurrent of self-critique, Bürgel's account of the
Castle's bureaucratic operation. Bürgel's official function is that of a
liaison secretary (*Verbindungssekretär*), one who builds working
relations between Castle officials and those stationed in the village
(C, 335). In his commentary, he is also a maker of connections, for he
elaborates the coincidences between the course of events that has
brought K. to his room at that moment and the most effective strategies for plying the organization. "There is, however, nevertheless, in
spite of all precautionary measures, a way in which it is possible for
the applicants to exploit this nocturnal weakness of the secretaries.
. . . It consists in the applicant's coming unannounced in the middle
of the night" (343). The connections between K.'s actions and Bürgel's
hypothetical strategy are so direct and transparent that their fabrication passes almost unnoticed.[13] In light of K.'s subsequent experience and the ending to the novel "passed on" to us by Brod, Bürgel's
ultimate prophecy, that the hypothetical party "has to do nothing

but in some way or another put forward his plea, for which fulfill-ment is already waiting" (350), is pure fantasy, but the fictiveness is almost lost in the explanation's self-certainty. Bürgel's commentary is most duplicitous in its simultaneity and affirmativeness, for these qualities obscure its functioning as a Fata Morgana of wish fulfill-ment. The completeness of the fulfillment reflects the desperation of the wishing. Sheathed in this invisibility and virtually sure to be passed over by the eye of a reader lulled into exhaustion by a narra-tive increasingly lacking in pauses and other forms of articulation, the text holds its violence in reserve. Correspondence may thus be added to the list of disjunctions that accompany, contrapuntally, the novel's ratios and correspondences. This intricate system is joined to the context of spatial and temporal disjunction present throughout the novel by the simultaneity, correspondence, and utter violence of commentary.

THE GEOMETRICIAN OF METAPHOR AND THE
HISTORIAN OF METAPHYSICS

That K.'s formal job description reads "Landvermesser" (Land/ vermesser = geo/metrician) stresses the spatial dimension of the movements for which he serves as a sometimes penetrating some-times blind medium. And yet, the historicity introduced most con-cretely in the Mayor's account of K.'s calling and in Olga's narrative also makes K. a surveyor of events unfolded along the discontinuum of time. Ironically, that we view these movements through the fictive entity identified as K. is the ultimate repudiation of the Castle's denial of license to practice his profession. In this sense, K.'s ultimate victory has been assured from even before the narrative begins.

The image of the Castle has served throughout the novel as an occasion for the realization of the limits expressed in spatial incoher-ence and temporal discontinuity. As the geometrician of these lim-its, K.'s work has consisted in surveying the dimensions of the image itself, the dimensions of metaphor.[14] In their spatial manifestations, these limits are not difficult to conceptualize. It suffices to say that spatially the boundary around the Castle determines the novel's movements of both inclusion and exclusion.

In their temporal manifestations, the limits for which the image of the Castle serves as a watershed have much in common with the movements of rise and fall, hope and desperation, and perdition and redemption at the poles of Judeo-Christian history and Western metaphysics. But the novel inscribes an at times hilarious unpredictability into the succession of these moments and throws disorder into any continuum of progress, any movement toward a fixed horizon.

The title of this chapter, "The Circle of Exclusion," is inadequate and perhaps misleading. The spatial and temporal movements staged by the novel confine themselves neither to circularity nor to exclusion. By favoring exclusion, however, I have drawn attention to the discovery of limit that emerges from the metaphor when it is elaborated in cognizance of its theoretical conditions and flaws. In comparison to this general delimitation of metaphoric and structural possibilities, the particular limits unearthed in the novel, such as that K. must confine himself to the *Herrenhof* taproom, are most monumental. The text is itself aware of this distinction when it describes the barriers that Barnabas, in the anguish of waiting for certification, confronts.

> And you mustn't imagine that these barriers are a definite dividing-line; Barnabas is always impressing that on me. There are barriers even at the entrance to the rooms where he's admitted, so you see there are barriers he can pass, and they're just the same as the ones he's never yet passed, which looks as if one ought not to suppose that behind the ultimate barriers the offices are any different from those Barnabas has already seen. Only that's what we do suppose in moments of depression. And the doubt doesn't stop there, we can't keep it within bounds. (*C*, 228–29)

Here, there is no particular limit, only limits known and unknown, visible and invisible, past and future, here and elsewhere.

The image of the circle serves as a convenient if reductive shorthand for the geometry of metaphor, for the possibilities of structure and structuralism. That it serves as a closed perimeter of exclusion is to be witnessed in the epigraph of this chapter. "Man schloss uns aus jedem Kreise aus" ("They . . . cut us off from the community forever"–Olga, [*C*, 273]). The German *Ausschliessen* also means "to lock out." The Castle appears here in perhaps a truer light, not as the assertion of the hierarchical order but as a lock (*Schloss*), the instrument of closure. The figure of the circle is also endless, like the novel, and although the endlessness of the novel may be unintentional, it certainly does have an ample context within the movements of the narrative. This endlessness is occasioned by nothing more formidable than a missing scrap or notation, a leftover, what cannot be placed and retained within the novel's fictive alignments and artificial memory.

As I have tried to hint at several points in this chapter, the disjunctions disordering the temporal and spatial dimensions of the novel have been anticipated in the functions assigned to figurative language in the history of rhetoric. In surveying the image of the Castle, K. surveys the geometry of language. He discovers language to inhabit a time and space vastly more complex than the symmetrical space bestowed upon science by Euclid, the patron saint of all surveyors. The time and space discovered by K. are, precisely, the time and space of analogy, metonymy, synechdoche, and metalepsis. And the discovery of these functions proceeds at the expense of the criteria according to which everyday existence is judged: order, consistency, continuity.

Through the at times noble and at times oblivious medium of K., we discover that metaphysics, in its inborn aporias, opens dimensions of time and space only to record the derangement of their coordinates. The time and space in which this history is played out is the novel, the text.

CHAPTER FIVE

The Text That Was
Never a Story: Symmetry
and Disaster in Kafka's
"Country Doctor"

Although organized, perhaps, by an intense Oedipal pain, Kafka's "Country Doctor" never becomes what might be properly called a story. The results are so inconclusive, the characters so blurred, as to deny any pretense to narrative cohesion on the part of this brief work. Twice the peasants who receive the doctor's judgments break out into incantations that, like the music throughout Kafka's writing, exemplified by Josephine's piping, are refrains of fugitive and unfulfilled desire. The doctor may indeed be stripped and placed beside the ailing young patient as the chants exhort, but he is "only a doctor, only a doctor" (CS, 224). The peasant song lending the text the air of an anthropological encounter declares the limits of its own expectations, as well as those of the patient.

But for all its declared and dramatized inconclusiveness, the tale is a suggestive allegory of how texts configure themselves. There is no lack of structure here. The text begins and ends in the forbidding winter landscape to which an aging doctor no less harsh and forlorn has been summoned by his vastly inferior clients. The scenic and thematic symmetry of the two scenes comprising the narrative framework is duplicated within the dramatic core. The text dramatizes not one diagnostic scene but two. Only after an initially unsympathetic examination of the sick boy—on the basis of which he concludes that "the boy was quite sound, something a little wrong with his circulation, saturated with coffee by his solicitous mother, but sound" (CS, 222)—is the doctor persuaded to admit "that the boy might be ill after all" (223). A reexamination, which the doctor undertakes almost whimsically, "out of mischief or out of absence of mind" ("The Knock at the Manor Gate" [418]), reveals the extent and nature of the illness as it affects both patient and healer.

The narrative ends with the doctor sitting in the same coach that brought him to his appointment, no longer wearing his coat perhaps, but facing the same climatic and personal bleakness with which the text began. If anything, the framework and organization of the narrative suggest structure: mirrored endpoints bracketing a doubled scene. And this structural symmetry, at least on the level of the text's widest components, is well suited to the doubling that takes place between characters, and which will be discussed more fully below. "A Country Doctor" is not reticent to admit the place of structure within its own encoding and decoding. Structure, however, does not so much account for or determine the allegory of the text as support or facilitate it. As I shall show, associations of a far more shifting nature disclose the qualities of this text, but within the format that structure provides. The text gathers its resonance at the point where its structure embraces something other, something transformational and anomalous. And here as throughout Kafka's fiction, the image bonding structure to theme, but precluding the narrative cohesion of a story, is nothing more than a metaphor.

Already in the narrative's first episode appear the major structural and thematic elements that will serve as a setting for its metaphoric transformation. When Rose, the maid who will become the source and object of the doctor's anxiety throughout the text, offers her comment on the scene—"You never know what you're going to find in your own house" (CS, 220)—she touches on the narrative's key psychoanalytical and sociological concerns. The well-equipped and generally efficient Country Doctor—"I had a gig, a light gig with big wheels, exactly right for our country roads" (220)—is in a frustrated rage. He cannot begin a house call to a neighboring village because his horse has died the previous night "Muffled in furs, my bag of instruments in my hand, I was in the courtyard all ready for the journey" (220). The bleak weather in which he waits with impotent anger only reinforces the sense that he is a man without a horse, a man who has lost his horse, or his kingdom for a horse, a victim of his own horse: "but there was no horse to be had, no horse" (220).

The motif of psychological repression examined by this text is reinforced by the dreamlike quality of its movements and transitions. The doctor arrives at the remote hamlet he is visiting instantaneously: "I was already there" (CS, 221). Just as suddenly emerge the apparent solutions to his predicament from an abandoned pigsty on his property that he kicks open in his desperation: a man whose open, blue-eyed face is reminiscent of other servants in Kafka's fiction, notably Barnabas of *The Castle*; and two horses, whose steaming bodies and powerful buttocks contrast sharply with the doctor's present capabilities. The doctor is well conditioned to make optimal use of his unexpected man- and horsepower. He commands Rose to help the groom (*Knecht*) hitch the horses to his wagon (the groom has emerged from the pigsty ready to serve), and he threatens the *Knecht* with whipping when the latter's attentions inexorably turn to Rose. This pugnaciousness turns to anxious despair when it becomes clear to him that Rose is fated to serve the groom's sexual whims, that his own home is to be the setting for the vigorous sexuality figured in the splitting and bursting of the door. The tormenting vision of the groom's sexual victory over Rose and himself returns to the doctor throughout the text with the force of obsessional thought as Freud defined it.[1] Until the groom declares, "I'm not coming with you anyway, I'm staying with Rose" (221), the doctor has treated her indifferently as "the pretty girl who had lived in my house for years almost without my noticing her" (223). In many senses, then, the narrative's first scene may be said to investigate repression as it operates in psychoanalytical theory. Distinctly sexual beings emerge from a repository in the house, a long-abandoned hiding place. Late-Oedipal competition stimulates a previously stunted desire for the girl. The psychological locus of the pigsty is repression in the unconscious.

This first scene is reminiscent of another repression, the sociopolitical sort dramatized and subverted in the section of *Phenomenology of Spirit* that Hegel entitled "Lordship and Bondage."[2] The doctor is not oblivious to his bullying and threatening his *Knecht* despite the fact that the latter "was a stranger; that I did not know where he came from, and that of his own free will he was helping me out when everyone else had failed me" (*CS*, 221). The groom is described as the sibling of the two horses, which he calls *Bruder* and *Schwester*. The groom's conquest of Rose thus completes a series of substitutions set into play by the upheaval of the doctor's authority. The groom's displacement of the doctor sexually results in a deflection of the threatened whipping from the horses to the groom. The ultimate victim in this sequence of power mongering is Rose, but the narrative curiously does not pursue this result.

The quick reversal of the doctor's mastery over his servants signals an ambiguity in characterization. Why is the doctor's sudden attachment to Rose so violent? The contest over her may be between two distinct male characters or, as is the case at other points in Kafka's fiction, may represent a conflict within a single fictive subject, a conflict here between active heterosexual lust and repressive asexuality.

More than any other major writer, Kafka exploited for twentieth-century esthetics the ambiguity between the intra- and intersubjective representations of dramatic interaction.[3] Perhaps his most notable follower in this regard is the film director Ingmar Bergman, above all in *Persona*, but also elsewhere. In the context of the intertwining and reversal of roles that will prevail between the doctor and the sick boy, it is perhaps not unreasonable to suggest that the doctor and the *Knecht* also exist as doubles in relation to each other. The doctor's doubling is doubled: he merges with his servants and patients. Doubling in characterization coincides with the doubling already observed in the scenic construction. As a case, the Country Doctor dispenses double medicine, but doubling, as Freud applies it to Hoffmann's "Sandman," is the mark of the uncanny as well as of the familiar.[4] As in familial relations, it is sometimes difficult to ascertain where one identity begins and another ends in Kafka's fiction. This soft border between fictive subjects becomes a major issue in the doctor's interaction with the peasant family.

For indeed, having arrived instantaneously at his patient's peasant cottage (this immediacy questioning again the status of distance and scale in the narrative), the doctor remains secure in the superiority and authority that have just been battered by the groom's conquest. (Repression, in Kafka's fiction, is not limited to unstated events from the characters' earlier lives, situated in the margins of the text and relegated to uncertainty. Characters such as the Country Doctor and the creature of "The Burrow" are quite capable of forgetting actions and realizations that occur to them in the course of the text at hand.) In deference to the doctor, the patient's sister sets a chair out for his instruments and takes charge of his fur coat. No higher honor does the family pay the doctor than the precious glass of rum the father pours out for him.

Throughout Kafka's fiction, above all in "The Knock at the Manor Gate," siblings are implicated in one anothers' guilts and torments. The air in the Kafkan familial scene is stifling. Not only can the siblings exchange identities, but the horses get into the act as well, the same horses to which the groom referred as brother and sister: "each of them had stuck a head in at a window and, quite unmoved by the startled cries of the family, stood eyeing the patient" (*CS*, 222). Throughout "A Country Doctor," but especially in the family setting, identities merge, making totemic distinctions useless. The highly visible horses in this text, at play in every aspect of the Country Doctor's interaction with the family, belong to a unique category of characters in Kafka's fiction: the mute and reactive figures who do not add to the action but comment upon it with their silent ges-tures.[5] The horses' status as animals in no way impedes their serving this metacritical function. Their siblings in the world of Kafka's writ-ing include K.'s servants, Arthur and Jeremias, in *The Castle*, the astonished villagers in "The Knock at the Manor Gate," and the onlookers who witness Joseph K.'s arrest in *The Trial*. In the medium of the film, the horses' closest relative is Harpo Marx, whose routines both mimic and intensify the actions of his less reti-cent brothers.

And yet, just as the doctor's mastery is undermined in the opening scene by the groom's (or his own) vibrant sexuality, so too does his encounter with the sick boy dissolve his air of superiority, his clini-cal detachment, his complacency, and his indifference. Intellectu-ally, the doctor grasps the limits of his position when he thinks, "To write prescriptions is easy, but to come to an understanding with peo-ple is hard" (*CS*, 223), but this formulation is only the weakest form of the lesson that the boy teaches him. (In this statement, the doctor takes over the Kafkan aphoristic voice from the maid, who has observed the paradoxes of distance — but the ultimate destination of this clipped, ironic mode of utterance is the patient). The doctor, dur-ing his initial examination of the boy, vacillates between two pos-tures: contempt for the entire family, buttressed by a kind of self-aggrandizing rationalization; and a compulsive, morbid interest in Rose's current status.

> I am no world reformer and so I let him lie. I was the district doctor and did my duty to the uttermost, to the point where it became almost too much. I was badly paid and yet generous and helpful to the poor. I had still to see that Rose was all right, and then the boy might have his way and I wanted to die too. What was I doing there in that endless winter! My horse was dead, and not a single person in the village would lend me another. I had to get my team out of the pigsty; if they hadn't chanced to be horses I should have had to travel with swine. That was how it was. (*CS*, 222–23)

This passage intertwines the doctor's dual roles as aggressor and victim. Having conceded his lack of philanthropic interest, the doc-tor dramatizes his self-sacrifices to himself in the way that a mani-pulative parent would attempt to induce guilt in his or her family. The climate is terrible, the pay is not good, he constantly makes con-cessions to his patients. The humor in the passage is that of uncon-trollable self-indulgence. If I hadn't found horses to bring me here, suggests the doctor, pigs would have had to do. (This projection becomes even more maudlin when considered in light of the taboo against pork in the Jewish dietary code.) The doctor thus places himself in the role of a temporary paterfamilias, whose bad conscience spurs him on to increasingly outrageous assertions of benevolence. But the doctor's martyrdom would not be real unless he faced some immediate and dire threat. The loss of Rose is not only *like* death; it is death itself ("I wanted to die"). The *form*, if not nature, of the doctor's fear is hypochondriacal. Not a condition but the self-representation of a condition threatens him. It is no accident that he ends up beside his patient. Kafka does not allow the aggression in all this posturing, the bad faith, guilt mongering, and hypochondriacal cries (at least to the reader) for help to remain implicit: "And I nodded to the family. They knew nothing about it, and, had they known, would not have believed it" (*CS*, 223). The doctor protects his posturing by endowing it with the aura of superior knowledge.

Thus far, then, we have a story structured in a way favorable to its themes of jealousy, displacement, ambivalence, ambiguity of character, and social conflict. The most prominent themes in turn lend themselves to interpretation in terms of two readily available models of repression: the psychoanalytical, and the Hegelian undermining of mastery through the more direct relation to material (including words) in labor. And yet it is only when the doctor, casually and almost by chance, condescends to review his diagnosis, that the text crystallized an emblem for its own operation as a text. The text locates its image only as the practitioner concedes some small margin of error. And it is far from insignificant that the insignia that the text inscribes upon itself (as the instrument of punishment of "In the Penal Colony" writes its sentence on the human body) is the external manifestation of a disease.

> And this time I discovered that the boy was indeed ill. In his right side, near the hip, was an open wound as big as the palm of my hand. Rose-red, in many variations of shade, dark in the hollows, lighter at the edges, softly granulated, with irregular clots of blood, open as a surface mine to the daylight. That was how it looked from a distance. But on a closer inspection there was another complication. I could not help a low whistle of surprise. Worms, as thick and long as my little finger, themselves rose-red and blood-spotted as well, were wriggling from their fastness in the interior of the wound toward the light, with small white heads and many legs. Poor boy, you were past helping. I had discovered your great wound; this blossom in your side was destroying you. (*CS*, 223)

Unapparent during the initial examination, the wound opens itself like a hitherto undisclosed secret, like a groom hiding in a neglected part of one's estate, or the desire for a servant girl that has lain dormant under daily ceremony. The wound announces itself like a secret to the doctor who discovers it, and who, as a competent practitioner, examines it both at a distance and in proximity.

Although located on the flank of a local boy, the wound is a metaphor for the secrets that have been disclosed to the doctor about himself. The festering wound, embellished with twisting, parasitic worms, is an image of the doctor's own festering sexuality. These worms, for all the revulsion that they might inspire, consummate an intensity of narrative description rare in Kafka's work. Like certain of the tumors and growths encountered by practicing physicians, the boy's wound radiates with a peculiar beauty, in this case, the beauty of vividness.

The wound is a displaced image for the doctor's sexual conflicts. While its color, "Rose," causes some syntactical ambiguity by virtue of its placement at the head of a sentence, the choice of hue relates the wound to the doctor's apparent competition with the groom over Rose dramatized in the framework. Kafka underscores the incorporation of the source of desire into the wound; he places the inscription of desire as the wound's very nature, in relief. The wound is rosy. The doctor describes it explicitly as a flower in the boy's side. The bloody worms have white heads. They thrive on red fluid but are themselves consumptive. In different ways, the doctor and patient are both consumed.

The wound is the flower of desire. Desire, as in Proust, is a disease. The boy, because he is affected with the festering wound of the doctor's desire, is the doctor's unlikely double. The bystanders are thus not being provincial when they place the two in the same bed, when they connect the doctor to his disease by means of metonymic contiguity. An aging man and an adolescent boy share a longing-sickness. In "First Sorrow" the tears of the constrained trapeze artist flow over the cheeks of his manager.

In the course of the story, then, the doctor is twice doubled, first in relation to the surprising groom, and then with the sick boy. And the image of the wound is both the mark and the agent of this doubling. It is that which connects the doubled framework to the doubled scene of medical speculation. The wound takes Rose out of the narrative's external shell, where she appears as a semi-autonomous bone of contention, and internalizes her within a scene of subjective ambivalence. As Rose passes from exteriority to interiority, so too does the narrative as a linguistic wound fold upon and consume itself. This text structures a desire for the resolution between its outside and inside, between its structure and its material. And the binding that it offers for its conflicts is the image of a wound. But a wound is traumatized tissue; it is the locus where the body capitulates to rather than resists dismemberment.

By virtue of its bruised texture, "A Country Doctor" may be taken as an instance of that weak cohesion that characterizes a literary work. It demonstrates that what binds texts need not be as tangible as themes, as abstract as ideas, or as systematic as logical schemes. The somewhat crumbly coherence of this text is concentrated around the signifier *rose*, which functions simultaneously as the name of a character, the color of a wound, and the name and color of a flower. The character, wound, and color are depicted within the text's representational field, while the flower hovers beyond the textual margins as a metaphorical icon, insignia, caption, or shorthand for the narrative's "events." The boy's wound becomes allegorical of the text because of the shifting permitted, even solicited, by *rose*. *Rose* marks the spot, precisely, where the text's dramatic scenario, its structure, its semantics, and its thematic underpinnings intertwine. By closely implicating a persona, Rose, within the metaphoric economy of a text, Kafka comes as close to any author to admitting the semiological rather than substantive nature of fictive "characters." Characters do not so much exist (or even act) as play within an ultimately deranged exchange of positions demarcated by Hegel as the speculative limit of the notion of force. They gather and abandon meaning in texts as signifiers pursue chains of displacement in the Lacanian imaginary.[6]

The overdetermination of the role of *rose* within the text helps account for the pronounced duplicity of the characterization and thematics. The self-referentiality dramatized by this signifier also serves as a precedent for the allegory of parasitism. A consumptive boy devoured by consumptive worms is a narrative representation of a metaphor that can both consume and fragment itself.

The boy is indeed correct, then, when he asserts, "A fine wound is all I brought into the world; that was my sole endowment" (*CS*, 225). For this brief work as well as for the sick character, a wound comprises the total equipment and production. The wound in the work as well as in the boy constitutes the fissure in the Moebius strip describing the text's configuration. Crowned by a rose, the wound is the site where the text endlessly folds and feeds upon itself.

It is no accident, then, that any departure from this domain must be abrupt and arbitrary. If the narrative framework results in an unresolved conflict over a woman between the doctor and his double, then in the core of the text the doctor's link to his second double, the sick boy, is ultimately complicitous.

"Do you know," said a voice in my ear, "I have very little confidence in you. Why, you were only blown in here, you didn't come on your own feet. Instead of helping me, you're cramping me on my death-bed. What I'd like best is to scratch your eyes out." "Right," I said, "it is a shame. And yet I am a doctor. What am I to do? Believe me, it is not too easy for me either." "Am I supposed to be content with this apology?" . . . "My young friend," said I, "your mistake is: you have not had a wide enough view . . . and I tell you: your wound is not so bad. Done in a tight corner with two strokes of the ax. Many a one proffers his side and can hardly hear the ax in the forest, far less that it is coming nearer to him." "Is that really so, or are you deluding me in my fever?" "It is really so, take the word of honor of an official doctor." And he took it and lay still. (CS, 224–25)

As this consultation commences, the boy has no confidence in the doctor, and the latter shows no sign of deviating from his general contempt for the surroundings. By the end of the interchange, the practitioner has been roused out of his indifference and the patient is calm, reassured, and perhaps prepared for death. The motive for this double reversal of positions may well come from the potentials offered by the ax and its relation to the image of the wound. If the wound figures the ambiguous textual intertwining afforded by the movement of the shifter between structural, thematic, and semantic levels, the ax promises release from the uncertainty by the excision of the function that loosens while its binds. A wound is all the text brings into the world to hold itself together. And yet precisely as a function of textuality, the wound marks the side of repression, desire, and internal and external conflict. It delimits the extent of life with surgical precision.

At the end of "A Crossbreed [A Sport]" both the marginal kitten/lamb and the narrator, the son for whom the creature and its intellectual conditions are an inescapable legacy, eye the butcher's knife as a possible escape from their despair. The execution of Joseph K. in The Trial may be described as the application of a penetrating instrument to the victim after it has playfully shuttled back and forth between the henchmen. In "A Country Doctor," as well, a sharp blade holds out the promise of resolution and acquires the thrust of a poignant wish. A double blow of the ax in a tight corner can free the patient from his inherited mark of Cain. Only in conceptually offering this instrument does the Country Doctor serve as a healer. The prescribed treatment involves, however, not a regeneration of tissue but amputation. Two decisive strokes of an ax can release the prisoner from his double bind, can free him, perhaps, from the narrow path upon which Oedipus meets his father. The ax strikes outward, beyond the confines of a constricting familial space, but in order to complete its task strikes inward, penetrating the superficial layers of the flesh.

The image of the ax is the sum total of the Country Doctor's reassurance. The wound is not so severe (*übel*): done (*geschaffen*) "with two strokes of the ax," both dispatched and created by the healing/incising ax. The ax is a messiah (or avenging angel) of resolution. Those who offer their sides to it, in reverence, may not hear it in the forest, but eventually its work is done, silently and implicitly (*geschweige*). The silent ax in the forest recalls the falling tree whose status is so crucial to ontology and to the hypothetical status of God. The ax, were there only an ax, would clarify, resolve, amputate, the duplicity and ambiguity whose locus is language and whose form is that of a congenital wound. But the closure provided by the ax can still be described only in terms of inscription: incision, marking, scarring. The poignant wish for a termination of involution and complexity is expressed by several of Kafka's characters; it hovers at the horizon of a good part of his fiction. This end-wish or wish to end wishes can be articulated only in terms of writing and the textual economy that writing both promises and renders bankrupt. The ax is only one moment of the wound that is both the flower and disease of writing.

Merely the invocation of the ax is sufficient to release the patient from his tension. To terminate a text whose insignia assumes the form of a Moebius strip is, however, not so simple. The Country Doctor's exit from the narrative stage necessarily takes the form of a desperate escape. Only the fall of an ax can truncate this text. The doctor's return trip home begins as abruptly as his arrival at his patient's house "as if my patient's farmyard had opened out just before [*unmittelbar*] my courtyard gate, I was already there" (*CS*, 221). And although these movements are as sudden as the shifts of location that Freud finds characteristic of dreams, the doctor's concerns are hardly dreamlike. The narrative ends with the doctor helplessly reaching for his fur coat at the back of his gig. He remains naked, having been stripped by the peasants and placed in bed next to his patient. He despairs of ever reaching home, at the collapse of his medical practice and being usurped by a successor, and of course, at the sacrifice of Rose and the groom's successful rage. "Betrayed! Betrayed!" moans the doctor as the text ends, "A false alarm on the night bell once answered—it cannot be made good, not ever" (225). The betrayal that the Country Doctor suffers is systematic and not merely sexual. Events are simply out of control. The arbitrary truncation of this text is merely one further manifestation of the loss of control that it has embellished. The losses and concerns that the text dramatizes are not to be recuperated. Betrayal, like the lines of sorrow indelibly inscribed on the trapeze artist's forehead at the end of "First Sorrow," cannot be undone. The "false alarms" that will disturb the doctor's sleep forever are not only a false alarm but the tones of absence whose textual manifestation is the figure of a wound.

Related contrapuntally to the rhythm of the eruption and amputation of ambiguity that may in fact comprise this text's only story is the music that twice breaks forth from the peasants. Although the text provides some psychosocial context for this singing, the sudden outbreak of music at all in the text is possessed of a shock value that cannot be reduced or assimilated. The peasants' incantations shift the narrative's setting to a world of primitive, obsessive, and ritualistic thought.

A school choir with the teacher at the head of it stood before the house and sang these words [*auf den Text*] to an utterly simple tune:
"Strip his clothes off, then he'll heal us,
If he doesn't kill him dead!
Only a doctor, only a doctor." (*CS,* 224)

The phrase *auf den Text* signals the ambiguity of the song's relationship to the remainder of the text: the melody not only sets the indicated lyrics to music but is inscribed *on* or *over* Kafka's writing. The performative dimension of this chant assumes the form of two imperatives and a judgment. The logic of the exhortations is the simple causality characteristic of infantile obsession. The stripping of the doctor is the initial phase of a sacrificial act. If we prepare the doctor for sacrifice, the logic runs, he will spare our martyr. If this fails, we will sacrifice him. The narrative rationalizes the singing in terms of the sociopolitical wish it expresses: to cut the doctor down to size, to strip him, literally, of his authority and paternalism. The song's prescriptions intertwine him with the boy. The doctor will suffer what he fails to cure. Because the doctor has been inscribed within the peasants' obsessive reasoning, the outcome of the boy's case is already fated to be his own condition. The peasant's final incantation celebrates the events that the initial one announces, and, with inexorable logic, fulfills, "O be joyful, all you patients, / The doctor's laid in bed beside you!" (*CS,* 225).

Symmetry and Disaster in Kafka's "Country Doctor"
133

The music in the text intensifies the arbitrariness of its events but also breaks free of the thematic networks that would seem to reinforce a sense of cohesion. The gestures celebrated by the music are precisely arbitrary: command, soothsaying, judgment, exaltation. The incantations become a counterpoint of arbitrariness arising out of the text but then floating above it with impunity, only tangentially related. The music hovers above the text as the doorbell tone floats beyond the confining domestic setting of "A Fratricide," "right over the town and up to heaven" (CS, 403). Music, in Kafka's fiction, diacritically annotates the directional aspirations of his writing. Of the text, it hovers above it, uncommitted to the apparent trends in which the thematic level has invested. Music underscores the constitutive role played by the metaphor in Kafka's writing: a fleeting refrain that sings of the difference between texts and stories.

CHAPTER SIX

Kafka in the Heart
of the Twentieth Century:
An Approach to Borges

A QUESTION OF INHERITANCE

The question of inheritance plagued Kafka. Guilt, familial relations, and even the activity of writing itself recur throughout his fiction as inevitable conditions, marks of Cain. Being an artist is a curse, a foregone conclusion no more negotiable than the identities of one's parents or siblings. Inheritance is among the primary metaphors that Kafka developed in order to house the concept of the arbitrary within a sociological context. Some of the bizarre hybrids that proliferate throughout the short fiction, including the kitten/lamb of "A Crossbreed" and Odradek of "The Cares of a Family Man," belong to a patrimony that the narrator cannot renounce. The kitten/lamb is a logical anomaly that the narrator explores with philosophical rigor. Odradek, an amalgam of organic and inorganic material, is doubly a creation of language: it is the product of an etymology and issues forth in speech as speech, a language divorced from the subjectivity commonsensically held to be the source of language. There is a strange complicity between these hybrids and the narrator who writes about them, as if they were siblings. Writing and the mark of writing, the anomalous image, are inherited traits. They may give rise to despair, but it is senseless to repress them. At the end of "A Crossbreed," the symbiotically linked hypothetical creature and the narrator both eye the sharp knife that is potentially an instrument of the former's sacrifice and the latter's suicide. The only escape from the inheritance of writing is the exaggerated definition that surgical steel might offer, and the tracery of the blade is merely a new form of inscription.

The curse of the Barnabas family in *The Castle* is inherited. So too, although suddenly, is the carapace of Gregor Samsa as *Mistkäfer*. Given the extreme significance of inheritance to Kafka as one guise for the arbitrary, a discussion of Kafka's future in the twentieth century, of the patrimony on which subsequent writers drew, cannot be casual. Indeed, this influence has assumed so many forms that any straightforward attempt to define it must be consigned to a certain arbitrariness. Kafkan elements may be detected across an astonishingly broad range of twentieth-century literary phenomena, encompassing the uncanny nostalgias of Elias Canetti and Bruno Schultz, Sartre's and Camus's existentialisms, Beckett's absurdism, the starkness of the *nouveau roman,* the disfiguration of conventional philosophy in the writings of Bataille and Blanchot, and the playful fictive inventiveness of the Latin American "school," exemplified by such writers as Borges and Cortázar.

The uniqueness of Kafka's work makes its mark on every element in that list. All of these phenomena can base their heritage on one or more distinct characteristics of Kafka's writing: its mood, its setting, its style, its humor, its characterization, its construction. As opposed to focusing on any particular Kafkan trait that may have been exploited by subsequent authors, however, this chapter will explore why Kafka's writing was so conducive to twentieth-century experimental fiction in general. The enterprise of mediating between the claims of Kafka's successors in determining his genuine "heirs" is fundamentally unsatisfactory because it presupposes a conception of literary works and authors as properties whose origin, value, and circulation can be determined. "Kafka" is not so much an asset or a critical cottage industry as a matrix of textual potentials. What Lévi-Strauss said about mythical structures applies to "him."[1] Kafka extends to any work in which Kafkan textual traits are deployed. Where these potentials are in play, every version of Kafka belongs to "Kafka." By the same token, the "final" texts by Kafka are themselves variations on the literary possibilities opened by their own sources, among which surely number Homer, Cervantes, Defoe, Kant, Kleist, Kierkegaard, and Dostoyevsky. Borges is sensitive to the regressive quality of this literary heritage. In "Kafka and His Precursors" and particularly in "Parable of Cervantes and the *Quixote,*" Borges demonstrates an uncannily demonic awareness of this process.[2]

TOWARD SCIENCE FICTION

Experiment differs from execution in the hypothetical nature of its premises and in the open-ended manner with which it tests its hypotheses. The performance of experiment is provisional; the performance of a definitive artwork is final.

An extraordinarily large segment of Kafka's fiction relies, for its programmatic element, on the structure of the hypothesis.[3] "What if there were such a thing as a kitten/lamb?" "A Crossbreed" demands and then systematically undertakes the investigation. Some of Kafka's most notorious works may be read as drafts of responses to hypotheses. "The Metamorphosis" is a case in point. "What if the most ordinary sort of a man woke up to find himself in the form of a giant insect?" ponders this text. In a sense, "The Judgment" elaborates the hypotheses of an Oedipal situation whose conventional teleological expectations are reversed, in which the father defeats the son, and this by means of a secret alliance with the son's supposedly eclipsed rival in Russia. "The Knock at the Manor Gate" takes as its premise an extreme judicial and ritual reaction to a minimal, and possibly nonexistent crime by someone tangential to the accused. The hypothetical structure of Kafka's works is not limited to his more fragmentary productions. It could be argued that the Castle, the center of power in the novel of that title, is identifiable primarily as an open hypothesis. A large portion of the action in the novel consists precisely in the testing of the logical, spatial, temporal, and communicative conditions of this central figure. As anomalous as they may be, such discoveries by Kafka as the success of unscheduled interactions with the bureaucracy or the sexual intimacy permitted between villagers and Castle officials serve a positive epistemological function: the demarcation of the conclusions permitted and not permitted by a possibly absurd hypothesis.

Among the most significant elements in the inheritance that Kafka bequeathed to subsequent writers must be counted the rigor with which his fiction tests its own hypotheses. Kafka is a major progenitor of the genre known as science fiction.[4] On the thematic level his invention and exploration of complex technological devices such as the Hotel Occidental telephone system and the execution machine in the Penal Colony opens a field of scientific interest in his work. It is in this respect that Kafka's writing shares a certain technological variety of uncanniness with such authors as E. T. A. Hoffman, Poe, and H. G. Wells.[5]

But Kafka is also an innovator of science fiction in a far more profound way. To the extent that many of his works are dedicated to the rigorous testing of fictive hypotheses, his fiction proceeds scientifically along the trajectory of experiment. Kafka's work is science fiction preeminently in its writerly dimensions. It matters little that many of the Kafkan texts in question eventually abandon the scientific pretensions of their structure and renounce the validity of their hypotheses. Even where everything goes wrong, where the execution machine in the Penal Colony breaks down and where none of the logical categories applied to the kitten/lamb works, vast portions of textual material are dedicated to scientific and pseudoscientific elaboration.

The beginning of "A Crossbreed," for example, sets forth the categories according to which the status of the anomolous beast may be determined.

> I have a curious [eigentümliches] animal, half kitten, half lamb. It is a legacy from my father [ein Erbstück aus meines Vaters Besitz]. But it only developed in my time; formerly it was far more lamb than kitten. Now it is both in about equal parts. From the cat it takes its head and claws, from the lamb its size and shape; from both its eyes, which are wild and flickering, its hair, which is soft, lying close to its body, its movements, which partake both of skipping and slinking. Lying on the window sill in the sun it curls up in a ball and purrs; out in the meadow it rushes about like mad and is scarcely to be caught. It flees from cats and makes to attack lambs. (CS, 426)

The creature is not merely a possession of the writer but a property (Eigentum), possibly of writing itself. This initial paragraph of the text is comprehensive in the logical categories that it affords the creature. In certain respects, this entity is either a kitten or a lamb, neither, or both of these animals. In different of its aspects, the creature sustains all of the following formulas: $A \land B$, $A \land \sim B$, $\sim A \land B$, $\sim A \land \sim B$. The creature has its head and claws from the cat, its size and shape from the lamb. It derives its eyes and movements from both, but certain of its antipathies (to rats and cats) question these very affiliations.

The fact that the text ultimately dismembers the logical matrix that it offers as an instrument for the creature's comprehension does not retract the resources that have been devoted to exploring the logical possibilities set into play. The high point of the creature's uncanniness assumes the form of a collaboration between attributes that are ostensibly mutually exclusive: "In long draughts [Zügen] it sucks the milk in through its fanglike teeth." The fangs here are indispensable to sucking but they also accentuate the uncanniness of the most innocent act, as it would be practiced by this hypothetical creature. Out of the calm logic of the text emerges a predatory suckling.

The dénouement of this fragmentary story consists of the disqualification of the very categories that have made it work. The metaphor of the kitten/lamb gathers a momentum that cannot be contained by any conceptual superstructure. The logic that has governed the narrative structure dissolves as the central metaphor hurtles toward the side, as it interacts with tangential categories and concerns.

> Sometimes I cannot help laughing when it sniffs around me and winds itself between my legs and simply will not be parted from me. Not content with being lamb and cat, it almost insists on being a dog as well. . . . I happened to glance down and saw tears dropping from its huge whiskers. Were they mine, or were they the animal's? Had this cat, along with the soul of a lamb, the ambitions of a human being? (*CS*, 427)

Once the possibility of the crossbreed, of the transposition and superimposition effected by metaphor, is broached, this trope need not be limited to a binary synthesis of elements. Extended, the logic of metaphor reaches a certain arbitrariness and unpredictability.[6] Pushed toward its limits, the logic of crossbreeds explored in this text encompasses animals not included in the original synthesis, such as dogs, and it approaches the most sensitive border of all, between the human and the animals. By virtue of the force of metaphor, the text that begins in games of logic ends up at the approach to the sciences of man.

In shorthand, "A Crossbreed" pursues one of the large vectors along which Kafka's fiction gathers itself. Science, as both a method and a thematic domain, steps forward in explanation of unanticipated anomalies but then succumbs as it is infected by the very irrationality that it has resisted. The act of writing fiction incorporates the scientific method that would detoxify the metaphoric germ at the heart of textual formation. Scientific method informs and even structures the text. But because the path of rigor cannot contain metaphoric disfiguration, scientific procedure as incorporated by the text relinquishes its pretentions to rationality and suffers mechanical failure. The superstructure provided by scientific method becomes a symptom of the belated and hopeless desire for control.

Science fiction is the fiction of science, describing the fate of scientificity within the textual domain and the textual quality of scientific reasoning. Technology, futurism, and the projection of the present into the remote past or future are merely secondary features of the science-fictive setting. Even while questioning rationality, Kafka pursues the potentials of fictive language scientifically. This unique quality of his writing, the isolation and then systematic exploration of the qualities of language responsible for literariness, is one of the most indelible of his fictive traces. While certain branches of the Kafka-inspired absurdism and existential vacuity seem already dated, a vibrant experimental fiction, whose experiment is its fascination with the qualities of fictive language, continues. This body of fiction does not comprise either a genre or a school. The devices and figures of speech emerging as exemplary of literary quality vary from writer to writer and from work to work. What forms the contours of such a body of literature is not a common vocabulary so much as the extension and intensity of an experimental posture.

Kafka's concern with the quality of language and the experimental development with which he endowed fiction have affected a body of literature so vast as to be beyond the scope of any reasonable study. Among the writers who exemplify the translation and prolongation of Kafka's unique attitude toward fiction in this regard must be counted Jorge Luis Borges and Italo Calvino. With enormous wit and rigor they extrapolate, as well as any other writers, Kafka's future in the twentieth century, the fate of the experimental fiction that he initiated. While unique in their own right, such works as *Ficciones* and *t zero* continue the rigor with which Kafka explored that unique border in fictive writing where science gives way to madness in an atmosphere of joyful discovery.

THE NEW WORLD OF BORGES' *Ficciones*

The setting of Jorge Luis Borges' fiction is a complex space in which labyrinths twist endlessly, leading nowhere, where railroad tracks proceed in straight lines until they abruptly disappear into the underbrush. No architecture is more characteristic of this domain than that of libraries, which expand internally through the proliferation of their galleries into an environment conducive to claustrophobia as well as agoraphobia. The compass of the Borgesian library dramatizes the textual involution continually expanding within and between the books that fill the shelves.

Borges' fiction first appeared in the United States in the pages of popular science fiction magazines.[7] This is a fitting historical commonplace, because Borges does engage in the hypothesizing of imaginary worlds that is one of the hallmarks of the genre. Yet new worlds, such as they exist in Borges' fiction, arise only in the margins between texts. The New World in Borges' fiction is not some external space, extraterrestrial, subterranean, submarine, or previously uncharted, inside whose perimeters the unusual may be projected. To the extent that Borges' imaginary places are outside the ordinary, they release the overlooked potentials in preexisting texts. As opposed to a science fiction that projects the concerns and historical idiosyncracies of a contemporary world into geographically or temporally alien settings, the New Worlds in Borges' fiction are constructed of textual potentials previously relegated to the margins of conceptual and interpretative systems. Reading and interpretation are the activities out of which alternative worlds emerge.[8]

Borges' imaginary world, then, is both nearer and farther away than the science-fictive settings modeled on the literatures of travel, adventure, and technological invention. His fiction is fated to remain within the confines of our universe because it never breaks the gravitational pull exerted by other, ultimately traceable texts. Yet at the same time, Borges establishes a symbiotic interdependency between established and alternate domains that is ultimately far more unsettling than the discernment of the familiar in settings of contrived remoteness. Borges' other worlds arise within the established tradition of Western thought and esthetics, which they then penetrate and derange. It is precisely the intimacy between the familiar and the Other in Borges' works that endows them with an uncanniness in excess of that inspired by the curious and the ingenious. The tension between the closed systems appropriated by Borges' texts and the margins that they engender is unending. This tension is the point at which Borges most closely approaches the activity of condensation, which, according to Freud, is the very crux of the distortion effected by jokes and dreams.[9] It is also what defines his most intense affinity to Kafka: Gregor Samsa's carapace is as integral and alien to his existence as Tlön is both an extension and distortion of the Western tradition.

The New World in Borges' fiction extends literacy, for it reveals the points of closure within traditions of logic, mathematical thought, psychology, and metaphysics so pervasive in Western thought as to have become tantamount to common sense. To understand where an accepted tradition gives way to a counterdomain in which it does not apply is to have read that tradition, and its seminal works, critically.

Borgesian literacy is not so much the transmission of various skills as the discernment and articulation of the limits within established systems. The library, as the site for the dissemination of literacy, is for Borges hallowed, if uncanny, ground.

Not only does Borges situate his fictive world within the library of proliferating textual complications, but he also evolves a lexicon of tropes and symbols that both account for his practice of fiction and serve as elements in the construction of increasingly daring compositions. Such phenomena as Borges' use of color, his exploration of geometrical shapes, and his invocation of chance in the chaining of events not only enrich the fictive landscape of his works. These devices also comprise a diacritical notation by means of which his writing accounts for its own style, obsessions, and construction. This is very different from Kafka's particular practice, but, sharing the earlier author's rigor, Borges' writing is thus scientific. Such uniquely Borgesian rhetorics as chance, neutrality, and bifurcation recur persistently from text to text. Different metatextual figures attain prominence in different *ficciones*. Borges' ability to combine and recombine the terms of his fictive rhetoric in different priorities, while playing on a wide variety of established literary genres, marks the corpus of his work with the character of the Library of Babel.

The contents were also deciphered: notions of combinational analysis [*analasis combinatorio*], illustrated by examples of variations [*variaciones*] with unlimited repetition. These examples made it possible for a librarian of genius to discover the fundamental law [*la ley fundamental*] of the Library. This thinker observed that all the books, however diverse, are made up of uniform elements: the period, the comma, the space [*el espacio, el punto, la coma*], adduced a circumstance confirmed by all travelers: *There are not, in the whole vast Library, two identical books.* From all these incontrovertible premises he deduced that the Library is total and that its shelves contain all the possible combinations of the twenty-odd orthographic symbols (whose number, though vast, is not infinite); that is, everything which can be expressed, in all languages. (*F,* 82–83)

Although in the Library everything is possible (the false with the true, the nonsensical as well as the reasoned), the individual works arise out of the relentless combination and recombination of the orthographic elements. In the library of Borges' fiction, a vocabulary of textual tropes takes on the function assumed by the alphabet in Babel.[10] Individual *ficciones* base their uniqueness on distinct combinations of textual tropes that reappear, although differently, throughout Borges' work. In the passage above, writing hovers between total knowledge and idiosyncratic trivia. The Library, though its resources are vast, does not fulfill the extent of its possibilities; the iterability of the alphabet prevents its works from lapsing into incoherence, the endlessness (as opposed to infinity) of combinatorial activity insures the Library against ever being complete. The Borgesian library, like the body of Borges' work, is an ever incomplete compendium of works themselves more devoted to the finalizing of particular plots. The books on the shelves of the Library have been produced by authors as idiosyncratic as Pierre Menard and Herbert Quain; like the novels of Tlön, they "are based on a single plot which runs through every imaginable permutation" (F, 28).

The literacy disseminated by the Library is an expansive process. It involves a discernment of the closure of the systems in which one operates, even as these systems themselves expand. It incorporates a differentiation between the instances of the particular. As a pedagogical tool in the acquisition of this literacy, Borges offers the reader little more than a list of textual functions, an index deciphering how written matter works. Yet this is more than an introduction to the Ficciones; it is a key to the quality of substantial, that is, densely written, texts.

CONE AND COMPASS

In only two of the Ficciones, "Tlön, Uqbar, Orbis Tertius" and "The Circular Ruins," does the discovery of new worlds figure decisively in the fictive drama. Yet even where the setting of the stories shifts to such venerable locations as ancient Babylon and China, the aura of fantastic literature pervades the volume. This is because the discovery taking place in the pages of the Ficciones is not of the extrinsic unknown so much as the marginally implicit. "Tlön, Uqbar, Orbis Tertius" is a particularly momentous text, within the confines of Ficciones, for Borges' work, and for twentieth-century literature in general, because of the concentration with which it fulfills its double program: to establish a motif of discovery and invasion, in which the fantastic appears to emerge from beyond; and, within this scenario, to dramatize the implications, marginal location, and textual nature of the phenomena conventionally associated with the fantastic and the imagination.

"Tlön, Uqbar, Orbis Tertius" is a framework story whose kernel, a detailed elaboration of a culture not bound by the ideological mainstays of Western thought, is encapsulated at both ends by an account of the discovery, history, and transmission of this culture. This story serves as a frontispiece to the remaining texts in Ficciones; any uncanniness that it achieves sets them in further relief. Toward its end, two strange objects are unearthed that offer material evidence of the existence of Tlön. In terms of the one facet of the fictive program that verges on fantastic literature, these objects represent "intrusion[s] of the fantastic world into the real one" (F, 32).[11]

Out of the recesses of a crate, stamped all over [rubricado] with international markings, fine immobile pieces were emerging—silver plate from Utrecht and Paris, with hard heraldic fauna, a samovar. Amongst them, trembling faintly, just perceptibly, like a sleeping bird, was a magnetic compass. It shivered mysteriously. The princess did not recognize it. The blue needle longed for magnetic north. The metal case was concave. The letters on the dial corresponded to one of the alphabets of Tlön. (F, 32)

We went to bed, but were kept from sleeping until dawn by the drunkenness of an invisible neighbor, who alternated between shouting indecipherable abuse and singing snatches of milongas, or rather, snatches of the same milonga. . . . At dawn, the man lay dead in the corridor. The coarseness of his voice had deceived us; he was a young boy. In his delirium, he had spilled a few coins [unas cuantas monedas] and a shining metal cone, of the diameter of a die [dado], from his heavy gaucho belt. A serving lad tried to pick up this cone—in vain. It was scarcely possible for a man to lift it. . . . This manifestation of an object which was so tiny and at the same time so heavy left me an unpleasant sense of abhorrence and fear. . . . No one knew anything of the dead man, only that "he came from the frontier." Those small and extremely heavy cones, made of a metal which does not exist in this world, are images of divinity in certain religions in Tlön. (F, 32–33)

Two objects, a compass and a cone, not only bridge the chasm between the "fantastic" and the "real." In them is concentrated the otherness given free reign in the domain (or philosophical space) designated by Tlön. The second object in question is an unusually dense cone. The extraordinary concentration of its material intensifies the final closure reached by its point. But the base of the cone is merely an arbitrary limit. The open end of a cone figures a hypothetically endless expansion. The heavy metal from Tlön assimilates nearly inconceivable density with unlimited expansion. If it is regarded as exemplary of the relationship between the "fantastic" and the "real," then the domain of Tlön is characterized by exceptional compression. There is a similar condensation in Borges' particular deployment of fictive language. Even the seemingly incidental in his descriptions, details of location, name, color, and number appear there by design, as I will have occasion to observe more fully below. While the figure of the dense cone is crucial to the text's fantastic program, as a trace of the inconceivable carried over to the real,[12] it is also emblematic of the relation between the language of *ficción* and the ordinary usages out of which it has been distilled and reduced. Not by accident does the cone share the dimensions of a die. In the concentrated fictive discourse that Borges is fashioning, the arbitrariness of chance is an integral element of hyperdesign, just as conceptual expansion begins at a point of total density. The cone is thus as crucial to the text's allegorization of its own language as it is to the fiction of alternate worlds.

The figure of the compass plays no less decisive a role in the story's internal and generic fictions. Although inscribed with letters from a secret alphabet, its needle points true north. Here the text admits that the space of *ficción* is coterminous with the space of an all-too-familiar world: both worlds, if they are indeed separate, share common directional coordinates. The otherness of Tlön, then, is not spatial. It is linguistic. Tlön has the status of an ambiguous language, partly inside and partly beyond the sphere of recognition. A spherical compass magnetically oriented to the north but inscribed with strange characters is a pointed instance of linguistic marginality.

The narrator's "discovery" of Uqbar (the "land" of which "Tlön" is an "imaginary region") at the very beginning of the story is couched in terms of this marginality.

I owe the discovery of Uqbar to the conjunction of a mirror and an encyclopedia. The unnerving mirror hung at the end of a corridor in a villa on Calle Goana, in Ramos Mejía; the misleading encyclopedia goes by the name of *The Anglo-American Cyclopaedia* (New York, 1917), and is a literal if inadequate reprint of the 1902 *Encyclopaedia Britannica*. . . . Bioy Casares had dined with me that night and talked to us at length about a great scheme [*polémica*] for writing a novel in the first person, using a narrator who omitted or corrupted [*desfigurara*] what happened and who ran into various contradictions, so that only a handful of readers, a very small handful, would be able to decipher [*la adivinación*] the horrible or banal reality behind the novel. From the far end of the corridor, the mirror was watching us. . . . Then Bioy Casares recalled that one of the heresiarchs of Uqbar had stated that mirrors and copulation are abominable, since they both multiply the numbers of man. (*F,* 17)

This passage establishes the "fantastic" scenario in which an article on an unknown world appears in a singular copy of a (pirated?) reprint of the *Britannica*. The additional pages, at the end of volume 46, appear literally in the binding of a reference work that evidently refuses to subscribe to the laws of mechanical reproduction as they apply to the printed medium. The intrusion of an alien world is akin to a mutation arising at the edges of a referential instrument. But Bioy Casares qualifies the uncanniness of this world as having a literary nature. The inaccessible and contradictory fiction that he proposes to write bears striking similarities to the history and literature of Tlön, the cultural agency of Uqbar. "Works of fiction," in Tlön, "are based on a single plot, which runs through every imaginable permutation" (F, 28). Not only can Bioy Casares, Borges' actual colleague and occasional coauthor, outline works of Tlönic complication for himself to write;[13] the elite audience that he envisions at the beginning of the story bears similarities to the "benevolent secret society" or "persecuted brotherhood" that evolves the culture of an alternate world over a period of three centuries.

The haphazard emergence of Uqbar is occasioned by a literary conversation during which Bioy recalls an aphorism by one of the country's heresiarchs (as opposed to a patriarch). The aphorism is significant because it outlines two alternate models for expansion available to fiction, one linear, one dialectical. Paternity combines repetitive and unrestrained linear extension. Fathers may produce multiple offspring, but each father (according to the fiction) is the starting point for a potentially endless sequence of reproductions. Fatherhood is merely one instance of linear extension in Borges' writing. Railroad tracks, lists, mathematical bases, and "the labyrinth made of the single straight line which is invisible and everlasting" (see "Death and the Compass" [F, 141]) are also prominent models of a literary expansion uncanny by virtue of its endlessness. The mirror, on the other hand, multiplies not by extension but (paradoxically) by division. The mirror of reflexivity enables the exterior to be internalized and vice versa. It serves as the frame of reference for irony. Tlön hovers between familiarity and alienation on its borders. Since expansion, in addition to penetration, is one of the decisive impacts of fiction upon the "real" world, the heresiarch's framing dictum is programmatic for Borgesian fiction.

Framed as it is by qualifications regarding the complication and expansiveness of literature, the discovery of Uqbar and Tlön take place as the unearthing of a lexicon partly inside and partly beyond the sphere of reference. "Of the fourteen names mentioned in the geographical section" of the Uqbar article that crops up in a single copy of the *Britannica* reprint, "we recognized only three—Khurasan, Armenia, and Erzurum—and they were dragged into the text in a strangely ambiguous way. Among the historical names, we recognized only one" (F, 19). For Borges, otherness and fiction are inextricably intertwined with the notion of referentiality. Fiction takes off where dependable reference begins to fail. Like the kitten/lamb in Kafka, Uqbar is a hybrid creation comprised of familiar and unknown elements.

Uqbar/Tlön is a New World and it is also a literary text. Borges thus links the genre of adventure literature and the position of the Latin American writer to the "discovery" or composition of an experimental text. The title of this story, as well as the geography of Uqbar, consists of familiar and unfamiliar elements. Only *Orbis Tertius* is immediately recognizable from Latin. This third element of the story's title appears cursorily near the conclusion as the name of a journal of Tlönic studies that appeared secretly over the years. It continues a sequence of displacements in the story, in which Uqbar precipitates itself out of "reality," Tlön is the unconscious of Uqbar, and Orbis Tertius is a gloss on Tlön. The primary importance of this last entry, however, is as an emblem of Borges' literary stance. If Europe is the locus where Western thought achieved its basic configuration, and if North America is the primordial New World whose potential is deeply embedded within that tradition, then Borges writes from the perspective of Orbis Tertius, the Third World that is not only involved in cultural otherness but about it as well. As opposed to such classical North American writers as Thoreau and Hawthorne, who can absorb themselves in cultural newness almost to the point of a certain naïveté, the Latin American writer writes from a deeply dialectical awareness of cultural deconstruction. The mirror indicated by the Heresiarch of Uqbar thus serves as a model for expansion available to all American writers, a critical-dialectical perspective embedded in their *stance*. Religious allegory and the thematic of traitorship, when they appear in Borges' writing, are invariably related to the issue of cultural generation by means of the mutual interpretation of "old" and "new" configurations. Just as Tlön emerges from the marginal hinterlands of Western thought and language, so too does the New Testament locate, predicate, and confirm itself in the margins of the Old.[14] The strategy by which a culture retrospectively discovers an origin for itself in an earlier ideology is in part what Heidegger designates by the term *appropriation*.[15] The theological dimension of this process structures another *ficción*, "Death and the Compass."

Cone and compass are thus telling images within the enterprise of Borgesian fiction. The cone mandates a fictive language that is denser, more concentrated, and more heavily designed than the language of other discourses, almost of a viscous quality.[16] The compass establishes a spatiality in which the everyday and the fantastic are coterminous, in which the parameters of established logical and metaphysical ideologies are continuously in a state of invasion, penetration, and subversion by an Other dwelling in the heart of the library of culture.

TLÖN AS COUNTERWORLD

"This plan is so vast that such individual contribution to it [*la contribución de cada escritor*] is infinitesimal. To begin with, Tlön was thought to be nothing more than a chaos, a free and irresponsible work [*licencia*] of the imagination; now it was clear that it is a complete cosmos, and that the strict laws which govern it have been carefully formulated, albeit provisionally" (*F,* 22). Only in one sense may Tlön be regarded as a coordinated domain: the attributes of its schools of thought, learned disciplines, and artworks all tend to the same sustained imbalance that is the effect of deconstruction. The paradoxes of complete chaos and ever provisional laws characterize a set whose single unity is its resistance to unity. As in the topological model for the mind that Freud first formulates late in the *Studies on Hysteria,* the hallmarks of Tlön form an involuted latticework of mutual confirmation as the narrative successively considers the disciplines of the culture (see *SE,* 2:288–98).

If those of us fated to lapse, at least occasionally, into non-Tlönic logic were to select a single attribute emblematic of the realm, my choice would be its *extreme idealism,* a term that Borges does not write without irony. Borges hardly suggests by this term that a counterworld to the traditions of Western thought, whose primary existence is textual, is organized by the structure of classical idealism, in which reality is subordinate to external, pure, and unattainable forms. On Tlön, idealism is at most one possibility among others, a hypothetical explanation for things, a minor deity in a cosmos overflowing with demons. Extreme idealism, with the stress on the first word, is the mode of expansion by which fiction pursues the appearance of logic to its limit. At this endpoint, self-contained order explodes, as in the universe a nova erupts out of the condensation of a white dwarf. Extreme idealism is a fictive compulsion toward and beyond limit. Borges expresses the sudden expansion that dramatizes the impact of fiction on the world as a shift from serial to exponential numbers; as the intervention of chance, personified as a mad deity, in the routine of everyday events; as perfume, which quite literally fills space. It is this compulsive expansion that characterizes the various disciplines, artworks, and folkways of Tlön.

Tlön is a counterdomain to the universe of Western thought primarily in its repudiation and implicit critique of two categories: Being and time.[17] For Borges, time is a broad rubric, implying not only succession and duration but also originality, determination, and truth. Tlön questions traditional assumptions made in Western thought about causation, the continuity of things in time, and the truth. Yet Tlön defines itself not only dialectically, as a foil to closed systems of thought beyond its purview: it also acts positively, specifically in literalizing the qualities of fictive language. Like the circular ruin in the story of that title, it serves as a dramatic space — in which the devices available to the writer act themselves out. The tangible qualities of Tlön assert themselves only as language whose predominant characteristic is the arbitrariness identified by Saussure.[18]

The nations of that planet are congenitally idealist. Language, with its derivatives — religion, literature, and metaphysics — presupposes idealism. For them, the world is not a concurrence of objects in space, but a heterogeneous series of independent acts. It is serial and temporal, but not spatial. There are no nouns [*sustantivos*] in the hypothetical *Ursprache* of Tlön. (*F,* 23)

The fact that no one believes that nouns refer to an actual reality means, paradoxically enough, that there is no limit [*sea interminable* to the numbers of them. . . . It is no exaggeration to state that in the classical culture of Tlön there is only one discipline, that of psychology. (*F,* 24)

The metaphysicians of Tlön are not looking for truth, nor even for an approximation of it [*la verosimilitude*]; they are after a kind of amazement. They consider metaphysics a branch of fantastic literature. (*F,* 25)

They recalled that any noun — *man, money, Thursday, Wednesday, rain* — has only metaphorical value. . . . They said that the heresiarch was motivated mainly by the blasphemous intention of attributing the divine category of *being* [*ser*] to some ordinary coins. (*F,* 27)

This collage of Tlönic extracts isolates certain of the fundaments of the culture. It is crucial to observe here how the critique of substantiality and Being as the basis for higher thought is interwoven with an exploration of time as the dimension in which variations on standard conceptual operations are free to emerge. For Borges as for Heidegger, Being is fundamentally a spatial category. If such primary systems of thought as religion and metaphysics are derivatives of language, Tlön is an instance of a linguistically structured field. Such a domain, implies Borges, is fundamentally at odds with belief systems based on substance. In this regard, Being, space, truth, and the noun all have something in common. In their respective areas of knowledge, each of these concepts serves as a stable ground of value. Throughout the history of philosophy, Being has been represented as a ground not only shoring up existence in a geological fashion but assuring personal identity and its continuity through time. Truth is the logical correlative to Being. The centrality of the noun to Indo-European syntax is the point at which Western culture has inscribed the idealistic structure of its thought processes within the deep structures of its very languages. In exploring the implications of and alternatives to the subject-verb equilibrium in Western languages, Borges is adapting some of the arguments that Ernest Fenollosa deployed in order to popularize Japanese poetry. Space alone does not bear the onus of substantiality. Truth-based systems of belief imply temporal attitudes as well. Models of simple determination and linear progression follow from the notion of an exclusive truth, but are not what interests Borges about time. If Borges values time above space, it is because time is the dimension of narrative, and narrative is the medium in which alternate models, routes, and explanations proliferate.

Borges' alternative to the substantiality and idealistic nature of Western thought consists of a world structured by linguistic operations. The lingua franca of each of the two hemispheres of Tlön presents an alternative to the division of labor between subject and object in Western tongues, itself predicated on the centrality and transparent domination of the verb *to be*. The language of the South, a privileged coordinate in Borges' literary geography, is strongly reminiscent of Chinese ideograms, as Fenollosa formulated their *Gestalt*.[19] It is a language of dynamic force refusing to be slowed or thickened into substantiality. "There are no nouns in the hypothetical *Ursprache* of Tlön. . . . There are impersonal verbs qualified by monosyllabic suffixes or prefixes which have the force of adverbs [*de valor adverbial*]. For example, there is no word corresponding to the noun *moon*, but there is a verb *to moon* or *to moondle* [*lunecer o lunar*]" (*F,* 23). The language of the North assimilates into its grammar two of Borges' most prevalent tropes for literary indeterminacy: synergy and endless metonymy. "The basic unit is not the verb, but the monosyllabic adjective. Nouns are formed by an accumulation of adjectives. One does not say moon; one says *airy-clear over dark-round* [*aéro-claro sobre oscuro-redondo*] or *orange-faint-of sky* [*anaranjado-tenue-del cielo*] or some other accumulation" (*F,* 23). Metonymy, a potentially endless chain of annexations, is fictive expansion carried to the semantic level. The antimaterialist bias of Tlönic culture limits the language of the North to an annexation of qualities, not things. Synergy, one of the effects of this grammar, may be characterized as a metonymy of qualities apprehended by different senses. "There are objects made up of two sense elements [*compuestos de dos términos*], one visual, the other auditory—the color of a sunrise and the distant call of a bird" (*F*, 24). Throughout Borges' fiction synergistic imagery appears as an important manifestation of the violence with which metonymy can derange classification and other logical acts. Synergy is, however, merely one instance of metonymic alogic in Borges' writing. Lists may be described as metonymic sets: Borges is notorious for the proliferation of uncanny lists throughout his works. Among the most striking must be numbered Funes' memories and the Chinese encyclopaedia in "The Analytical Language of John Wilkes."[20]

Given the alternatives that Borges provides for language on Tlön— a choice between verbal dynamism to the point of the dissolution of nouns and an endless annexation of logically unordered qualities— and given the derivation of other Tlönic disciplines from the language, it can come as little surprise that in related disciplines conditions for the orderly conduct of business are less than ideal. In these circumstances, the isolation of an exclusive truth is a futile enterprise. Mathematics is based on fluctuation rather than fixed concepts of value. (For this reason, Herbert Ashe, one of the demiurges of Tlönic culture, is "transcribing some duodecimal tables . . . into sexagesimals," in some of the narrator's "fading" memories of him; hence, railroads, which function concretely and metaphorically as sliding scales of value, are set in relief on the Borgesian map of fiction.)

> The foundation [*la base*] of visual geometry is the surface, not the point. . . . The arithmetical system is based on the idea of indefinite numbers. It emphasizes the importance of the concepts *greater* and *lesser*, which our mathematicians symbolize as > and < . . . . The fact that several individuals counting the same quantity arrive at the same result is, say their psychologists, an example of the association of ideas or the good use of memory. (*F*, 28)

Only in its relativism may Tlön be said to be comprehensive. In a counterdomain, the concepts essential to orderly business in systematic thought appear as myths or whimsical demons. Basic philosophical concepts such as identity and time on Tlön possess differentiated and even contrary meanings, while conventional philosophy would impose consistency on their usage. The notion of identity is a case in point. The parable of the coins demonstrates that the sustained identity of things in time is as questionable as that of people. Tlönic culture makes different approaches to identity, as a composite, "indivisible individual," which is "every one of the separate beings in the universe" (F, 27), and as a null set: "The concept of plagiarism does not exist; it has been established that all books are the work of one single writer, who is timeless and anonymous" (F, 28). Just as the books of Tlön are not attributable to any single author, they are not content to limit themselves to any monolithic story line. They run instead "through every imaginable" plot permutation.

Identities and works of literature on Tlön are thus collective in nature. They derive not from any mystical principle of unity so much as from the impersonal set of linguistic capabilities that Saussure called *langue*, the slowly evolving resources available to a community of speakers.[21] It is not inappropriate that the culture of this realm should be preserved and disseminated by a secret society as anonymous as the authors and personalities of Tlön. The scenario of a cultic awareness of the counterdomain to the Western tradition implies a model of literary history as well. Here Borges comes closest to the Derridean scenario of a counterpoint to the dominant Western trends of ideational, deterministic, and teleological thought inscribed by "major" authors in the margins of their own texts, or historically subjected to political and scholarly suppression.[22] The Tlönists who undertook "to define a country" comprise a hypothetical collectivity with the deconstructive apprehension that emerges every time contemporary critical theory addresses a different body of texts. Although such *ficciones* as "The Garden of Forking Paths" and "The Secret Miracle" are specifically colored by the historical circumstances of the great World Wars, the secret society of Tlönists is strictly amoral in nature. The "millionaire ascetic," Ezra Buckley, "was a freethinker, a fatalist, and an apologist for slavery" (F, 31). Despite an explicit personal repugnance for the events of the war, Borges insists that a textual counterdomain is as void of clear moral coordinates as it is of fixed mathematical values.[23] By virtue of the Nietzschean moral indeterminacy that pervades Tlön, Borges' heroes, like John Vincent Moon in "The Form of the Sword," are indistinguishable from traitors. Borgesian characters are subject to every moral gradation in the same sense that Tlönic novels undergo all permutations of plot.

Chance emerges as a Borgesian rubric indicative of the multifaceted indeterminacy prevailing on Tlön.[24] The proliferation of texts in the "Library of Babel" and of human fates in "The Babylon Lottery" dramatize fictive expansion in terms of probability theory. No allegory in "Tlön, Uqbar, Orbis Tertius" is more indicative of the confluence between chance, a critique of time, and the counter-tenets of Western culture than the parable of the *hrönir*. These "secondary objects" are situated in the margin where "centuries and centuries of idealism have not failed to influence reality" (*F,* 29). *Hrönir* are hypothetical objects produced by thought. They can arise in Tlön rather than in the domain governed by (Western) common sense because there reality and fiction are continuous rather than mutually exclusive. *Hrönir* are the concrete products of realized desire. "Until recently, the *hrönir* were the accidental children of absent-mindedness and forgetfulness. It seems that the methodical production of them has been going on for almost a hundred years. . . . The first attempts were fruitless" (*F,* 29). Randomly, a *hrön* could be generated by an individual in search of a pencil; systematically, they are produced by a state-run experiment in which prisoners are offered freedom in return for their success at duplicating objects shown to them in photographs. *Hrönir* are not merely emblems for the influence of fiction on reality in a domain eschewing transcendental categories and oppositional classification. They are units of derivation as well and are thus illustrative of the historical and temporal conditions prevailing in a counterdomain.

> These secondary objects are called *hrönir* and, even though awkward in form, are a little larger than the originals. . . . One curious fact: the *hrönir* of the second and third degrees [*grado*] — that is, the *hrönir* derived from a second *hrön,* and the *hrönir* derived from the *hrön* of a *hrön* — exaggerate the flaws [*aberraciones*] of the original; those of the fifth degree are almost uniform; those of the ninth can be confused with those of the second; and those of the eleventh degree have a purity of form [*pureza de líneas*] which the originals do not possess. (*F,* 29–30)

Neither history nor the derivation of secondary objects in Tlön may be characterized exactly as a progressive sequence. The degrees of fidelity in reproduction pursue an arbitrary and zigzag path, declining in quality in the earlier stages and then superseding the originals in quality. This model of derivation is a splendid parody of the Platonic theory of forms. When it is applied to the histories of art and ideas in Tlön, such notions as influence, imitation, development, and evolution become maddening in their arbitrariness. By implication, generations are easily passed over in the history of an idea, and the most tangible instances of poetic influence are often the most circuitous ones (as when Pound owes more to haiku and the troubadours than to Hopkins and Tennyson). And yet, in the actual practice of literature, this model of derivation and influence is less far-fetched than certain of the sequential developments posited by critics and art historians. As systematically as Borges elaborates the parameters of a counterdomain in his text, there is a strong element of parody throughout, whose target is the etiquette of scholarship. Not only is the elucidation of the sequence of *hrönir* a bit too much *de rigeur:* the hilarious account of the popularization of Tlönic studies at the end of the story anticipates the scholarly responses to Borges' writing, which the present interpretation joins. The allegory of the *hrönir* is a corollary of the critique of time reified in Tlön. The concept of time, like identity, becomes phantasmatic and differentiated within the counterdomain.

> One of the schools in Tlön has reached the point of denying time. It reasons that the present is undefined, that the future has no other reality than as present hope, that the past is no more than present memory. Another school declares that the *whole of time* has already happened and that our life is a vague memory or dim reflection, doubtless false and fragmented, of an irrevocable process. Another school has it that the history of the universe, which contains the history of our lives and the most tenuous details of them, is the hand-writing [*escritura*] reproduced by a minor god [*dios subalterno*] in order to communicate with a demon. Another maintains that the universe is comparable to those code systems [*criptografías*] in which not all the symbols have meaning, and in which only that which happens every three hundredth night is true. Another believes that, while we are asleep here, we are awake somewhere else, and that thus every man is two men. (*F,* 25–26)

This brief catalogue of four theories of time is characterized by the categorical problems attending all Borgesian lists. The first two theories approach time by suspending it and placing it at a certain point along the temporal continuum, where it absorbs all other time frames. The denial of the time amounts to a flattening of the past and future within the present. The metonymic language of the northern hemisphere of Tlön, as well as Ireneo Funes' memory, are literary instances of this absorbing present, which by its nature questions the assumptions underlying narrative sequencing devices in fiction. The theory that "the *whole of time* has already happened" locates the all-absorbing time frame in the past. There is a mystical quality to this hypothesis, because according to it, present experiences are merely derivatives of an indefinitely prior aggregation of time. It is within the framework of this "always-alreadiness" of language and experience that Pierre Menard can, by dint of meticulous scholarship and an ability to project himself into the past, compose during this century a bit more than two chapters of Don Quixote without having read the text.[25] The complementary denials of time in the beginning of the list are supplemented by three explanations having nothing to do with time. The one that interprets history as the handwriting of a minor god to a demon cosmologizes a conventionally philosophical category and designates time as a medium for writing. The penultimate theory interpolates randomness into the continuum of time, declaring that only certain moments and events can be "real," and the final entry has a psychoanalytical tinge, implying that time is an effect of "split consciousness," approximating the distinction between primary and secondary process (see SE, 2:12, 24, 33–34, 215–20, 225–31).

If the passage quoted above denies time, it is not because of the predominance of any particular theory but because of the multiplicity of temporal attitudes that Tlönic culture sustains and the decisiveness of these positions within the architecture of Borges' fiction. Appealing to chance, exploring the splits or bifurcations that take place in narrative, observing the impact of metonymy on logic, and hypothesizing demonic explanations for commonplace events are all ways in which Borges resists the tyranny of time in fiction. For Borges this oppression assumes the form of causal explanations, monolithic plots, arbitrary temporalizing devices, and "single" meanings. Tlön is a domain in which Borges challenges the assumptions of Being and time and whose characteristics articulate positively the implications of a language-based reality.

SCIENCE *Ficción*

"Tlön, Uqbar, Orbis Tertius" occupies a pivotal position in Borges' writing, not because it is more profound than other texts in its awareness of linguistic and literary potentials but because it is a work in which Borges introduces virtually the entire battery of textual tropes endowing this writing with its distinctive character. Were one to permit oneself a textual violence that would never be tolerated by the heresiarchs of Tlön, one could, taking off from this story, enumerate the textual tropes that Borges develops in *Ficciones* and combines throughout his writing as he explores the scientific madness of fiction. In keeping with a Borgesian esthetic, the compendium of textual tropes would take the form of a list, and, as a reputable scholarly instrument, this list would be substantiated by examples from the text and their page numbers. Such a catalogue could hardly claim to read or interpret Borges' writing, but it might delineate a set of operations in his work combined in multiple permutations under radically different thematic and circumstantial conditions.

Tropes of Textuality in Borges' Ficciones

1. Endless proliferation of interpretations (symbol: the labyrinth) (e.g., F, 28, 76, 79, 83, 87)
2. Bifurcation (forking) (e.g., F, 28, 75–76, 93, 96, 98)
3. Relativism (free-floating values)
   (a) Amoral (traitorship, etc.) (e.g., F, 31, 66, 75, 90, 119)
   (b) Quantitative (e.g., F, 21, 113)
   (c) Philosophical (color: gray) (e.g., F, 20 [*Ashe*], 93, 95, 117, 129)
4. Restructuring of language, breakdown of representation (e.g., F, 23, 81–82)
5. Theology (the ascendancy of language, *logos*, over *theos*, God) (e.g., F, 28, 31, 34, 61, 81, 85)
6. The negation of Being, the inhumanity of the text (e.g., F, 27, 34, 109)
7. Temporal disordering
   (a) Break in the continuity of the flow of time (e.g., F, 26, 100)
   (b) Cyclical recurrence in time (e.g., F, 62–63, 87, 100, 141)
   (c) Expansion of the present to encompass all time (e.g., F, 25, 70, 90, 112, 121, 124)
   (d) Endless bifurcation, and hence suspension of the present (e.g., F, 70, 97–98, 100, 149)
   (e) Inversion of past and future, i.e., reversal of cause and effect, i.e., retrospective crystallization of the past (e.g., F, 62–63, 75, 124–25, 138–41)
8. Derangement of spatial coordinates (e.g., F, 23, 89–91, 101)
9. Intrusion of arbitrary orders (e.g., chess) into everyday life (e.g., F, 34, 69–72, 75, 79)
10. Chance (e.g., F, 26, 29, 32, 46, 68–72, 82–84)
11. Abolition of selfhood, identity, authority (e.g., F, 28–30, 48, 65, 77, 83, 117–22)
12. "*Extreme* idealism" (the idealism of following phenomena to their extremes, the intimation of a matrix encompassing the totality of possibilities, the expansion from particular to system) (e.g., F, 28–29, 57, 78, 120)

Kafka in the Heart of the Twentieth Century

13. The New World
(e.g., in particular, "Tlön, Uqbar, Orbis Tertius," "The Circular
Ruins," and "The Garden of Forking Paths")

Two other *ficciones* are particularly noteworthy for the ingenuity
with which they combine and, in so doing, expand Borges' lexicon of
textual practices. Interestingly, both are allegories of reading that
dramatize the complex interaction between literal and ironic levels
of interpretation. "The Garden of Forking Paths" is one of the stories
in *Ficciones* set amid the circumstances of World War I. Yu Tsun, the
narrator, counts among his ancestors the Mandarin author of a labyrinthine novel. He has, however, renounced his cultural heritage.
He is a racist, working to disprove the racial prejudices of the Germans by aiding their cause. He succeeds in his mission, which is to
transmit from London to Berlin the name of a "new British artillery
park," by murdering someone sharing its name. His approach to language, then, is brutally concrete.

Stephen Albert, Yu Tsun's adversary and prey, is an Englishman
who has preserved the glory of Chinese culture, including the "invisible labyrinth of time" composed by his murderer's forebear. With
his grey features and a bearing that synthesizes the saintliness of a
priest and earthliness of a sailor, Albert belongs to the neutral readers in Borges' fiction whose attitudes toward language and time
could well characterize the world order of Tlön. These personal qualities are displaced to the name of the railroad station closest to his
home, Ashgrove. His death, then, dramatizes the killing of a sophisticated method of interpretation that does not resolve paradoxes and
reduce indeterminacies by a much more utilitarian approach to language. Simplicity kills. World War I is not merely a historical event
but becomes a cultural moment as well. The story becomes an allegory of the relation between politics and language. Political action is
predicated on a certain closure applied to language, while for Borges,
fiction resists, and must resist, this type of flattening: through its
proliferation of meanings and possibilities and in the indeterminacy
that it sustains.

As can easily be inferred from the plot summary above, Borges luxuriates in the spatial ambiguities generated by the story. The setting
is a Mandarin China superimposed on modern England. The paths
followed in the story are tortuous and labyrinthine. Rather than existing at opposite poles, East and West merge indifferently and sometimes uncannily. As a child, Yu Tsun frequented the symmetrical
gardens of Hai Feng. Albert's suburb is Fenton. "The damp path zig-

zagged like those of my childhood. When we reached the house, we went into a library filled with books from both East and West. I recognized some large volumes bound in yellow silk. . . . A phonograph record was spinning near a bronze phoenix" (F, 95).

For all the story's historical urgency, its most significant events play themselves out in interpretative and writerly terms. The artillery battery that the Germans wish to destroy is located on the Ancre River, a play on the French words for anchor (ancre) and ink (encre). A writing instrument is inscribed into the name of the narrator's exceptionally literate ancestor, Ts'ui Pên. The narrative states that its central topic is declared just as Albert's name is transmitted to Berlin, through its explicit elimination. The story ends in an indication of the only recompense that literature can offer in the wake of monstrous events: through the endless bifurcation of time that enlightened texts record and enact, there may come a moment when the forces of literacy and the toleration of ambiguity that it involves will prevail over the brutal *execution* of language. "I leave to various future times, but not to all, my garden of forking paths" (F, 97).

One leaves Borges' uniquely complex fictive space, however, at "the labyrinth made of the single straight line which is invisible and ever-lasting" (F, 141). It is to this point that Lönnrot, the truly well-informed reader of "Death and the Compass," who has deciphered the Talmudic argument linking a triad of murders, has been drawn in time to become the fourth and culminating victim.[26] His predator, the devisor of the geometrical scheme of murders, is Scharlach, a Jew whose aim is not merely to avenge the loss of a brother but to reverse the critical ascendency that the New Testament once established over the Old.[27] (Hence, the first in the string of murders occurs at a Talmudic conference set in the diaspora). Early in the story, Lönnrot[28] demonstrates the inventiveness of his exegetical method in comparison with the prosaic approach of the police chief, Treviranus (or "three-turn-anus"), who can follow the first three murders in a triangle as they occur—after the fact—but cannot intuit the mystical square in which they are joined. In the closing moments of the text, one is reminded that its two archreaders, Lönnrot and Scharlach, will pursue each other through its contortions forever, that the text will remain suspended between two alternate fates: being penetrated by its readers and swallowing them.

"Death and the Compass" is a supreme work of science fiction, as worthy an aftereffect as Kafka could hope to produce, because it eventuates in a moment of uncanny fictive expansion after having undergone rigorous patterning to the point of overdetermination. The story is structured theologically, geometrically, numerically, and in terms of color code. It is dense with synthetic creations: a hotel that "most manifestly unites the hateful whiteness of a sanatorium, the numbered divisibility of a prison, and the general appearance of a bawdy house"; a Talmudic scholar with the name of Marcel Yarmolinsky; a murder occurring at 11:03 A.M., a time linking the repeated unity of the Jewish God to the triple manifestation of the Christian deity. And yet the violence of this story invariably breaks out at the limit of its patterns, where a synthetic balance no longer holds, where closed patterns undergo both enlargement and metamorphosis through the inclusion of yet another serial integer.

Scharlach, the avenging angel or prodigal son of the Jews, weaves a text of murders that take place on the third days of, respectively, December, January, and February in a city whose geographical site belongs to Buenos Aires but whose place names derive from Paris. The crimes form "the perfect vertices of an equilateral and mystic triangle" in the northern, eastern, and western sectors of the city. All three victims derive from the no man's land between Judaism and Christianity: the emigré Talmudist, the bandit Daniel Simon Azevedo, whose name echoes the Hebrew verb *azavtani* in Jesus' final lament, "Why hast thou forsaken me?" and Gryphius-Ginzberg-Ginsburg, a decoy whose murder narrative involves painted rhombs and Irish revolution (this victim frequents a "Liverpool House" owned by "Black Finnegan").

What passes for resolution amid such a tight grid of determinations can only be, here and throughout Borges' fiction, a vertiginous expansion. Lönnrot, the fourth and final victim in the sequence and the only non-Jew, encounters this possibility as he prepares himself to decipher the crimes through scholarship. In the calendrical scheme, his death coincides with Easter, making him the sacrificial lamb.

> A large octavo volume revealed to him the teachings of Israel Baal Shem-Tob, founder of the sect of the Pious; another volume, the virtues and terrors of the Tetragrammaton, which is the ineffable name of god; another, the thesis that God has a secret name, in which is epitomized [*compendiado*] . . . his ninth attribute, eternity. . . . Tradition numbers ninety-nine names of God; the Hebraists attribute this imperfect number to the magical fear of even numbers; the Hasidim reason that this hiatus indicates a hundredth name — the Absolute Name. (*F,* 131–32)

"Death and the Compass" intensifies an evasive point of orientation that shimmers above the *Ficciones*—the moment at which a finite series reaches a perfect number, when lines explode into spatial geometry, when letters spell out the name of God, when a little story opens into the plot of plots. This moment is the *telos* of Borgesian fiction, inasmuch as there can be one. The fourth murder in the story, Lönnrot's own, relates to prior circumstances as the final letter completes the Tetragrammaton, as the square, one hundred, absorbs the sequential and even interesting number, ninety-nine, as the resolution to a triad of murders could be an exacting, but endless, line. It is almost predictable, then, that the final murder should take place in the South, the Latin American equivalent of the North American West. Lönnrot encounters his adversary "amid the boundless odor of the eucalypti" (*F,* 122), in a setting of "maniacal repetitions" (*F,* 137). Lönnrot's life and his reading culminate in the possibility for endless linguistic expansion that is the drift of Borges' work and one of the afterworlds in which Kafka's writing still flourishes.

CHAPTER SEVEN

The Modern/Postmodern:
On the Plain of Indifference

A BROKEN CONTRACT: THE DISCOURSE
OF HALF-REFERENCE

One of the most telling ways in which a particular cultural moment declares its uniqueness and opens the setting for its discourse is through the standing contracts that it refuses to honor. In this respect the period of high modernism, with its unprecedented experiments in style, organization, and cultural pastiche across the spectrum of the arts, comprised an excruciatingly difficult act to follow. After Mallarmé and Pound what new horizons are there to open in a poetic space that has already been exploded from within? After *Ulysses* what additional play on grammar, narrative, syntax, and genre can be introduced within the form of the novel? After Schönberg and Stravinsky what new liberties can be taken with musical harmony, form, and resolution?

The most brilliant modernists addressed such questions even as, in their exuberant *bricolage*, they improvised new forms with the debris of inherited productions. They allowed themselves to teeter on the cusp of the modern/postmodern. The act itself of distinguishing between these moments is fraught with the most fundamental philosophical and methodological problems. Even to speak in these terms may be, to paraphrase Hegel, a distinction that is, in the end, no distinction at all. Or possibly, the difference we experience when we pass from the modern to its Other or successor may be merely one of mood, like the shadow on the face of the depressed even while it rests on the most familiar features.

JAMES JOYCE. I would argue that any distinction the postmodern can claim is neither more nor less tangible than a mood, a bearing, an address. And as an instance of this transition, I would propose the sea change that takes place when we move between the worlds of Joyce's *Ulysses* and *Finnegans Wake*. The latter novel joins Kafka's late animal narratives, key passages in the writing of Samuel Beckett, and the contemporary fiction of Thomas Bernhard as a work in which language builds toward new thresholds of association at the same time that it obliterates any vestiges of structure surviving from kaleidoscopic experimentation.

To the extent that he occupies the position of the player-god and the Artist-Son, Joyce repudiates many aspects of the filial duty to represent—with fidelity or even clarity. A nose-thumbing, a conspicuous taunting of the classical etiquettes of representation, is one of the characteristic gestures of his fiction after *The Dubliners*. In *Ulysses* he ranges freely over the history of the English language, taking a bit here and there. Particularly in such episodes as "Proteus," "Aeolus," "The Wandering Rocks," "Cyclops," "The Oxen of the Sun," "Circe," and "Ithaca," Joyce explodes conventional forms of styles of writing from within. Through Molly's monologue in "Penelope"— with its lifting, its suspension of the conventional markers of thought, logic, and conceptual super- and subordination—the novel moves toward a demonstration of pure textuality: the configuration of text out of text. The thematics out of which this particular episode spins itself are not overwhelming in number: clothing, flowers, music, marriage, adultery, sexuality, child rearing, animals, Spain, and religion. Yet the combination of these motifs in the thoughts of Molly—whose fluidity is both a slur upon and tribute to her gender— builds toward an *ouverture* of meaning rather than any definitive crystallization. Playing on the musicality of Molly's thought and activity, the Penelope chapter serves as a coda to the novel as a whole. It assures a convergence of certain themes that might otherwise have functioned separately; it furnishes a certain symmetry in recalling key details of the beginning. The Penelope chapter is the novel's retrospective musical *ouverture*. It might also seem to be rehearsal for, a bridge leading in the direction of, Joyce's next— postmodern?—phase.

In *Finnegans Wake*, I would argue, the filial refusals that achieve prominence throughout *Ulysses* achieve a new qualitative plateau. If in *Ulysses* fiction could violate its conventions with the belligerent joy of the bull in the china shop, in *Finnegans Wake*, language in general refuses to represent; it curtails or partially shuts down its most basic function, the *sine qua non* of its other effects. A variety of devices instruments this referential slowdown—a rhetoric of labor relations enters my commentary—the most prominent of which is the half-reference. A half-reference, as opposed to a full one, is both more and less than what one expects from ordinary language. A half-reference may well obscure a word's meaning, and hence its relation to other signifiers in the contexts of its signification; in this sense it means less than it does in a clearer representational mode. The distortions taking place in half-reference may also, however, open the associations leading between a signifier and its cognates, synonyms, and homonyms. To the extent that the subliminal domain of half-reference is polysemous, it augments the associative value of words while it diminishes their lucidity. Half-references may be described as terms that almost simulate other signifiers, but not quite. What they leave "up for grabs" is more important than what they establish. They intensify reference, by meaning one thing and implying others, but they also verge on a referential limit, the variant meanings for which they cannot exhaustively account. Precisely in its multifaceted ambiguity, half-reference constitutes a serious disruption to the most fundamental linguistic contract: the assumptions and functions pertaining to reference.

Half-reference opens up a subliminal domain of meaning, in which relations are hazy, unsure, tentative. It ushers in the night of the novel and the conventions that have contributed to its history. The nocturnal ambiance and setting of *Finnegans Wake* are the theatrical correlatives to a convention of half-reference. Molly Bloom's musings are similarly nocturnal; but, although a lifting of the end-stops of thought and phrasing characterizes her discourse, her words' referential function is not called into any fundamental question.

On the level of affect the half-reference corresponds to the writerson's passive aggression; not an assertive act but a refusal, the breaking of an agreement; injury through absence. The refusal installed in the half-reference colors the universe of *Finnegans Wake*. The half-reference consummates other of the formal inventions that Joyce rehearses in *Ulysses* and elsewhere: run-ons, an obsessive piling of puns and word plays, unannounced and unexplained allusions and grafts. It extends the other half-hearted gestures abounding in Joyce's fiction: half-allusions, half-entendres, half-implications.

In *Ulysses*, Joyce succeeded in bringing the conventions of the novel to a point of self-dismantling fullness. In his subsequent writing, he did more than any other author to explore the performance of language at the level of the less-than-optimal, the below-standard-specifications.[1] As I shall show below, the adjusted expectations of the half-referential comprise the enabling legislation for a set of other textual experiments that one tends to associate with the postmodern. Half-reference facilitates these departures, these stress tests on the metal of language, both in the later Joyce and in the authors who succeeded him, including Beckett, Artaud, Bataille, and Derrida. When one arrives at the fictive discourse that has to some extent abdicated its obligation to refer, one's sense of departure is, nonetheless—and for lack of a better word—tangible. It is in keeping with the postmodern esthetic of the textuality of language—the precedence of linguistic texture and material over discrete works or their units—that a plethora of passages from *Finnegans Wake* will be illustrative of this entry into the half-referential.

What *Finnegans Wake* does not afford in the way of plot, story line, and overarching structure is as important as what it does offer. To the extent that the novel dedicates itself to a questioning of the expectations surrounding literature, it offers a plot, mythological scenario, and characterological interaction that are at most minimal. In place of a structure or framework, it furnishes soft structure, what Rodolphe Gasché calls, in relation to philosophy and theory, infrastructure.[2] If the novel demarcates the end of literature, to the extent there can be such, soft structure, or slippery structure is an integral element of its strategy. The *Odyssey* is indeed a centering context for *Ulysses*. Each autonomous episode is grafted onto a telling episode from the classical source. Characters such as the Citizen draw their significance in part from the appropriated ur-text (this example corresponds to Polyphemus, the cyclops). In *Finnegans Wake* there is only the loosest plot, the vaguest characters, the most subliminal events. The haziness of the story line enables it to spin around itself, further frustrating any resolution of events. It is in this sense that, according to Clive Hart, some sections of the text are "dreams" of other sections.[3]

Ulysses traces the meandering of two—somewhat dialectically related—characters through an Odyssey confined to one day in Dublin. *Finnegans Wake* grafts the situation of one HCE and his family onto the fate of the mythological character Finn MacCool. Adaline Glasheen quotes Joyce saying that "Finnegans Wake was 'about' Finn MacCool lying dying beside the Liffey, while history cycles through his mind."[4] The cycles of Earwicker and Finn vaguely correspond to different moments along the arc of fall and redemption: Finnegans death and resurrection is in some sense emblematic of possibilities available to Earwicker. Yet Earwicker, as an encompassing hypothetical subjectivity for the novel, is a multiple and shifting character, also appearing in the form of fish and other animals. The twin sons, Shem and Shaun, as much figure the self-displacing structure of rivalry itself as any particular conflict, although Shem tends to be a creature of writing and Shaun of reductive pragmatism. Anna Livia

Plurabella is a woman and a river, a geological river and a river of language. She is the river of language in which the writer delves, according to a venerable tradition of gendrification, the *matter formed*. She partakes in some of the same esthetic ambivalence surrounding Molly Bloom—privileged as inspiration, denigrated as material. The least formed of these already vast and unformed characters is Issy, whose name underscores the hovering ground of Being. From a biographical point of view, it is said, Issy corresponds to Joyce's daughter Lucia, whose increasingly schizophrenic language comprised a major model for the novel's discourse.

Vague, protean characters are thus set within a ho-hum, almost "nothing" plot, surrounded by the loosest archetypal fluctuation from death to life, fall to redemption, ignorance to revelation and vice versa. A loose templating of *Finnegans Wake* onto the sequence of *Ulysses* characterizes the novel in the sense that book 3, roughly corresponding to the Nighttown episode, effects a loosening of the loosening. It takes place between midnight and dawn. Clive Hart situates it in the innermost two circles of internalized dreaming.[5] It contains Shem and Shaun's "watches" and their musings on sexuality. Book 4, like "Penelope," is a moment of synthesis and release, a release from life at the same time that it is an affirmation of writing. As in *Ulysses*, the beginning of the novel, the first two books, consists of slightly more measured and pointed chapters—although there is a tendency for the chapters in *Finnegans Wake* to end in the emptying of the thematic threads they wove together, a decoupling from their own manifestly absurd attempts at structure. The individual chapters reenact the novel's placement at the *end* of literature, during its long night, by themselves ending in a shadow realm.

In a very limited sense, then, the novel does provide wider structural units, whether these are called its books or its cycles. The range of activity in the novel, however, takes place at the microscopic level, the setting of locality and singularity. The relationship between this theater of particularity and such wider structural patterns as fall-redemption or sibling rivalry is tenuous at best.

The novel's language, to take one vital instance of this emphasis, is at all times a disfigured simulacrum of itself. It mounts an ongoing resistance to its referential function. Its effect is to proliferate association while limiting specific signification. This disfiguration raises serious questions about the syntax of words. Syntax is the *role* that words, viewed as characters, assume in a sentence. The questioning of syntax comprises, on a microscopic level, a radical critique of identity and characterization. The gravitation toward disfigured syntax in *Finnegans Wake* is so powerful that Joyce's occasional reversions to standard speech patterns amount to stunning surprises and innovations in themselves. A sentence such as "To anyone who knew and loved the christlikeness of the big cleanminded giant H. C. Earwicker throughout his excellency long vicefreegal existence the mere suggestion of him as a lustsleuth nosing for trouble in a boobytrap rings particularly preposterous" (*FW*, 33) befuddles the reader—in the context of Joyce's systematic syntactic disfiguration—as much by its apparent transparency as by the pages of distortions that have preceded it.

The discourse of *Finnegans Wake* is, by virtue of this highly unusual linguistic facility of suggestibility, unusually receptive to the incursion of foreign languages. If Noam Chomsky is correct that the ability to separate different languages or keep them straight is an inborn deep structure, then philologically, at least, *Finnegans Wake* performs a monumental regression. In its conflation of a remarkably large set of ancient and modern languages, it would undo a language-differentiating function that is, according to Chomsky, innate.[6] In *Finnegans Wake* the integrity and the national identity of languages dissolve. There is a reversion to a cultural as well as a psycholinguistic Babel; this biblical episode becomes an ongoing motif in the novel (for example, *FW*, 15). Interlinguistic punning is a compulsive and ubiquitous feature of this text, on the microscopic level. It forces the reader to be both pre- and superlinguistic, to be a philological if not theoretical comparatist.

Paradoxically, many of the novel's most important and suggestive motifs are introduced by means of linguistic disfiguration. Disfiguration becomes a pivotal means not only to open and close reference but also to introduce themes subliminally. Themes or narrative ideas do not emanate from a narrator who serves as a brain or idea source for the text. Ideas, such as they occur in *Finnegans Wake,* are accidental, the happenstance of language.

One of the crucial tasks in reading *Finnegans Wake* is simply discerning these subliminal themes or subtexts amid the cloud-chamber of linguistic distortion, and understanding their sequence and chaining-off from one another. Each chapter and major passage in the novel marks a certain coincidence between theme, time, place, character, and action or its absence. The text of *Finnegans Wake* is "made" of these constellations or coincidences. To understand why themes emerge in the text when they do and in relation to which characters and incidents is to read *Finnegans Wake.* The big mythic-archetypal structures are not always decisive in this regard. An allegorical understanding of how this text constitutes and performs itself begins with the questioning of what converges and why. *Finnegans Wake* is at all times a performance. Its substantive elements verge into a performance of linguistico-textual allegory. The understanding of how the constellation of disjunctive factors performs the act of writing constitutes the allegorical reading of this book.

Finnegans Wake is a splendid example of the degree to which a literary work predicates the body of criticism that arises to elucidate and amplify it. The encyclopedic works of the early twentieth century, including *Ulysses, Finnegans Wake,* and *The Cantos of Ezra Pound,* demanded keys and guides almost simultaneously with their publication. Eliot's *Wasteland* comes equipped with its own footnotes. *Finnegans Wake* is a mass of allusions, characters, and nonevents. Hence, some of its scholarly responses pursue the characters (Adeline Glasheens' *Second Census of Finnegans Wake;* John Gordon's *Finnegans Wake: A Plot Summary*), codifying the allusions (James Atherton's *Books at the Wake*), synthesizing the megastructures (Clive Hart's *Structure and Motif in Finnegans Wake*), and furnishing a plot summary (Glasheen, Gordon; and Joseph Campbell and Henry Morton Robinson's *Skeleton Key to Finnegans Wake*). Certain other compendia pursue the sequence of the text in furnishing "marginal" annotations (Roland McHugh's *Annotations to Finnegans Wake*).[7] In effect, a significant and extremely productive portion of the critical literature has structured itself by addressing specific dimensions of the novel's chaos needing to be unscrambled. This segment of the critical literature may be visualized as a set of enigma machines or code unscramblers organized according to different principles. In this sense the novel's criticism reflects the profound unease that readers feel when addressing texts manifestly nontotalizable. Like the posture of deconstruction, *Finnegans Wake* constitutes a literary psychoanalysis, an unmasking of the expectations and structures that readers bring to reading.

One cannot speak of any overall schematism of *Finnegans Wake* to parallel the superimposition of times and places, colors, art forms, and classical antecedents that characterizes *Ulysses.* The various segments of *Finnegans Wake* are nonetheless heavily colored in their local difference. Chapter 1.1 is hilariously historical; chapter 2.1 heavily theatrical; and, a section to which I will now turn, chapter 1.5 formatively scriptural. The reading of *Finnegans Wake* is at all times a doubled process: interpreting a specific constellation or configuration of themes, allusions, characters, puns, and esthetic models; and accounting for the implicit textual allegory in this performance. No segment of this work combines its elements more interestingly and is more indicative of its performance of itself as a text than chapter 1.5.

In addition, no chapter is more tenacious in setting out the novel's writerly dimension. It is a focal point for the letters that abound throughout the novel. It comes even replete with directions on how to read itself. "Now, patience; and remember patience is a great thing, and above all things else we must avoid anything like being or becoming out of patience" (FW, 108). According to Glasheen, the central epistle of the novel has been gathered by a pecking hen on page 11 and is buried by HCE's servant Kate on page 80. Its text appears on page 111, in chapter 1.5.

This chapter begins with a "mamafesta" by Anna Livia Plurabella "memorializing the Most highest"—God? HCE?—an unreadable list of titles, many with the ring of book or popular song titles. The chapter's ur-text is thus an incoherent list, by another Joycean woman. The body of the chapter is thus a gloss of this impossible text. No sooner is the manifesto ended than that chapter takes up the issue of writing: "The proteiform graph itself is a polyhedron of scripture" (FW, 107). Reading the chapter indeed consists in exploring a polyhedron of figures that emerge from Joyce's disfigured language by pursuing the proteiform of writing, the leaps between figures permitted by the associative volatility of language. Joyce's significant subtexts emerge as repetitions within the open-ended sequence of distortions. The body of chapter 1.5 proceeds from the motif of writing ("scripture") to that of letters, both as epistles and alphabet characters ("naif alphabetters," "personalities inflicted in the documents" [107]), and on into envelopes ("a quite everydaylooking stamped addressed envelope" [109]), clothing ("the facts of feminine clothiering are there all the time or that the feminine fiction, stranger than the facts" [109]), photography ("almost any photoist worth his chemicots will tip anyone asking him the teaser that if a negative of a horse happens to melt enough while drying" [111], hens and birds in general ("About that original hen," "The bird in the case was Belinda of the Dorans" [110–11]), the police ("if you police, after you, policepolice, pardoning mein" [113]), war and politics ("what we have perused from the pages of I was a Gemral, that Showting up of bulsklivism by 'Schottenboum'" [116]), sounds ("variously inflected, differently pronounced, otherwise spelled, changeably meaning vocable scriptsigns" [118]), drink, orality, and kissing ("nor since Roe's Distillery burn'd have quaff'd Night's firefill'd Cup . . . whang, whack on his pigsking's Kisser for him" [122]), and back to a lengthy excursis on letters as written and phonic characters ("and begin again to make soundsense and sensesound kin . . . those haughtypitched disdotted aiches easily of the rariest inasdroll as most of the jaywalking eyes we do plough into halve" [121]).

Reading this chapter, then, which so much concerns itself with the phonic and graphic dimensions of writing, demands first the discernment out of linguistic disfiguration of the operative motifs in the text and then an understanding of their interconnection. What do letters have to do with female clothing, or photographs with hens? Letters as epistles are dressed in envelopes and clothing envelops us all ("Yet to concentrate solely on the literal sense or even the psychological content of any document to the sore neglect of the enveloping facts . . . is just as hurtful to sound sense" [FW, 109]). In its visual dimension, writing depends as much on light as does photography. The involutions of its meaning allow for volatile fluctuations between the semantic as well as photographic positive and negative. Yet throughout *Finnegans Wake*, Joyce is equally concerned with the aural dimension of the scriptural medium. This is why chapter 1.5 concerns itself so much not only with pronunciation and mispronunciation but also with eating, pecking, drinking, and kissing. Joyce highlights rather than suppresses the subtle differences between his text's *soundsense* and its visually decoded meaning.

Chapter 1.5 provides a demonstration of the novel's decoding at the same time that it explores its written medium. *Finnegans Wake* does not abdicate the need for interpretation; it does, however, radically shift the demands and expectations of reading. The aims or orientations of reading have become open-ended. A suspension of the demand for finality and specificity has taken place. It is in this sense that I have described a referential slowdown in the novel.

The beginning of *Finnegans Wake* is surely as full (and devoid) of a sense of initiation as any novel or narrative may be. Although the reader is reminded that the text's formal beginning, its first sentence, is a carry-over from its conclusion, *Finnegans Wake*'s outset is replete with a geological and cosmological overview, biblical (and Koranic) references, and a comprehensive, if parodic historical background. While radically questioning the conditions of narrative and conceptual origins, this novel (or counternovel) nonetheless arises in a dramatic flourish accentuating its own beginning(s). Continuing in the litany of grammatical and conceptual markers that is the great stylistic contribution of the Penelope episode of *Ulysses*, the river of the counternovel's language, having run "past Eve and Adam," quickly incorporates a heterogeneous mélange of contexts: the Old Testament (the Fall and "a bland old isaac"), "christian minstrelsy," European folklore (Sir Tristram weds the Germanic to the insular), and the specifically Irish ("thuartpeatrick," "the pftjschute of Finnegan"—all FW, 3).

Such predictable historical and cultural contexts are immediately intertwined in a network of not yet intelligible internal references and in a widely heteroclite external web of associations. Out of the sequence of interchangeable male characters emerges "Wassaily Booslaeugh of Riesengeborg," a Germanic-Gaelic-alcoholic hybrid (FW, 5). The communal "cubehouse" (clubhouse?) "still rocks to the thunder of his" (Finnegan's?) "arafatas but we hear also through successive ages that shebby choruysh of unkalified muzzlenimiissilehims that would blackguardize the whitestone ever hurtleturtled out of heaven" (5). Half-reference and linguistic disfiguration afford Joyce the ongoing opportunity to interpolate different supplementary referential codes, hidden agendas, situated at the edge of the description or action at hand—into the fictive discourse of *Finnegans Wake*. In the sentence cited immediately above, a string of Islamic associations insinuates itself into the explanation of Finn's "tragoady," at the same time consolidating the mock-heroic assertion of "canonical" authority. "Shebby choruysh" inserts an as yet unidentified character, one of the son figures, into the description. The phrase "unkalified muzzlenimiissilehims"—whose hidden calif, muslin, and missiles enrich and qualify a parodic account of a multiple fall—indicates the rich play and wit that the ambiguity of half-reference affords.

In its own idiosyncratic way, then, the first chapter of *Finnegans Wake* furnishes a mythical, theological, cultural, and allusive foundation for the novel—or rather it elaborates specifically the only foundation a counternovel to the tradition of this genre could have. (If the occasion for the novel's *Wake* is indeed a physical as well as spiritual fall on the part of Finnegan, in its narrative structure, at least, the text bears a certain resemblance to *The Cantos of Ezra Pound*, whose mythological framework sets out from the fatal fall of another character, Elpenor.) Yet already in the novel's introduction to itself, there are passages amounting to tangents within a discourse structured by indirection; interjections consummating, to the extent this is possible, the Shandean tradition of the digression. Such passages amount to metadigressions; they epitomize the potentials opened by half-reference, explored by Joyce and the other modernists who accompanied him into the postmodern.

With Finnegan duly introduced and dispatched to the other world, the reader happens upon the following interjection:

This the way to the museyroom. Mind your hats goan in! Now yiz are in the Willingdone Museyroom. This is a Prooshious gunn. This is a ffrinch. Tip. This is the flag of the Prooshious, the Cap and Soracer. This is the bullet that byng the flag of the Prooshious. This is the ffrinch that fire on the Bull that bang the flag of the Prooshious. Saloos the Crossgunn! Up with your pike and fork! Tip. (Bullsfoot! Fine!) This is the triplewon hat of Lipoleum. Tip. Lipoleumhat. This is the Willingdone on his same white harse, the Cokenhape. This is the big Sraughter Willingdone, grand and magentic in his goldtin spurs and his ironed dux and his quarterbrass woodyshoes and his magnate's gharters and his bangkok's best and goliar's goloshes and his pulluponeasyan wartrews. This is his big wide harse. Tip. This is the three lipoleum boyne grouching down in the living detch. This is an inimyskilling inglis, this is a scotcher grey, this is a davy, stooping. This is the bog lipoleum mordering the lipoleum beg. A Gallawghurs argaumunt. This is the petty lipoleum boy that was nayther bag nor bug. Assaye, assaye! Touchole Fitz Tuomush. Dirty MacDyke. And Hairy O'Hurry. All of them arminus-varminus. This is Delian alps. This is Mont Tivel, this is Mont Tipsey, this is the Grand Mons Injun. This is the crimealine of the alps hopping to sheltershock the three lipoleums. This is the jinnies with their legahorns feinting to read in their handmade's book of stralegy while making their war undisides the Willingdone. The jinnies is a cooin her hand and the jinnies is a ravin her hair and the Willingdone git the band up. This is big Willingdone mormorial tallowscoop Wounderworker obscides on the flanks of the jinnies. Sexcaliber hrosspower. Tip. This is me Belchum sneaking his phillippy out of his most Awful Grimmest Sunshat Cromwelly. Looted. This is the jinnies' hastings dispatch for to irrigate the Willingdone. Dispatch in thin red lines cross the shortfront of me Belchum. Yaw, yaw, yaw! Leaper Orthor. Fear siecken! Fieldgaze thy tiny frow. Hugacting. Nap. That was the tictacs of the jinnies for to fontannoy the Willingdone. Shee, shee, shee! The jinnies is jillous agincourting all the lipoleums. And the lipoleums is gonn boycottoncrezy onto the one Willingdone. And the Willingdone git the band up. This is bode Belchum, bonnet to busby, breaking his secred word with a ball up his ear to the Willingdone. This is the Willingdone's hurold dispitchback. Dispitch desployed on the regions rare of me Belchum. Salamangra! Ayi, ayi, ayi! Cherry jinnies. Figtreeyou! Damn fairy ann, Voutre. Willingdone. That was the first joke of Willingdone, tic for tac. Hee, hee, hee! (*FW,* 8–9)

Even within a novel as polymorphous and playful as *Finnegans Wake,* this passage is as unmotivated as any digression could be. In light of the novel's mythological and biblical beginnings, how does one suddenly find oneself in the midst of a "museyroom," where a "speaker" identified only through an economic demand for "Tips" and stylistic repetitiveness, points out such wonders as "a Prooshious gunn," the "Lipoleumhat," and "Willingdone on his . . . white horse"? At the same time that the passage initiates a vertiginous tangent, it discloses the assumptions one must make and inferences one must draw even in order to decode it. If "Lipoleum" is Napoleon, if "Willingdone" corresponds to Wellington, and if a "museyroom" is a museum, the passage launches a linguistically wild escape from the novel's already tenuous groundings: a guided tour of a Wellington museum replete with hats, weapons, depictions of horses, and dispatches. Yet so unmotivated are certain tangents in this digression that it explicitly underscores the identifications and other reductive operations in which we necessarily engage in order to decode this less-and-more-than-referential text.

There are indeed certain interests militating for the at least provisional toleration of these identifications: the novel wants to be read; the critical literature has established certain of the interpretative traditions suggested above. A rigorous reading of the passage must also, however, take its operative terms at their own word. What is specific to Lipoleum, museyroom, and Willingdone? Is there lip service and flooring in the first, affirmation in the last, and rumination in the middle term? What happens to the passage's coherence if these signifiers merely are what they are and do not translate into an intelligible "original" meaning.

The three terms in question belong to the reluctant order of the half-reference. Only half-heartedly do they man their stations in the social and literary contracts of language. As they go, so go the other ambiguous and possibly disfigured signifiers with which the text of *Finnegans Wake* is heavily laced. The digression adds precisely nothing to the action of a novel or the development of a narrative. What it adds is at most a demonstration: of the linguistic determinations or points of fixity operative in conventional narrative, and the vertigo resulting from their cumulative release.

The preponderant language game of the passage in question is simple indication. "This is a Prooshious gunn. . . . This is the petty lipoleum boy that was nayther bag nor bug. . . . That was the first joke of Willingdone, tic for tac." The narrative not only presents a transcript of the discourse of a quirky and simple-minded character: it stages a *mise en abîme* of the acts and assumptions surrounding indication itself. The absurdity of the guided tour attaches to the presumptions of novelistic identification, equation, and reproduction. The half-reference not only liberates the signification of words and sentences: it subjects the foundations of novelistic representation to a devastating, if hilarious critique. As a unified linguistic field, every novel is a "museyroom" of objects, actions, and memories of the past.

Half-reference adds through the process of subtraction. It releases metonymic possibilities while it detracts from the certainty of semiological value. The misspelling of "gharters" (as in *Gurkha*) opens a path for the description of "Willingdone's" galoshes as "bangkok's best." "Belchum," if it indeed corresponds to Belgium, introduces the after-effects of digestion into the setting of the Battle of Waterloo. Where sustained phrases transpire under the semiology of half-reference, the experience of reading becomes uncannily alienated from itself. The reader submits to the flow of decoding, but without the support that conventional usage customarily provides. The impact of this pursuit of chains of signification no longer fully qualified by the *parole* is the linguistic equivalent of getting lost or taking the wrong turn. So many variables are left open in the syntax of *Finnegans Wake* that the reader stumbles upon this vertigo from every direction. "This is the Willingdone branlish his same marmorial tallowscoop Sophy-Key-Po for his royal divorsion on the rinaway jinnes. Gambariste della porca! Dalaveras fimmieras!," continues the "museyroom" passage. This fragment not only describes runaway horses; it also constitutes a runaway sentence. Syntactical ambiguity (should "this" be "thus"?) combines with grammatical distortion (if Willingdone is the sentence's subject, "branlish'—brandish— should be "branlishes") and imprecise diction to generate an irreducible ambiguity, a hovering between sense and non-sense. Careful exegesis and scholarship may eventually identify all but a few of the individual elements in such a sentence, but even so, the links between unknowns are so tenuous that the statement never eventuates at any linguistic grounding or "earth." The mode of half-reference thus guarantees, at certain points, the illegibility of its discourse through the unpinning of multiple simultaneous variables.

The distinctive postmodern discourse of *Finnegans Wake* is, by the same token, the result of a concurrence of factors. It arises, above all, from the conjunction of a refusal and an overwhelming, a repudiation of standing literary contracts and conventions, and the overrunning of grammatical, syntactical, conceptual, and lexicographical markers and rules. Neologisms and disfigurations of an etymological and syntactical nature combine with run-on sentences, the obsessive piling of puns and other wordplays, and unannounced, unmotivated allusions and grafts. The mode of half-reference opens up a false etymological bottom through which the text exercises its freedom to interpolate new and tangential themes. An undercurrent of river imagery insinuates itself into the least expected strata of "Anna Livia Plurabella": "My wrists are wrusty rubbing the mouldaw stains. And the dneepers of wet and the gangres of sin in it!" (*FW*, 196). "She was? Gotta pot! Yssel that the limmat? As El Negro winced when he winced in La Plate. . . . Tell us in franca langua. And call a spate a spate" (198). The not terribly well-hidden agenda of rivers in these examples transforms mildew into Moldau stains and "Isn't that the limit?" into an impossible confluence of Dutch and Swiss rivers (the Ijssel and Limmat). Through the same type of thematic introjection, Shem the Penman's breakfast emerges from the oven as a deluge, a nightmare of eggs: "his cantraps of fermented words, abracadabra calubra culorum, (his oewfs à la Madame Gabrielle de l'Eglise, his avgs à la Mistress B. de B. Meinefelde, his eiers Usquadmala à la pomme de ciel, his uoves, oves and uves à la Sulphate de Soude, his ochiuri sowtay sowmmonay à la Monseigneur, his soufflosion of oogs with somekat on toyast à la Mère Puard" (184).

Amid the fulminating murkiness of half-reference, national languages, as I have shown, do not even have to be faithful to themselves. Half-reference opens up a vast space for interlinguistic punning that Joyce exuberantly invades, making it henceforth impossible to "tell us in franca langua." Finnegan's fall is his "pftjschute," a Germanized version of the French *chute* with extra consonants added for measure. Shem's soufflé becomes a "soufflosion." An interlinguistic construction is not quite at home in any of the languages that it spans. It occupies the position of the alien that is nonetheless a catalyst of unexpected meaning. It is *of* both none and all of its languages.

On a thematic level, Molly's monologue in *Ulysses* opens, stylistically and through its allusions to garters, drawers, and smells, the forbidden path into the anus and anal sex. In *Finnegans Wake*, the artwork becomes, above all, a composite, a distinctive substance or stuff, whose texture and consistency mean more than its form or resolution. Although at the highest level of literary sensibility, *Finnegans Wake* effects the digestion of its thematic, historical, and allusive materials. The affective correlative to this digestion is indifference, a retrospective detachment from the "day" of action, representation, conceptual lucidity, and volition. Surely it is with a certain degree of rage that *Finnegans Wake* witnesses and enacts the violation of the basic contracts governing representation and the novelistic genre. Yet the end product of this multifaceted retraction is a certain active indifference, a tolerance for the emptying of linguistic content and motivation.

The discourse of *Finnegans Wake* is thus *décontracté*—relaxed or un-tensed—in the full sense of the French word. Its associative proliferation surely exceeds the capacities of the structuralist kaleidoscope. This instrument, despite its affinities for modernist *bricolage*, is ultimately motivated by what Wallace Stevens called "the blessed rage for order." In this sense, *Finnegans Wake* comprises an affront as well as a delight to commentators.

The product of Joyce's experimentation and toying with the contractual assumptions of linguistic usage was a text of surplus meaning, association, and inference challenging the assumptions as well as the practices of organized knowledge. The discourse of *Finnegans Wake* is indifferent to the compulsions and schemes to control it. It indicates both a mode and an ambiance of textual production bypassing the often exuberant anxiety in which structures are crystallized and applied. Though this counterdomain to the turnings of the structuralist kaleidoscope may be most compellingly illustrated by *Finnegans Wake*, it is also inhabited, in different ways, by the late Kafka, Benjamin, and Adorno; it inspires as well a still-growing body of fictive and theoretical texts.

ON THE PLAIN OF INDIFFERENCE

And the smaller rooms, each familiar to me, so familiar that in spite of their complete similarity I can clearly distinguish one from the other with my eyes shut by the mere feel of the wall: they enclose me more peacefully and warmly than a bird is enclosed in its nest. —Kafka, "The Burrow"

I did my best to go in a circle, hoping in this way to go in a straight line. For I stopped being half-witted and became sly, whenever I took the trouble. And my head was a storehouse of useful knowledge. And if I did not go in a rigorously straight line, with my system of going in a circle, at least I did not go in a circle, and that was something. And by going on doing this, day after day, and night after night, I looked forward to getting out of the forest, some day. —Beckett, *Molloy*

In his text, the writer sets up house. Just as he trundles papers, books, pencils, documents untidily from room to room, he creates the same disorder in his thoughts. They become pieces of furniture that he sinks into, content or irritable. . . . For a man who no longer has a homeland, writing becomes a place to live. In it he inevitably produces, as his family once did, refuse and lumber. But now he lacks a store-room, and it is hard in any case to part from left-overs. —Adorno, *Minima Moralia*

The meditation chamber is so constructed as to make it possible to meditate there for several days in a row, and it's intended for no other use but meditation, it's totally devoid of any objects, there's not to be a single object in the meditation chamber, nor any light either. A red dot in the center of the meditation chamber indicates the actual center of the meditation chamber, which is also the true center of the cone. The radius from the center in every direction is fourteen meters long. —Bernhard, *Correction*

The postmodern, then, does not transcend or leave behind the modern. It is always already inscribed within the modern. It obliterates and effaces the structures upon which modernism must rely for its own improvisations and for its unanticipated grafts, appropriations, and retrospective realignments.

As I have elsewhere suggested, certain of the structures gaining particular prominence in modernism come with venerable traditions in the history of philosophy. Performatively, the explosion of structure by postmodernism assumes the form of a multifaceted violation of contractual obligations (Bataille's term is transgression).[8] In pursuing the developments making the final phase of Joyce's fiction possible, I have focused on the flaunting of what is perhaps the most fundamental contract: the referential imperative making all other representation possible. Wherever this kind of open-ended disfiguration appears, whether in Laurence Sterne or in works in or outside the period, the overall thrust is postmodern.[9] The postmodern plays at the violation of multiple secondary linguistic contracts as well. These conventions may be grammatical, rhetorical, logical, or stylistic in nature. Molly Bloom's monologue in the Penelope episode of *Ulysses*—with its seemingly endless run-ons, its refusal to introduce or close the logical units of thought, and its dearth of transitional devices—comprises a privileged but by no means exclusive site for this multifaceted postmodern violation of linguistic conventions.

Affectively, a certain indifference coincides with the postmodern effacement of structure, which is also prefigured in the vast Proustian arc of utterance and in the sustained ruminations of Kafka's animal characters. It would be reductive to draw any clinical inferences as to where, on the emotional spectrum, this indifference stands. The universe of Freudian neurosis is largely accommodated by hysteria (or anxiety) and its complementary syndrome, which Freud calls obsessional neurosis. Freud characterizes this domain in terms of disquieting thoughts that refuse to be blocked out and in terms of miscues within the economy of sexual object-choice. In elaborating the countersyndrome to anxiety, he generally avoids the term *depression*.

The indifference of postmodernity is anxious-depressive, fusing an endless annexation of qualifications with a fatal resignation to the predetermination of an entropic universe. Postmodern discourse is suspended between the terror underlying statements that can never be made perfect enough and a sense of the absurdity surrounding the endeavor. It is placed in the hands and mouths of entities whose resemblance to humans grows increasingly tenuous. These creatures of the text ruminate obsessively on a range of possibly insubstantial issues, often hopelessly after the fact. They meditate with a mixture of Wittgensteinian rigor and deconstructive awareness of the arbitrariness of all formulations. The discourse of the postmodern character or surrogate is framed both by a sensibility to the closed operations making discourse possible and by a commitment, however absurd it may seem, to conceptual rigor. It is thus possible both for the often hilarious disfigurations of *Finnegans Wake* and for the fatalistic enclosure of Beckett's characters within the limits of their knowledge to arise within the context of postmodern indifference. In a sense, the creatures of postmodernity are at home in the relentlessly logical, functionally divided world of Wittgenstein's *Tractatus*. This work, typeset as a single extended paragraph, without the sequence and subordination furnished by its numeration, would comprise an exemplary postmodern text.

The indifference of postmodernity emerges when the structures and differences joyously and anxiously discovered by modernism have ceased to make a difference. The philosophical parameters of this movement have been meticulously set out in recent work by Rodolphe Gasché.[10] Irreducible to any stylistic manifestation or affective content, postmodern indifference is, in Gasché's sense of the word, systematic: it is installed throughout the discourse and mode of postmodernity.

The truly distinctive works of twentieth-century literature straddle a modal and, in Foucault's sense, archaeological divide. What happens when one crosses over into the counterdomain demarcated by *Finnegans Wake*, Beckett's plays and novels, the fictive and discursive prose of Georges Bataille and Maurice Blanchot, and the theoretical writing of Jacques Derrida? Above all, there has been a loss or relinquishing of a certain nostalgia, a weaning from the presumptions of total intimacy and possession. The Angel of History no longer stares longingly into the past. The past is no longer an origin, a time more authentic than others because a greater degree of intimacy once prevailed there. It is, rather, a relative position along an indifferent continuum—one might say tedium—of time. Sexuality ceases to be an exclusive or privileged proving ground of Being but is one activity among others, something that people do. They *do sex* for a variety of motives—sometimes with no motive at all—and with a number of different results. Sex means inherently nothing in its own right; its variants are devoid of any implicit moral, political, or esthetic value.

The literary implications of this slight shift are multifaceted: In the conception of literary characters, the role of surrogation diminishes in favor of functionality. Characters do not so much embody subjects, real or imagined, as they perform functions, within language and throughout the range of philosophical, sociopolitical and psychological economies. The shift from a subjective to a functional model for character representation is no more suggestively ambiguous —placed squarely between the two—than in Musil's *Man without Qualities*, whose characters play simultaneously in an interlocked story and a vast philosophical scheme.[11] In his short prose, Kafka had already experimented with treating characters as the hypothetical agents of logical and mathematical word problems, a practice subsequently exploited above all by Italo Calvino.[12]

SAMUEL BECKETT. The rules of psychological hygiene—such as consistency, unity, and integrity—apply less to literary characters when they have been liberated from the analogical imperative to imitate subjectivity. The literature of postmodernity thus toys with the fictive conventions by which each character claims a uniqueness of essence and purpose. I have already pointed out the absence of boundaries separating the human and animal family members in Kafka's "Country Doctor." The pronounced doubling of characters in twentieth-century literature—the revelation or suggestion that two distinct fictive agents could be the same character or share the same subjectivity—arises in the context of this critique of the presuppositions underlying surrogation. If characters are nothing other than constructions of the text, why do they have to be discrete? Why can't they overlap? What "actions" are they obliged to complete? It is precisely such questions that Samuel Beckett, in a postmodern climate, is free to pursue. For this reason the experience, physical traits, and language ascribed to the agent Jacques Moran and to Molloy in the novel named after the latter character turn out to be remarkably similar. To enforce its illusion of characterological integrity, the novel is divided in two parts, the second ostensibly introducing a different perspective, corresponding to the action and thoughts of a new character, one more purposive and socially integrated than Molloy. By the end of the novel, however, its division, motives, and adversarial drama are most tenuous: *Molloy* thus continues the questioning of characterological status initiated by Kafka in, among other texts,

"First Sorrow," "A Common Confusion," "Description of a Struggle," and *The Castle*.

Just as character representation relinquishes its attachment to the model of subjectivity, literary form, in a postmodern climate, relaxes its fidelity to the representation of events. Not only must "events" no longer be brought to fruition or completion: in a strict sense, there is no necessity for them even to occur. The only events taking place in the enclosed subterranean environment of Kafka's "Burrow" correspond to the hypotheses of a somewhat crazed burrowing rodent. *Molloy* sets the stage for an interrogation, an escape, and a pursuit, but these actions, in the strict sense of the word, never eventuate. Molloy and Moran, to the extent they are distinct characters, both end up "on the road." The motives for Molloy's departure and Moran's assignment are never clarified. More importantly, although the characters do cross paths, no decisive cooperation between them ever takes place. The events of the novel, to the extent they can be named as such, consist in a language of imagery eventually penetrating the discourse of both characters: bicycles, legs, crutches, dogs, smells, circles. In this sense the plot of the postmodern novel is no longer an organizing framework whose formal necessities shape the narrative artwork; plot assumes instead a figural, often ironic posture.

What applies to the novel's events applies to its coherence. In the postmodern setting, no dominant result or resolution need emerge. Rather than completing any story, Calvino's *If on a winter's night a traveller* tells the same one several times over, each time parodying different styles and fictive conventions.[13] Postmodern fiction neither emulates nor instruments actions. It submerges the structural apparatus on which actions and events are arranged and placed in sequence. (Section and chapter divisions, as well as the devices attributing dialogue and thoughts to characters, contribute in part to this apparatus.) The effacement of this structure may explain the infirmity of Molloy's skeleton—why this central character cannot perform actions without prosthetic devices such as crutches and (chainless) bicycles.

The discourse of postmodernity is closer to a distinctive fabric or material than to formed objects. It continues relentlessly, often devoid of action and resolution, to no predetermined end. What holds true for plot in the postmodern novel holds true for the argument in contemporaneous discursive prose. Development is not measured in terms of conclusion, inference, or resolution, but rather through the associative involution that language constructs out of itself. No sooner is there a single line of plot or association than multiple parallel or skewed pathways emerge. The postmodern relinquishes its developmental thrust to the accumulated reverberations and dissonances that the linguistic medium unleashes. To the extent that deconstruction arranges variegated materials according to an ongoing concern or conceptual matrix—the status of language in systematic thought—it contains a structuralist moment; to the extent that its discourse is idiosyncratically configured by complex tropes deriving from the texts it addresses, it is poststructuralist and hence postmodern. A vibrant parallelism prevails between the stylistic improvisations of postmodernism and the conceptual dismantling and recasting furnished by poststructuralism.

Acceptance, resignation, and indifference—these attitudes comprise the esthetic, conceptual, and thematic atmosphere in which the sea changes of postmodernism arise. These terms share the limitations inherent in all generalizations, including those presuming to account for wide bodies of literary works. The attitudes of indifference, to the extent that they capture nothing more substantial than an atmosphere of textual production, anticipate, ever so briefly and inadequately, the spontaneous afterimage of an accelerated and fast disappearing century.

For a novel organized around an unmotivated chase between two characters who are never more remote than when they are together, a novel whose structure and resolution are as soft as its central characters' legs are gimpy, Samuel Beckett's *Molloy* is surprisingly concerned with the law. Indeed, the second syllable of its title character's name corresponds to an archaic variant for the French word for law, a point all the more compelling since the novel originally appeared in that language. Phonically, in English as well as French, "Molloy" is *my law, ma loi*. Etymologically, it is "soft law," combining law with the Latin *mollis*, surviving in the German musical notation for flat or "weak" notes and keys and also in the French *mou, mol/le:* "soft," "feeble," "weak," "mellow."

And how could any novel be more illustrative of the "soft law" than *Molloy?* After fatally running over a dog with his chainless bicycle, Molloy is released by the authorities in the custody of its owner. His pursuer, agent Jacques Moran may be a churchgoer, a home owner, and a father, but his relations to his colleagues, son, and servant are as vague as Molloy's senses of placement and identity. (Molloy's greatest achievement during an initial—unmotivated—interview with the police is to recall his name, to furnish his own signature: "And suddenly I remembered my name, Molloy. My name is

Molloy, I cried, all of a sudden, now I remember. Nothing compelled me to give this information, but I gave it, hoping to please I suppose. They let me keep my hat on" [M, 29].) The law is tested to the limit by the uncanny doubling that ultimately ascribes Molloy's distinctive attributes to its "agent."

After killing a dog with a bicycle explicitly described as a mechanical supplement to his defective endoskeleton, Molloy is taken home by the animal's owner, an individual of indefinite sexual identity named Lousse. (The homonymy linking this name to the English *loose* only reinforces the caption of a "soft law.") An immediate affinity springs up between Lousse and Molloy:

> It was she made me acquainted with love. She went by the peaceful name of Ruth I think, but I can't say for certain. Perhaps the name was Edith. She had a hole between her legs, oh not the bunghole I had always imagined, but a slit, and in this I put, or rather she put, my so-called virile member, not without difficulty, and I toiled and moiled until I discharged or gave up trying or was begged by her to stop. A mug's game in my opinion and tiring on top of that, in the long run. But I lent myself to it with a good enough grace, knowing it was love, for she had told me so. She bent over the couch, because of her rheumatism, and in I went from behind. It was the only position she could bear, because of her lumbago. It seemed all right to me, for I had seen dogs, and I was astonished when she confided that you could go about it differently. I wonder what she meant exactly. Perhaps after all she put me in her rectum. A matter of complete indifference to me, I needn't tell you. But is it true love, in the rectum? That's what bothers me sometimes. Have I never known true love, after all? She too was an eminently flat woman and she moved with short stiff steps, leaning on an ebony stick. Perhaps she too was a man, yet another of them. But in that case surely our testicles would have collided, while we writhed. (M, 75–76)

Such are love and sexuality in the postmodern world: conducted with remarkable detachment, devoid of romantic delusions as of emotions, veering sharply toward the forbidden path of the anus. It scant matters whether Lousse, "a woman of extraordinary flatness" is a man or a woman: "she, undertaking me from behind, thrust her stick between my legs and began to titillate my privates." Sexuality — in the Freudian system as in the history of the novel the very crucible of identity and fate — has become "a matter of complete indifference ... I needn't tell you." Molloy departs from this setting of domestic bliss as abruptly and arbitrarily as he arrived.

Molloy has pursued Molly Bloom's ruminations on smells and anality (does the Molloy-Molly pairing further justify his name?). Known to his mother, dead at the outset of the novel, by his smells, "I don't diffuse the perfumes of Araby myself," Molloy muses. The anus is for Molloy the locus of sexual indifference, as excrement, for Freud, reduces the variegated substances of the world to a single composite.[14] Beckett underscores the atmospheric detachment in which postmodern love, one completely weaned from metaphysical delusions, is consummated. "The other thing that bothers me, in this connection, is the indifference with which I learned of [Lousse's] death, one black night I was crawling towards her, an indifference softened indeed by the pain of losing a source of revenue" (M, 78). Even Molloy's remorse at his indifference is tenuous and heavily qualified.

In its distinctively loose way, Molloy is a twentieth-century descendant of Kierkegaards' Either/Or. Within the novel's conspicuously aborted plan, Jacques Moran, to whom the second segment is dedicated, would furnish the authority, measure, and purpose lacking in Molloy and more forcefully advocated by Judge William in Or.[15] Molloy would occupy the place of Kierkegaard's esthete, with one decisive difference: Moran's adversarial relation to Molloy is as questionable as, in the end, the judge's is to the esthete; but Beckett has transformed the esthete's musical effervescence, a bubbling energy epitomizing the realm of art, into an autistic confinement to silence and monotony. "To restore silence is the role of objects" (M, 16). There are sensations in Molloy's world, above all, sounds and smells, but these are relentless, almost inarticulate.

> I listen, and the voice is of a world collapsing endlessly, a frozen world, under a faint untroubled sky, enough to see by, yes, and frozen too. And I hear it murmur that all wilts and yields, as if loaded down, but here there are no loads. . . . For what possible end to these wastes where true light never was, nor any upright thing, nor any true foundation, but only these leaning things, forever lapsing and crumbling away, beneath a sky without memory of morning or hope of night. . . . Yes, a world at an end, in spite of appearances.
> (M, 53)

Molloy's universe is in an endless state of entropy. Its limp objects bend, although they are burdened with no weight. Molloy's infirmity, the stiffness of a leg, fuses an inorganic rigidity to this torpor.

The single constructive force in this world may well consist in the ability of the written thing to furnish an account of its own production. Molloy shares with the subterranean enclosure of Kafka's "Burrow" a concurrence between the ruminations of postmodern subcharacters and the text emerging on the page. The locations of

Molloy may shift, from hamlets to forests and swamps; the activities narrated, however, never stray far from the moves deployed in the composition of this text. Molloy the character may warn "that you would do better, at least no worse, to obliterate texts than to blacken margins, to fill in the holes of words till all is blank and flat and the whole ghastly business looks like what it is, senseless, speechless, issueless misery" (*M*, 16)—yet he is incapable of couching his activities in terms that are not intimately bound up with writing. The novel's sustained coincidence between its narrated events and its scene of writing allows a free access to characters from Beckett's other novels, although they have not figured in the actions. Molloy and Moran are not only sources for the novel's narrative: they comment freely on their own compositional options: "But in order to blacken a few more pages may I say I spent some time at the seaside, without incident," qualifies Molloy (92), and Moran informs us, "I had to suffer other molestations that this, other offences, but I shall not record them" (236). However the novel's surrogates characterize their activities, they are at all times internal writers in the text, occupying the place of Derrida's stage prompter.[16] "I lost interest in my patients, once I had finished with them," concedes Moran. "I may even truthfully say I never saw one of them again, subsequently, not a single one. No conclusions need be drawn from this. Oh the stories I could tell you, if I were easy. What a rabble in my head, what a gallery of moribunds. Murphy, Watt, Yerk, Mercier and all the others" (188).

The characters of *Molloy*, then, walk, stumble, ride bicycles, and crawl through a variety of settings allegorical of textual production and rhetorical figuration and disfiguration. They are agents, creatures of the text, at the same time as they are actors. From a pragmatic point of view, their plans and activities are fruitless, absurd. The only meaning their actions can have is within a scene of writing. Appropriating the structure of a detective novel in the loosest possible sense, Beckett has extended the amorphous and self-sustaining ruminations arising in Kafka's Burrow to an existential setting. As in the epigraph to this section from Beckett, the characters describe certain shapes as they stumble through the novel's forests and swamps. Molloy circles back on himself. He arrives at crossroads (*M*, 98, 112, 115); he steals a silver object in the form of an ×️ from Lousse (85). He reaches impasses: "Yes, my progress reduced me to stopping more and more often, it was the only way to progress, to stop" (105). These movements extend the faint hope of structure in the form of geometrical figures: "I altered course, which permitted me to describe, if not a circle, at least a great polygon, perfection is not of this world" (122). Such movements across an allegorical landscape describe, if anything, moments in the process of writing itself: repetitions, chainings, abrupt endings that lines of association reach. Fictive composition is itself a shaky ride on "a chainless bicycle, with a free-wheel, if such a bicycle exists" (19).

In a postmodern setting, Beckett conspicuously dismantles the machinery of the novel. He deprives his characters of identity and motivation. He displays the action on a hopelessly broken, impotent framework. An affective environment of remorseless indifference mutes the emotional music that has come to accompany works of fiction as well as operas. He has opened literature to the much more silent and disquieting noise — a static — that writing generates out of its friction with itself. With great rigor, scientifically shifting them from pocket to pocket, Molloy sucks stones (M, 93–100). This modest and sterile act describes the aspirations and pretensions of literature when they have been tempered by their postmodern climate.

THEODOR ADORNO. How ironic: Theodor Adorno, writing during and after the war that had released his culture's barbarism, that had obliterated virtually his entire intellectual and artistic generation, finds in dialectics, perhaps best exemplified by Hegel, the most hopeful remainder of a conceptual tradition whose other cultural products included Nazism. Adorno's writing admits of a certain quirkiness, perhaps because it has been so directly mitigated by historical circumstances. Much of French structuralism, particularly Barthes and Foucault, is unthinkable without the Frankfurt school. But by 1977, one finds the Barthes of A Lover's Discourse combing comfortable Paris for trinkets of affection, whereas thirty years before, Adorno had been making difficult, and not always even, choices.[17]

Adorno takes on the monumental task of somehow explaining how World War II could follow in the wake of a highly sophisticated, indeed exemplary, philosophical tradition. He combs Western philosophy for an understanding of how it might have rationalized an unthinkable historical outcome. He sounds its depths to locate the foundations of totalitarian thought, the evolution toward individualism and personal freedom, the self-perpetuating generalizations underlying genocide. This target is as much the excesses and subtle repressions of commodity-driven capitalism as it is totalitarian dictatorship. In Kant, Adorno finds an inflexible proponent of a ubiquitous morality, one preempting individual choice and initiative. "Kant's every concretion of morality bears repressive features. Its abstractness is a matter of substance, eliminating from the subject whatever does not conform with its pure concept. . . . As he honors freedom, however, seeking to cleanse it of all impairments, Kant simultaneously condemns the person to unfreedom in principle (*ND*, 256). Any play in Kantian thought, according to Adorno, is crushed under the weight of principle. Principle becomes the substance as well as the form of systematic thought. The consideration of substance and material relations is itself shunted aside in favor of a homogenizing unity: "Opposed to this, Kant's entire philosophy stands in the sign of unity. This lends it the character of a system, despite the heavy accentuation of 'material' not derived from pure forms; Kant expected no less from a system than did his successors. The governing unity is the concept of reason itself, and eventually the logical reason of pure noncontradictoriness" (234).

In different ways, Nietzsche and Heidegger pose the problem of an uncontainable, subjectively based arbitrariness and willfulness. "The doctrine of *Dasein*—of subjectivity—as the royal road to ontology resurrects the old subjective inquiry that had been humbled by ontological pathos. The phenomenological method claims to strip the tradition of Western philosophizing of its power, but it is at home in that tradition and well aware of the fact" (*ND*, 86). "Heidegger's cult of Being, his polemic against the idealistic cult of the mind, does of course presuppose a critique of the deification of Being. But Heidegger's Being, all but indistinguishable from its antipode, the mind, is no less repressive than the mind. It is only less transparent than the mind, whose principle was transparency" (98). "Under the weight of tradition, which Heidegger wants to shake off, the unexpressible becomes explicit and compact in the word 'Being,' while the protest against reification becomes reified, divorced from thinking, and irrational" (110). "Ideology lies in wait for the mind which delights in itself like Nietzsche's Zarathustra" (*ND*, 30). The road of Western philosophy is, then, for Adorno a double gauntlet beset on one side by a technical virtuosity in the violence of abstractions and on the other by calculated mystification and arbitrariness. The systematic thought that may be extrapolated from this tradition is severely flawed: it resolves or reconciles opposed elements, instead of exploring their differences (6, 24); it fosters a relativism, whose ultimate extension is dangerous anomie (40); it fosters antiintellectualism, which may be equated with a certain illiteracy or blindness to the incommensurate (44–45); it represses individuality and language (44–45, 55).

For all its rootedness in this tradition, dialectical thought harbors a decisive saving grace. Surveying the rubble of a philosophical tradition as of a war, Adorno finds in dialectics the single conceptual model capable of correcting his own potential flaws. A negative dialectics would pose the critical questioning of negativity against dialectics itself. It would in this way be equipped with internal correctives, implicit safeguards against conceptual barbarism. At the expense of certain grumpiness, a negative as opposed to a positive dialectics would effect the rectification, the settling of horribly skewed accounts, by means of the internal correctives with which it has been innoculated.

Dialectics is the single philosophical manifestation in Adorno's survey equipped with this corrective potential.

> As early as the Introduction to *Phenomenology of Mind*, Hegel comes close to a sense of the negativity of the dialectical logic he is expounding. That Introduction bids us purely observe each concept until it starts moving, until it becomes unidentical with itself by virtue of its own meaning—in other words, of its identity. This is a commandment to analyze, not to synthesize. . . . Objectively, dialectics means to break the compulsion to achieve identity, and to break it by means of the energy stored up in that compulsion and congealed in its objectifications. . . . As the concept is experienced as nonidentical, as inwardly in motion, it is no longer purely itself; in Hegel's terminology, it leads to its otherness without absorbing that otherness. . . . This is where the claim of their identity obtains that restlessness, which Hegel calls Becoming. (*ND*, 156–57)

As much as Adorno respects dialectics' conceptual integrity, he admires the dynamic force it contains and unleashes. His appreciations of dialectical suppleness are in the modernist spirit: they are reminiscent of Poundian vorticism and Fenollosa's tributes to the Chinese written character.[18] Negative dialectics retains a dynamic energy and flexibility; it maintains a resistance to identity and a generosity toward otherness. It would hope to avoid Hegel's weakness, a shrinking "from his own conception" (*ND*, 173). "In negative dialectics not even the transmission of essence and phenomenality, of essence and thing, will remain what it was" (170).

Although marked by historical circumstance and subjective values, the enterprise of negative dialectics opens a broad philosophical purview, similar in scope to the deconstructive critique of the ongoing status of language. For Adorno as well, at least in one facet of his work, language epitomizes the individual, the singular, and the irreducible: "In its dependence—patent or latent—on texts, philosophy admits its linguistic nature which the ideal of the method leads it to deny in vain. . . . In despising rhetoric, philosophy atoned for a guilt incurred ever since Antiquity by its detachment from things" (*ND*, 55). Drawing on Benjamin, Adorno has pursued the linguistic implications of a degraded experience on their own terms in earlier work, notably *Minima Moralia*. The task to which he addresses himself in *Negative Dialectics*, the installation of a preventive corrective in Western thought, remains a dialectical one. In light of the difficulties to which the Hegelian system is itself party—above all, a certain blind formalism, destructive of context—Adorno offers Hegel's philosophizing its most sympathetic twentieth-century rehabilitation. However receptive *Negative Dialectics* may be to the negative, it remains a structuralist exercise, retrospectively aligning material from different conceptual moments in accordance with a matrix of common concerns: freedom, individuality, totalitarianism. By virtue of its unique historical circumstances and mission and its structural program, *Negative Dialectics* necessarily misreads Heidegger and Nietzsche. Adorno's remorseful review of the Western philosophical tradition forces him to equate the linguistic indeterminacy explored by both philosophers with occultism, a potential for political madness. Adorno is a vigilant reader, and the misreading of *Negative Dialectics* takes place not on the level of substantive observations but on that of an *address*, a tangible relation to the material.

Adorno has, at other moments in his work, however, dedicated himself to the dismantling of structure in the wake of the unprecedented nineteenth- and twentieth-century disclosures of shock. He thus furnishes us with an instance of a writer whose modernist phase succeeded his postmodernism. Modernism and postmodernism are not necessarily aligned in a developmental sequence. *Minima Moralia* is written in the shadow of World War II. Fragmented and alternately laced with rage and despair, *Minima Moralia* is an important model for subsequent postmodern discursive prose. It occupies a position analogous to that of Benjamin's "On Some Motifs in Baudelaire." At the same time that it pursues the decline of twentieth-century experience through a range of contexts—the entertainment industry, social conventions, the state, and the family, as well as the modern city—it shatters its internal framework of intelligibility. Composed during and shortly after the liquidation of its community and intended audience, *Minima Moralia* shares something of the exhausting relentlessness of Beckett's ruminating prose.

The stylistic correlative to negative dialectics that Adorno explores in *Minima Moralia* is the sudden and undigestible nugget of language crammed down the gullet (or input) of an assimilation machine. If Benjamin's characteristic stylistic gesture is "the tightening of the knot," the emergence of concentrated, complex images out of initially loose strands of association, Adorno transforms his prose into an inferential minefield strewn with aphorisms instead of explosives—but with relatively the same effect. (Of contemporary writers, the film critic Pauline Kael indulges in this surprise technique to the best advantage.) *Minima Moralia* consists of 153 brief sections that reverberate off each other, not always in the most harmonious way. Of these, three consist entirely of aphorisms, of formulae reduced to their highest linguistic density (numbers 29, 72, and 122). Among the most memorable formulations exploding from these passages are the following: "in psycho-analysis nothing is true except the exaggerations" (*MM*, 49); "the first and only principle of sexual ethics: the accuser is always in the wrong" (50); and "every work of art is an uncommitted crime" (111). More important than any single statement, however, is the cumulative dissonance of a prose receptive to rhetorical and conceptual bombshells.

Adorno's tribute to Walter Benjamin in *Minima Moralia* is multifaceted, implicit and explicit. It may be said of this volume that it is loosely held together by a continuation of the Benjaminian probing of the decline of experience in a world of technological as well as political totalitarianism. The scope of Adorno's critique is vertiginous, ranging from modern architecture ("Modern man wishes to sleep close to the ground like an animal, a German magazine decreed with prophetic masochism before Hitler" [*MM*, 38]) to the family ("Marriage as a community of interests unfailingly means the degradation of the interested parties" [31]) to mass culture ("But the tone adopted by every film is that of the witch handing food to the child she wants to enchant or devour, while mumbling horribly: 'Lovely, lovely soup. How you're going to enjoy it!'" [201]). The uncompromising rigor of the hard look Adorno takes at his contemporary world is nowhere more evident than his introspections regarding the intellectual profession. "For [intellectuals] get to know each other in the most degrading and shameful of all situations, that of competing supplicants, and are thus virtually compelled to show each other their most repulsive sides" (28).

Adorno's allegiance is surely to the aptness of the observation rather than to the logical integrity of the encompassing framework. The form of his scattered critiques is often the double message, cognitive dissonance, the "can't do with or without" of ambivalence. This double bind is the logical correlative to negative dialectics, transported in *Minima Moralia* to the domain of a discontinuous and open-ended discursive medium. Thus, the family in *Minima Moralia* is hopeless, but divorce, "even between good-natured, amiable, educated people, is apt to stir up a dust-cloud that covers and discolours all it touches" (*MM*, 31). Adorno deplores the depersonalization and reductiveness of kitsch but insists on a certain distance (or self-detachment) in cultural life as the basis for "the mental life" and creative "tension" (80). He condemns the subtle but nonetheless pervasive repression of a commodity-driven economy while mourning the disappearance of luxury, grand hotels, and the exchange of gifts (42–43, 117–19, 217). He recognizes the obsolescence of the traditional gender roles but deplores the ridicule to which "he who respectfully kisses the hand of a well-connected girl who is somewhat too young" exposes himself (93, 171, 180). These seeming contradictions in no way comprise logical or mental lapses; they are, rather, constitutive of any radical force the critical text generates as its author assumes the insurmountable task of memory and correction. *Minima Moralia* is the open horizon in which the tricks of negative dialectics configure constellations, similar to Benjamin's mosaic. The constellation "illuminates the specific side of the object, the side to which a classifying procedure is either a matter of indifference or a burden" (*ND*, 162).

Qualified by the irreducible difference of its fragments and observations, *Minima Moralia* is situated at the postmodern flank of Adorno's writing. To be sure, a very distinctive energy arises from the conceptual collisions that Adorno generates, from the treacherous contradictions that he plants within his reasoning. But there are rigorous constraints on the newness and reform such a critique can promise. *Minima Moralia*, situated at the bottom line of expectation, arises hopelessly after the fact. Its historical circumstances bespeak the exhaustion of a system and a tradition. The rubble through which Adorno rummages is devoid of the lost cultural gems, the hints of a prior age that tantalize Pound, Stevens, and the other modernists. Newness is itself a bauble, a child's trinket created by the popularizers who pacify the public. A passage treating the despair of the new must suffice as one final instance of Adorno's complex and painful attitude toward the twentieth-century.

> For a 'pre-history of modernity' it would be instructive to analyze the change in the meaning of the word sensation, the exoteric synonym for the Baudelairian *nouveau*. The word became familiar to the educated European through epistemology. . . . Thus the historical emancipation from being-in-itself is converted into the form of perception.

... Baudelaire's poetry, however, is full of those lightning flashes seen by a closed eye that has received a blow. As phantasmagoric as these lights is the idea of newness itself. (*MM*, 235–36)

Even at a time of destruction, Adorno remains the philosopher. He begins his overview of the notion of modernity with Locke. He then follows the footsteps of the Benjaminian *flâneur* through the nineteenth-century as he teases out further implications from the explosive shock structure. Ever brilliant, ever conjuring unexpected "lightning flashes" from his material, Adorno nevertheless arrives at an unmitigated cul-de-sac, a great emptiness.

The new, sought for its own sake, a kind of laboratory product, petrified into a conceptual scheme, becomes in its sudden apparition a compulsive return of the old, not unlike that in traumatic neuroses. To the dazzled vision the veil of temporal succession is rent to reveal the archetypes of perpetual sameness: this is why the discovery of the new is satanic, an eternal recurrence of damnation. Poe's allegory of the 'novel' is that of the breathlessly spinning yet in a sense stationary movement of the helpless boat in the eye of the maelstrom. The sensations in which the masochist abandons himself to the new are as many regressions. So much is true in psychoanalysis that the ontology of Baudelairean modernity, like all those that followed it, answers the description of infantile partial-instincts. Its pluralism is the many-coloured *fata morgana* in which the monism of bourgeois reason sees its self-destruction glitter deceptively as hope. This false promise makes up the idea of modernity. . . . Fascism was the absolute sensation: in a statement at the time of the first pogroms, Goebbels boasted that at least the National Socialists were not boring. (*MM*, 236–37)

This passage opens the associative potential of the modernist kaleidoscope full throttle. It marshals literary history, psychoanalysis, and social criticism in gaining a philosophical overview of modernity. Particularly striking is the aptness with which it can bring sophisticated literary productions by Poe and Baudelaire to bear on concrete historical circumstances. Also impressive is its placement of psychoanalysis, which elsewhere in the book Adorno has decried for its passivity and acceptance of the status quo (*MM*, 58–63) within conceptual and literary histories. Such a passage, then, achieves an apotheosis of insight, brilliance, and critical commitment achieved by the Frankfurt school. It relies on certain assumptions that have since been questioned, above all on experience and subjectivity, but the range of its account and its combination of phenomena overshadow any naïveté in its presuppositions.

This conceptual and metonymic sparkling, however, arrives only at dead ends, empty illusions, and factual brutalities. If Adorno observes the obliteration of the traditions and structures lending his work, and that of his colleagues, its effervescence, he does so less with fascination than with despair, indifference, exhaustion. In the passage above, the concept of modernity, the very essence of novelty and hopefulness, achieves a decisive emptying. Adorno links it to the nineteenth-century esthetic of decadence and to the masochistic excesses of psychoanalysis. Modernity is a bourgeois Fata Morgana. For all its rich allusiveness, the passage eventuates at a night, in which the prevailing myths have been voided, where the facilitating illusions of culture have lost their force and direction as well as their content. As modernity and novelty are demystified, so too does the momentum of expectation lose its force. At this standstill Adorno enters the affective environment of postmodernism.

Negative Dialectics may schematize the knowledge of *Minima Moralia*, but ultimately this knowledge betrays any attempt to package it. What curricular schematization can there be in the wake of the revelation that National Socialism provided a diversion, an entertainment for the German nation, that, at a certain level, the interests of the entertainment industry and militaristic avarice mesh? Adorno's postmodern discourse is intensely aware of the constraints upon its structuralist combinations, of the night in which its acrobatic fireworks have already been extinguished. The work of gathering, assembly, and intellectual extension go on, but qualified by this darkness. Adorno's writing begins in the heart of our systematic heritage; it ends, however, where texts achieve obliviousness to their uses and future prospects. The text of *Minima Moralia* exists precisely at this threshold: where texts diverge from the teleology of purpose, where they configure even though the great night has begun. It is thus situated at the threshold, the minimum, the zero point of presumption. *Minima Moralia* is an epitome of constrained brilliance, illumination narrowed to a fragile beam. The constellations it configures in spite of these constitute its own indifference and herald a relentlessly detached critical prose, whose prominent contributors included Artaud, Bataille, and Blanchot.[19]

THOMAS BERNHARD. It may well be appropriate to conclude this preliminary overview of the shifting border between modernism and its implicit countermovement with a brief discussion of Thomas Bernhard, the Austrian novelist and playwright whose recent death in no way diminishes his importance. Bernhard's 1975 *Correction* (*Korrek-*

tur) describes a construction project of virtually impossible perfection conducted by a Cambridge scientist of Austrian origin, whose commitment to analytical rigor rivals Wittgenstein's own. Roithamer's collaboration with his sister on the erection of a cone (*Kegel*) situated in the exact geometrical center of the Kobernausser forest is reminiscent of the house that, in 1926–28, Wittgenstein personally designed and built for one of his sisters.[20] In the novel's scenario, design, and theoretical concerns, Bernhard has produced a text returning us to the convergence of analytical rigor and deconstructive dismantling already discernible in the fiction of Kafka. This seemingly incongruous collaboration between conceptual minimalism and expansiveness both sets the stage for and epitomizes the modern/postmodern.

Correction is narrated by an unnamed Austrian mathematician who, like Roithamer, constructor of the cone, has fled the intellectual stultification of his native land for England. As children, the narrator and Roithamer attended the same remote school. They would be joined on their silent morning and afternoon treks through the woods by Hoeller, who in adult life became a taxidermist. The consummation of Roithamer's plans to build a cone in the midst of a forest is considered to be one factor at play in the suicide of his sister, to whom the Cone was dedicated. Roithamer shortly follows his sister's suicide with his own: he hangs himself in a forest clearing (*Lichtung*). The narrator, after a serious bout of pneumonia (disease is an ongoing motif in the novel), settles into a garret in Hoeller's house in order to complete his task as executor of Roithamer's intellectual legacy, whose remains include a text: "About Altensam and everything connected with Altensam, with special attention to the Cone" (*K*, 3). It was in the same garret that Roithamer, revolted by the ostentation and intrigues surrounding his family's estate at Altensam, had done exhaustive research and calculations for the Cone. Uncannily, then, the narrator enters Roithamer's space after several significant coincidences. This is not the only way that the characters in the novel are intertwined, almost to the point of nonidentity, or at least seriously qualified identity. The garret where Roithamer and the narrator spend much of the novel belongs to the third friend, Hoeller, who devotes a considerable part of his efforts to stuffing a cavernous black bird. Hoeller's garret, the scene of writing for the novel and the setting for Roithamer's last major undertaking, in its stark simplicity is one of only two spaces in the novel resembling the Cone.

Like *Molloy*, *Correction* is divided into two sections. The first, "Hoeller's Garret," clearly issues from the narrator and describes the set of circumstances culminating in the construction of the Cone and the deaths of Roithamer and his sister. The second, "Sifting and Sorting," is in a sense the product of the narrator's editorial and curatorial labors. Yet it is so heavily laced with extracts from Roithamer's notebooks that authorship and agency are left entirely ambiguous. The citations from Roithamer's writings in the second segment of the novel are often dense and aphoristic. They share the closure and contraction of Wittgenstein's prose style.

A postmodern work, *Correction* is about the intellectual and discursive conditions under which a fictive construction and a text arise far more than it is concerned with a sequence of events joining a set of fictional surrogates. What it offers in circumstantial details is far less weighty than what it demonstrates—of the conjunction between literature, construction, and confinement. What this novel provides, then, in the way of existential circumstances is minimal, but important. The reader knows that, in general, Roithamer's relations to his family are at best strained. His mother, who embodies his country's antiintellectuality (*K*, 18), holds his work in contempt. He and his mother set traps for each other; their rapport is predatory. Roithamer's brothers, in response to the Cone and Roithamer's desire to devote his fortune to rehabilitating ex-convicts, attempt to have him declared mentally incompetent. His father, a local landlord and hunter, wills him the Altensam estate out of spite. Only with the sister, the sister to whom the Cone is dedicated—whose pervasiveness is accepted as a given but who resides at the site of frustrated incestuous desire—is there some emotional and intellectual sharing. These siblings commiserate in an Altensam attic that is the second model for the Cone.

As the child of a wealthy family, Roithamer must bring two pieces of wood for heating each day, not one, and it must be hardwood (*K*, 97–98). At the same school, during childhood, a teacher hanged himself "because of a vulgar slander against him" (106). At a music festival, with a suddenness that is one of the novel's prominent images for creativity, Roithamer spontaneously shoots two dozen paper roses in a row at a shooting gallery, although he has always eschewed his family's enthusiasm for hunting.

Such "facts" of the novel are strongly overshadowed, however, by its few sustained images and by the discursive performance of its issues. The novel's existential grounding is minimalist; its images, as in postmodern drama, are few, but elaborated meticulously, elaborated toward the perfection that the Cone would consummate.[21] The primary architectural feat achieved by this work is the breathless suspension of its images as they evolve over seemingly endless sentences. The text's consummate performance is at the level of discourse itself: ultimately, it is in the pacing, texture, consistency, and feel of its discourse that the novel says whatever it has to say.

Correction is, if any "voice," the voice of language itself—devoid of spatial and temporal markers, of characterological agents and unities—as it hurtles forward with no certain end, with all the force of the Aurach torrent, endlessly building upon, extending, qualifying, *correcting* itself. *Correction* does not merely give this novel a title; it describes the vast expansiveness of a language accounting for its closures and biases at the same time that it would presume to say, to relate. I have already associated this open-ended expansion, this refusal of language to succumb to its end, with the discursive style assumed by modern phenomenology in its delving. Phenomenology bequeaths this plumbing of the depths to deconstruction. In the text he has composed as a supplement to his Cone, Roithamer writes,

> Actually I'm quite shocked by everything I've just written . . . I'll correct it all when the time for such correction has come and then I'll correct the corrections and correct again the resulting corrections and so forth, so Roithamer. We're constantly correcting [*korrigieren*], and correcting ourselves, most rigorously, because we recognize at every moment that we did it all wrong (wrote it, thought it, made it all wrong), acted all wrong, how we acted all wrong, that everything to this point of time is a falsification, so we correct this falsification, and then we again correct the correction of this falsification and we correct the result of the correction of a correction andsoforth, so Roithamer. But *the ultimate correction* is one we keep delaying. (*K*, 242)

This "ultimate" correction may well be suicide. The first sentence in this extract is unusually brief for this novel. Set off by the refrain "so Roithamer," the sentence clearly derives from the central character's final and unfinished study. The source of the second sentence is left ambiguous, and the distinction between Roithamer and the narrator, between characters, is truly a matter of indifference. In these sentences the novel thematizes a correction deeply imprinted within its discourse. One might say that correction, open-ended and endless qualification, comprises the operating system for its implicit cybernetic program. The breathless sentences of *Correction* are densely impregnated with dependent clauses rarely set off from each other by means of punctuation. So compulsive is this qualification that the difference between phrases is often invisible. The text of *Correction* overflows with redundancies: "That a man who lets such an idea as that of building the Cone develop in his head, then uses his inherited fortune . . . to turn this idea into a reality, and actually goes ahead . . . with his project to build the Cone, still does not prove, after all, that the man is crazy, even though the majority of bystanders and relatives believe that such a man is crazy, that he simply *must* be crazy" (*K*, 13). Hoeller "considered it an honor that Roithamer could use this garret, otherwise completely unused and used by no one, for his own purposes" (46–47). "Wherever we turn in this world, all we see is nothing but destroyed ideas, all there is, as any reasonable person must admit, is nothing but destroyed ideas, just as everything is only a fragment, it's always only an abandoned intention, so Roithamer" (263). *Correction* situates itself in the gradations, not the exclusivity, of statement. Intensely sensitive to subtle distinctions between statements, its discourse ultimately admits shades of meaning *all but the same*. In the examples above, the "man is crazy" by virtue of his interests in several grammatical senses; the text distinguishes between "completely unused" and "used by no one"; and, in the third case, the futility of ideation and intention reaches a stalemate at which "nothing but destroyed ideas" can only be repeated.

Written some fifty years after Kafka's "Burrow" ("Der Bau"), *Correction* joins the earlier work as a relentless transcription of the constructive and destructive forces at play in the act of writing itself. *Correction* may be read as a postmodern fictive exegesis and extension of Kafka's text, which had already in its consistency and style entered the precinct of postmodernity.[22] Both texts are themselves products of a construction to which they have confined themselves with obsessive fascination. "Like Roithamer we resorted to words such as master builder or building or the art of building; that the word B U I L D [*Bauen*] is one of the most beautiful in the language, we knew ever since Roithamer had spoken about it, in that same garret where I have now installed myself" (*K*, 8). The product of the rodent's burrowing in Kafka may be a subterranean labyrinth, whereas Roithamer's Cone rises among the trees in a forest, but in both cases production is inextricably linked with literary composition. Language consists in constructions, and constructions are, above all, configurations of language.

In a sense, then, the tidal undertow of postmodern literature may be situated between the ruminations of Kafka's animals and Bernhard's corrections. The "commerce" between these authors intensifies, but by no means exhausts, a writerly experiment also incorporating the fiction of Joyce, Beckett, and Flann O'Brien; the discursive prose, above all of Bataille and Blanchot. Within this postmodern undercurrent, literary production consists in involution and complication. Literature is a rumination, proving and implementing nothing. It is an interior monologue as external as immanent, within nothing so unified, distinct, or integrated as a "subject."

Whereas Kafka's literature is fated to end, and his burrowing creature to die, within the involutions of a subterranean enclosure, Bernhard takes greater liberty to sketch out the political and affective environment in which intellection and literary production transpire. Roithamer's Cone is not merely an architectural aberration, an intellectual hypothesis imposed upon a forest; it is situated at the interstice between writing, madness, and death, specifically suicide. *Correction* is a corrective text: the text that would exhaustively account for its conditions while telling its story does not omit the stresses and fatal impulses that emerge within the intensity of writing.

"The idea demands fulfillment, it demands realization and never stops demanding to be realized" (*K*, 201). It is with good reason that construction of the Cone, like that of Kafka's Burrow, takes place within an aura of confinement and imprisonment—"Total isolation in Cambridge alternated with total isolation in the Kobernausser forest" (249)—for the project arises between an impossible perfection and an intolerable monstrosity. "I must assume," on the one hand, "that the Cone is ideal for my sister" (158). "The Cone is the logical consequence of [my] nature" (166). "To build is the most wonderful thing in the world, it's the supreme gratification, 'supreme gratification' underlined" (200). There is at the same time, however, something monstrous in a calling of such momentousness. "One is called upon to approach and realize and complete the monstrousness, and everyone has some such enormity in his life, or else to be destroyed by this monstrousness even before one has entered into it. . . . The matured idea is enough in itself to destroy most people, so Roithamer" (202–3).

Bernhard's cone figure, like that of Borges, fuses open-endedness with an intolerable concentration. The cone of *Correction* is a map of its characters' lives: "How we moved from our different points of departure, our positions, toward one single point, the single acceptable point, death" (*K*, 122). With its enclosure, concentration, and single-minded dedication, existence at the point of writing is vulnerable indeed. The Kafka of "The Burrow" elaborates the dangers as they would appear to an impossible fictive rodent: there are scratching noises, threats to repositories of supplies, in the deep. Bernhard, on the other hand, is free to extend the paranoia of writing into more familiar terms. The threats to writing are all the more pernicious because its conditions are so delicate, so tenuous. The form of these threats is invariably human: jealousy, plagiarism, cultural illiteracy, and hostility: "An idea, always an extraordinary idea, attracts hundreds of parasites who hook onto it and suck it dry and ruthlessly capitalize on it, always to the loss of the person who had the idea in the first place. Keep thought and idea immured as long as possible" (156). "We're constantly badgered by insinuations by those who don't want us to accomplish our aim because they begrudge us our achievement, so we're constantly subjected to their meanness, their spying presence which only fills us with disgust, they never cease their vulgar spying. Most of the time we have to deal with human filth, so Roithamer" (161).

The text of the novel explicitly associates the construction of the Cone with writing: "my chance after my return to devote some time to this work, a writing job, 'writing job' underlined, in retreat" (K, 198). Writing thus verges on a treacherous point of isolation, surrounded and constantly qualified by attempts to appropriate and stifle it. Writing can be stolen—even worse, muffled. Its enemies are personified by Roithamer's mother, "the Eferding woman." Creative innovation is despised as much as it is copied.

Writing is thus saturated with frustration. It invariably confronts, and ultimately succumbs to, limits. Frustration is the wearing, entropic strain against limits. Distractions, cultural indifference, and intellectual competitiveness are some of the frustrations to writing that Bernhard explores. The special attraction that Roithamer feels toward his sister may hint at another mode of stifling in the novel.

The point of concentration toward which sustained frustration inevitably lends is self-inflicted death. The extended allegory of writing in *Correction* is engulfed on two sides by death, the brain death of an indifferent culture and the suicide that culminates prolonged intellectual and emotional frustration. Suicide demarcates an indifference in its own right, an inclusion of death among the acceptable immediate outcomes. "He had, in the end, forgotten the essay altogether, when he killed himself, because *in the end nothing matters all that much*, as he also wrote on another slip, and on his last slip he'd written, *it's all the same [es ist alles gleich]*" (K, 62). So infused is Roithamer's culture with suicide, clarifies the narrator in one of his rare moments of assertiveness, that biological death need not necessarily proceed from it.

On the Plain of Indifference

197

It's a folk art of sorts, I said to Hoeller, always longing to kill oneself
. . . so that the condition is stabilized in the form of lifelong controlled suffering, it's an art possessed only by this people and those
belonging to it. We're a nation of suicides, I said, but only a small per-
centage actually kill themselves, even though ours is the highest per-
centage of suicides in the world. . . . What mainly goes on in this
country and among these people is thinking about suicide, everywhere, in the big cities, in the towns, in the country, a basic trait of
this country's population is the constant thought of suicide, they
might be said to take pleasure in thinking constantly, steadily, without allowing anything to distract them, about how to do away with
themselves at any time. It's their way of keeping their balance. (K,
108)

Although localized in this passage, the nation of suicide is one without borders. Suicide, in this passage, functions as a margin, a
between-space infusing a certain give or tolerance within local existence. As a margin, a release valve, a variable factor injected into an
only too familiar certainty, suicide is to the locals what the Cone is
to Roithamer: the clearing (Lichtung) or opening of possibility. It is
in this sense that the mathematician describes suicide, whether
actualized or not, as a folk art. Suicide is that flank of Roithamer's
perfectionist obsession accessible to the general population.

While Roithamer imposes a perfect Cone upon the Kobernausser
forest—his construction consists in filling space; the Cone is a
projection—Hoeller occupies himself with stuffing dead animals.
The Cone may lead to the finite point where life ends, but the life of
taxidermy is beset by its own variety of morbidity. Hoeller's black
bird is a gaping cavern of death; it is a mocking necrophiliac hole
that no living man (or woman) can fill in the symbolic sense. Mor-
bidness overcomes the novel, then, both in the ever-narrowing path
of rigor and depression and in the hysteria of an insatiable morbid
solicitation.

Viewed as a system of life, not a single act, suicide veers toward a
point of no return. The general system of suicide thus assumes the
form of a cone. Roithamer's Cone is the scene of writing and the
point of death. "When I said to my sister," writes Roithamer, "the
Cone is yours, it belongs to you, I built it for you, and specifically in
the Kobernausser forest, I saw that the effect of the Cone on my sister was devastating" (K, 267). The Cone ultimately becomes an instrument of death. It is where death and writing merge. Its foundation is
impossible desire. Its planning has been based on the observation of
"everything connected with my sister. . . . The Cone's interior cor-

responding to my sister's inner being, the Cone's exterior to her outward being, and together her whole being expressed as the *Cone's
character"* (158). The Cone kills the sister not as a plan, projection, or
blueprint, but when it is executed. So suicide.

Roithamer dies, kills himself, in a clearing, the forest clearing
where Heidegger discloses the traits of Being as language.[23] A clearing is an opening of possibility; it makes everything possible, but it
is also deadly: there is something inimical to human life where language abandons itself to its full disclosure. At certain points in the
discourse of *Correction* the main characters become the verbs, to
whose conjugation and variants the text surrenders itself. I think particularly of how Roithamer's father "lets go" (*nachlassen*) and "gives
up" (*sich aufgeben*) to "the Eferding woman," his second wife. The
clearing where Roithamer chooses to die is an opening of possibility,
based on extreme philosophical rigor, so relentless as to be indifferent to existential concerns, including the border between life and
death.

Roithamer's Cone marks the convergence of writing, death, and
the impossibility of desire. It is both the product of stringent mathematical rigor—"After all it took me six years to build the cone" (*K*,
161)—and the locus of great violence: rage, despair, suicide. In this
sense, *Correction* encompasses the major literary countertraditions
of its century. It embraces both the spare logic of analysis and an
excessive prolixity overwhelming structure by the sheer mass of possibility. As the fiction of Kafka and Musil demonstrates, these two
modes of critical questioning could be joined as the century began.
If they diverged, they did so as much in the interest of the academic
division of labor as of any other factor. Tremendous rage and detachment join in the construction of the Cone. Bernhard's fiction thus
extends the postmodern undercurrent of twentieth-century literature, one that has coincided with, not supplanted, our most recent
modernity. The distinctive mark of this postmodernity is not a plan,
an ideological bias, an architectural design, or a set of particular
works or authors. Postmodernity announces and performs itself,
rather, in a discourse: a self-engendering, endlessly suspenseful rumination whose subjects, messages, implications, and effects are yet
uncertain.

AFTERWORD: WHAT THEORY GOT FROM LITERATURE

At a moment when the study of literature has gained a new force,
direction, and vitality from its placement in the context of parallel

and contemporaneous developments in the history of philosophy, it becomes possible for literature to be placed in a secondary and subordinate position in the inevitable comparisons that arise between the modes of discourse. During a phase when the study of literature has never been more philosophical and the discipline of philosophy has perhaps never given itself more freely to literary devices and attitudes, the relation between the two becomes a matter of major significance. To be sure, the interstice between philosophy and literature has, at certain decisive moments if not always, been a seminal if volatile frontier. Though philosophy is capable of formulating models of the beautiful, the sublime, and the esthetic characterizing (and possibly mystifying) artworks produced down to the present day, a pronounced literariness has entered and reshaped philosophical discourse since its inception. (The *Tao Teh Ching*, the pre-Socratics, Platonic allegories, Kierkegaard's tracts, and Nietzsche's *Zarathustra* are surely among the most notable philosophical works to approach this watershed; on the literary side, they are countered by such works as *Tristram Shandy*, *La Nouvelle Heloïse*, *The Elective Affinities*, and *Moby-Dick*.)

Let us employ the phrase *mutually encompassing frameworks* to denote those parallel endeavors that would absorb and contain at the same time as they would illuminate each other. Thus, rigorous theory can formulate the various biases or torques that sociological analysis imposes on its data; while sociological analysis can extrapolate the socioeconomic positions and aspirations of theorists. Mutually encompassing frameworks exist in an intense and uneasy relation to each other. They both embrace and are bracketed by each other. They cannibalize, assimilate, and digest each other (these can be hostile acts). The most concrete image for the interpenetration of mutually encompassing frameworks may well derive from the world of games. The oriental game go terminates in vertiginous fluctuations of power as the white and black stones of the opponents outflank and surround each other with every successive move.

It is in the interest of no inquisitive mind either for literature to restore its primacy or for philosophy irrefutably to establish its authenticity in the reciprocal qualification that prevails between the two discursive modes. Among the major contributions of the movement known as contemporary critical theory has been its receptivity both in extending the literariness of philosophical discourse and the philosophizing of literature. To the extent that deconstructive criticism addresses itself to and articulates itself around the tropes configuring specific texts, it arises within a postmodern environment. Concerned as it is with questioning and performing the acts constitutive of language and the scientific uses to which it is put, the discourse of deconstruction is, relatively speaking, indifferent to establishing origin, essence, or influence, to proving or refuting arguments, or to reinforcing the established divisions of knowledge. Though texts in every age articulate and perform their constitutive tropes to some degree, in a postmodern environment the relentless elaboration, qualification, and correction of the conditions of writing achieve a unique degree of sufficiency: this endless elaboration, in which there is a simultaneity between ostensible description and critical commentary, defines the acceptable achievement of literary works.

Among the major achievements of Jacques Derrida must surely be numbered the epochs and discourses he has brought into communication with one another through his ongoing concern with the status of language. Deconstruction has, on the one hand, facilitated a more rigorous and precise interlocking than was previously possible between the wide range of literary manifestations and the philosophical interrogations in which they arose and which, to some extent, structured them. The philosophical extensions that deconstruction has inspired, by authors including Philippe Lacoue-Labarthe, Jean-Luc Nancy, and Rodolphe Gasché (of which Gasché's *Tain of the Mirror: Derrida and the Philosophy of Reflection* is a splendid example) have been able to specify and formulate the philosophical traditions at play (or work) in the linguistic radicality remarked by Derrida. Such work has also accounted, in a precise way, for the conditions of the asystematic philosophical, linguistic, and rhetorical figures that epitomize a double movement: the dismantling of systems formulated in language, by the traces of the linguistic and conceptual indeterminacy that systems cannot assimilate. Drawing on the Derridean terminology, Gasché designates as infrastructures those conceptual aberrations that are at once constitutive of intellectual systems and upon which they founder. Gasché defines infrastructures rigorously, as much according to what they are not as in terms of any positive manifestation. Though as pervasive as structures, infrastructures do not share their closure or formation. Gasché separates them from the ontology of being or essence; they circumvent the "opposition of sense and non-sense;" they do not annul or neutralize differences. In a formulation particularly close to the present discussion, Gasché insists that infrastructures evade both "florid language" and "fallacious reasoning—as simultaneously grounds and ungrounds, as conditions of possibility and impossibility."[24]

According to Gasché, then, infrastructures are the astructural possibilities for heterogeneity, asymmetry, difference, and open-endedness in conceptual and, for that matter, literary texts. He arranges five of the pivotal infrastructures in Derrida's philosophy in a provisional but by no means negligible sequence of increasing complexity beginning with the "arche-trace" and passing through "differance," supplementarity, iterability and the re-mark. "The infrastructure is what knots together all the threads of correspondence among certain heterogeneous *points of presence* within a discourse or text. It must be understood as the *medium of differentiation* in general of the heterogeneous possibilities, contradictory strata, lexicological disparities, and so on."[25]

Gasché's notion of infrastructures is no less than decisive in explaining how deconstruction could both extend longstanding philosophical debates and traditions and be receptive to conceptual and esthetic aberrations. Indeed, the infrastructure is precisely the polymorphic but persistent factor that could enable philosophy both to entrench its traditions and, in cataclysmic fashion, to dismantle them. While in no way reducing the radicality of infrastructures, Gasché devotes considerable attention to establishing their grounding in speculative philosophy and phenomenology. Infrastructures play the role of radicals in the dismantling of systems. As such, their relation to deconstruction is privileged; they are both its "outcome"[26] and its possibility:

Deconstruction *starts* with an interrogation of a variety of contradictions and aporias in the discourse of philosophy. These are not contradictions and aporias proper, however, since the discourse of philosophy accommodates them without difficulty. In addition to these contradictions and aporias, which pertain to the formation of concepts and to the development of philosophical arguments, deconstruction addresses many other discursive and conceptual inequalities that have never before been questioned by philosophy. All these aporias, differences of levels, inequalities of developments, and disparities characteristic of the discourse of philosophy, yet which do not seem to disturb the logic of philosophy, also contribute to the establishment of that logic. All the gestures of philosophy— reflection and transcendentalization, all the themes of philosophy, but primarily those of subjectivity, transcendentality, freedom, origin, truth, presence, and the proper—are impossible without the differences and discrepancies that permeate philosophical texts.

Deconstruction is an attempt to account for these various and essentially heterogeneous aporias and discursive inequalities with what I have called infrastructures. These minimal structures are both the grounds of possibilities of the canonical philosophical gestures and themes and their ungrounds, that is, that which makes them impossible. These structures limit what they make possible by rendering its rigor and purity impossible. The infrastructures are the internal limit from which classical philosophical concepts and themes take their force and necessity. Deconstruction does not merely destroy metaphysical concepts; it shows how these concepts and themes draw their possibility from that which ultimately makes them impossible. The infrastructures achieve this double task.[27]

Systematic thought arrives at infrastructures both in its expansion and in its contraction. They are the bases for dissymetry and heterogeneity, but they also comprise an internal limit. They thus straddle both the diffuse and the rigorous modes of twentieth-century expression.

Such work makes it possible to account precisely for philosophy's receptivity to what might otherwise appear disordered, monstrous, or comprehensive only under special conditions such as the esthetic or sublime. It is at the same time sensitive to the fact that Derrida's achievement is as unthinkable in the absence of certain pivotal literary texts and figures as it would be divorced from the works of major philosophers, notably Plato, Descartes, Kant, Hegel, Nietzsche, Husserl, and Heidegger. For all the philosophical rigor permeating the deconstructive project, however, I would argue, in its own terms, that literary texts comprise a supplement without which deconstruction would be impossible. They constitute the critical difference between a gifted restructuring of the history of philosophy and the generation of a radical hybrid discourse, of unpredictable quality and effects, whose implications and applications remain far from exhaustion. From the literary side, deconstruction's great innovation may be characterized as the configuration of philosophical discourse in accordance with literary tropes and distortions, a literary performance coinciding with a theoretical exploration of literary manifestations.

It is a distinctively postmodern literature that constitutes at least one major difference in the Derridean enterprise, between historical reorientation and the devising of a radically important genre and discursive instrument. For instances of what Gasché calls infrastructures, Derrida gravitates toward the productions of postmodernism: heralded by Mallarmé's poetry, the texts of Kafka, Joyce, Bataille, Blanchot, Artaud, Genet, Celan, Jabès, and Ponge become the loci where the moves of literature and philosophy intersect. Although

Derrida would rigorously and rightly question the assumptions underlying any literary corpus, in such writings as Mallarmé's "Or," Blanchot's "Folie du jour," and Ponge's "Fable," he has assembled a subset of texts approaching pure textuality, in which few, if any, resources are *not* involved in the articulation of infrastructural and textual possibilities. It may well be that in such works, Derrida discerns the literary correlatives to the limits that philosophy has broached and in some senses exceeded. It may well be that the time is ripe for a literary parallel to Gasché's exploration of the roots of the Derridean enterprise in the philosophy of reflection. What are the literary sources of deconstruction? Why does Derrida select the particular literary works that he elucidates and cites? Is there something productive to be said about the body of literary texts his writing has incorporated? It must suffice to say, in the scope of the present discussion, that Derrida's literary debt is a large one, and that in assembling sources and instances of infrastructures, he gravitates, almost inevitably, to works recognizable within the current purview of postmodernism: texts concentrating on and constructed around their textual nature, qualities, and movements, texts achieving simultaneity between their performative and constative functions, texts having reached, in the rigorous sense of the word, their indifference. It is in the works of postmodernity that we find a particularly fecund field for infrastructures: the elucidations in this book of Joyce, Wittgenstein, Kafka, Borges, and Bernhard have necessarily invoked such infrastructural issues as supplementarity, doubling, iterability, and displacement. One could well argue that infrastructures are the enduring possibilities released in the play between modernism and postmodernism; that the discourse of deconstruction achieves its full expansive potential, the expansiveness of Borgesian perfumes and numbers, only because such infrastructural exploration took place within the literary field. The ongoing go game in which literature and philosophy are involved has reached particular intensity during the twentieth century in part because the two discursive modes have so knowingly entered a relationship of supplementarity and mutual inscription and re-marking.

The literature of postmodernity describes not so much the productions of a particular historical moment as a set of texts in which the motors of systematic thought—identity, determination, subjectivity, intention, consistency, completion—have undergone a severe, if often humorous, demystification. By implication, the exegesis of works not achieving, in different degrees, their postmodernity forces deconstruction to address constructs, among them plot, character, and action, with which literary critics have long contended. When deconstructive discourse sets out to account for such literary phenomena, it enters upon a domain not thoroughly unfamiliar to literary criticism. A growing list of critics demonstrates that the philosophical inquiry orchestrated by deconstruction has a great deal of light to shed on the standard literary categories. There is a pronounced affinity between postmodern literature and the conceptually open space that deconstruction would delimit. Literature harbors the traces of theory that would illuminate it, if only its reading can be rigorous to the point of concentration, expansive to the degree of endlessness. Roithamer's Cone figures concretely the narrowing and clearing between which the postmodern arises.

Notes

PREFACE

1. Ihab Hassan, *The Dismemberment of Orpheus* (Madison: University of Wisconsin Press, 1982).

2. Renato Poggioli, *The Theory of the Avant-Garde*, trans. Gerald Fitzgerald (Cambridge: Harvard University Press, 1968).

3. Peter Brüger, *Theory of the Avant-Garde*, intro. Jochen Schulte-Sasse (Minneapolis: University of Minnesota Press, 1984), vii–viii, 8, 20–22, 27–29, 35–53, 63–66, 90–91.

4. Stanley Trachtenberg, ed., *The Postmodern Moment* (Westport, Conn.: Greenwood Press, 1985).

5. Marshall Berman, *All That Is Solid Melts into Air: The Experience of Modernity* (New York: Penguin, 1988).

6. Jean-François Lyotard, *The Postmodern Condition: A Report on Knowledge*, trans. Geoff Bennington and Brian Massumi (Minneapolis: University of Minnesota Press, 1984).

ONE. A MODERN CLIMATE

1. See Ferdinand de Saussure, *Course in General Linguistics*, trans. Wade Baskin (New York: McGraw-Hill, 1966), 6–11.

2. Ibid., 78, 120.

3. Ibid., 9, 14–15, 73–78.

4. In this sense, Monod's biological scenario in which the communication and replication of a genetic code takes place is at least in large part a structuralist endeavor. Structures comprise a major share of what the genetic material communicates. See Jacques Monod, *Chance and Necessity*, trans. Austryn Wainhouse (New York: Alfred A. Knopf, 1971), 10–3, 28, 34–35, 100–25, 133–37.

5. See Roland Barthes, *Mythologies*, trans. Annette Lavers (New York: Hill and Wang, 1986), 110, 123, 125, 154, 154–55.

6. See Claude Lévi-Strauss, *Tristes Tropiques*, trans. John Weightman and Doreen Weightman (New York: Antheneum, 1974), 17–19, 43–44, 129–30, 143–45, 149–50.

7. Cf. Michel Foucault, *The Order of Things* (New York: Random House, 1973), 280–94.

8. Cf. Claude Lévi-Strauss, *The Savage Mind* (Chicago: University of Chicago Press, 1973), 2–3, 8–9, 11–20–22, 35–36, 63–69; also Lévi-Strauss, *Tristes Tropiques*, 178–80, 190–97, 219–29.

9. Claude Lévi-Strauss, "The Structural Study of Myth," in his *Structural Anthropology*, trans. Claire Jacobson and Brooke Grundfest Schoepf (New York: Basic Books, 1963), 211, 213–16.

10. Ibid., 216–17.

11. Ibid., 229.

12. Barthes, *Mythologies*, 125, 131.

13. Ibid., 119–21, 142–44, 150, 153.

14. See Roland Barthes, *S/Z*, trans. Richard Miller (New York: Hill and Wang, 1986), 5.

15. See Roland Barthes, *A Lover's Discourse: Fragments*, trans. Richard Howard (New York: Hill and Wang, 1984), 45–47.

16. See Martin Heidegger, *Identity and Difference*, trans. Joan Stambaugh (New York: Harper and Row), 35–39, 99–103.

17. See Homer, *The Odyssey of Homer*, trans. Richmond Lattimore (New York: Harper and Row, 1975), 157–67, ll. 210–574).

18. Marcel Proust, *A la recherche du temps perdu*, ed. Pierre Clarac and André Ferré (Paris: Pléiade, 1954), 1:9–10.

19. See Freud, "The 'Mystic Writing-Pad'" (*SE*, 19:225–32). Freud writes of this device, "But if it is examined more closely it will be found that its construction shows a remarkable agreement with my hypothetical structure of our perceptual apparatus and that it can in fact provide both an ever-ready receptive surface and permanent traces of the notes that have been made upon it" (228).

20. See Thomas Mann, *The Magic Mountain*, trans. H. T. Loew-Porter (New York: Vintage, 1969), 214–19.

21. Characterizing "primitive" science, for example, Lévi-Strauss writes: "This logic works rather like a kaleidoscope, an instrument which also contains bits and pieces by means of which structural patterns are realized. The fragments are products of a process of breaking up and destroying, in itself a contingent matter, but they have to be homologous in many respects. . . . They can no longer be considered entities in their own right in relation to the manufactured objects of whose 'discourse' they have become the indefinable debris, but they must be so considered from a different point of view if they are to participate usefully in the formation of a new type of entity" (*Savage Mind*, 36). On the fictive side, can it be entirely accidental that visual instruments—a stereoscope, a kaleidoscope, and a cinematographic drum—comprise the salon diversions in the sanatorium on the magic mountain? Cf. Mann, *Magic Mountain*, 84. Eddington, in his characterization of a physical universe operating in accordance with relativistic laws, invokes both the kaleidoscope and the deck of cards as figures for the sequential effacement of structure. See Sir Arthur Eddington, *The Nature of the Physical World: The Gifford Lectures* (1927) (New York: Macmillan, 1929), 63–65, 68, 78–79.

22. Walter Benjamin, "On Some Motifs in Baudelaire," in his *Illuminations*, trans. Harry Zohn, ed. Hannah Arendt (New York: Schocken, 1969), 174–75. My association between the Benjaminian aura and the Derridean signature is not entirely fortuitous.

23. Ibid., 159, 155.

24. For the notion of the signature, see Jacques Derrida, *Writing and Difference*, trans. Alan Bass (Chicago: University of Chicago Press, 1978), 293–300. Also see Derrida, in *Glyph* 1, ed. Samuel Weber and Henry Sussman (Baltimore: Johns Hopkins University Press, 1977), 193–96, and Derrida, "Limited Inc," in *Glyph* 2, ed. Samuel Weber and Henry Sussman (Baltimore: Johns Hopkins University Press, 1977), 162–68.

25. Benjamin, "Baudelaire," 161, after Freud, *SE*, 18:27.

26. Ibid., 176–79.

27. See Proust, *A la recherche*, 1:206–14; 3:248–64, 274–77.

28. Ibid., 1:322–33.

29. Cf. Ezra Pound, *The Cantos of Ezra Pound* (New York: New Directions, 1973), 28–57 (cantos 7–12); 61–67 (cantos 14–15); 80–100 (cantos 18–21); 209–22 (cantos

42–43); 229–35 (cantos 45–46). I have written extensively on Pound's protectiveness toward a hypothetical cultural and linguistic purity in "The University of Verse: The Economies of Modern American Poetry," in my *High Resolution: Critical Theory and the Problem of Literacy* (New York: Oxford University Press, 1989), 115–96.

30. Lévi-Strauss, *Savage Mind*, 17. I have elsewhere argued, in my *High Resolution*, 131–37, that the notion of *bricolage* is essential to an aware reading of modernist poetry.

31. Lévi-Strauss, *Savage Mind*, 21, 22.

32. Ibid., 30.

33. I think of such sculptures by Picasso as *Guitar* (1912), *Violin* (1913–14), *Guitar* (1914), *Still Life* (1914), *Musical Instruments* (1914), *Woman in the Garden* (1929–30), and *Head of a Woman* (1931). Among composers, the work of Charles Ives may well exemplify musical bricolage. I think particularly of *Decoration Day* (1912), the First Piano Sonata (1901–9), the First Violin sonata (1899–1902), and the Second Symphony (1900–1902).

34. See Walter Benjamin, *The Origin of German Tragic Drama*, trans. John Osborne (London: New Left Books, 1977), 29.

TWO. JOYCE'S MUSICAL COMEDY

1. Friedrich Nietzsche, *The Birth of Tragedy and the Case of Wagner*, trans. Walter Kaufmann (New York: Random House, 1967), 54–56.

2. Walter Benjamin, "Theses on the Philosophy of History," in *Illuminations*, trans. Harry Zohn, ed. Hannah Arendt (New York: Schocken, 1969), 257–58.

3. Marcel Proust, *A la recherche du temps perdu*, ed. Pierre Clarac and André Ferré (Paris: Pléiade, 1954), 1:10–3, 15–17, 147–49.

4. See Paul de Man, "Literary History and Literary Modernity," in his *Blindness and Insight: Essays in the Rhetoric of Contemporary Criticism* (Minneapolis: University of Minnesota Press, 1983), 142–65.

5. Ibid., 148.

6. Ibid., 150.

7. Ibid., 152.

8. Ibid., 164–65.

9. Bruno Schulz, *Sanitarium under the Sign of the Hourglass* (New York: Penguin, 1979), 116–17.

10. The *mise en abime*, the "placement in an abyss," is a French term applied to internal stagings, the play-within-a-play.

11. The term *theatricality*, as I use it, has been considerably informed by the work of Jonathan Baldo. I think of his excellent doctoral dissertation, "Theatricality and Drama" (State University of New York at Buffalo, 1981), as well as the essays he has published, including "'His form and cause conjoin'd': Reflections on 'Cause' in Hamlet," in *Renaissance Drama*, XVI, ed. Leonard Barkan (Evanston: Northwestern University Press, 1985), 75–94.

12. William Butler Yeats, "Who Goes with Fergus?" in *The Collected Poems of W. B. Yeats* (New York: Macmillan, 1956), 43.

13. Cheryl Herr exhaustively explores the interaction between different art forms and media in Joyce's work in *Joyce's Anatomy of Culture* (Urbana: University of Illinois Press, 1986), 1–6, 33–38, 96–118, 189–216.

14. See Marshall McLuhan, *Understanding Media* (New York: McGraw-Hill,

1964), 36–39, 145–50, 156–62, 217–32; Walter J. Ong, *Orality and Literacy* (New York: Methuen, 1982), 117–38.

15. James Joyce, "The Dead," in his *Dubliners* (New York: Penguin, 1986), 223.

16. I employ the term *pastiche* in the Proustian sense of "stylistic parody," not as a substitute for *collage* or *bricolage*. For a specific stylistic analysis of *Ulysses* proceeding from chapter to chapter, see Karen Lawrence, *The Odyssey of Style in Ulysses* (Princeton, N.J.: Princeton University Press, 1981), 38–54, 59–75, 80–88, 101–9, 146–59, 203–9.

17. For information of this type I am indebted to Weldon Thornton, *Allusions in Ulysses* (Chapel Hill: University of North Carolina Press, 1968).

18. The *begats* take up the main part of Genesis 5.

19. Dusty Rhodes, according to Thornton, *Allusions in Ulysses*, was "an American cartoon character belonging to the period around 1900" (355) and is not to be confused with the baseball player of the same name.

20. For a most suggestive discussion of singularity, see William Beatty Warner, *Chance and the Text of Experience* (Ithaca, N.Y.: Cornell University Press, 1986), 73–74, 96–97, 104–9, 153–55, 184, 291–98.

21. See Kafka, "The Truth about Sancho Panza" (*CS*, 429); also see Borges, "Pierre Menard, Author of Don Quixote" (45–56).

22. James Joyce, *A Portrait of the Artist as a Young Man* (New York: Penguin, 1976), 15–16, 103, 191.

23. Walter Benjamin, "The Image of Proust," in his *Illuminations*, 201.

24. The term *disfiguration*, explored in an essay by Paul de Man on Shelley, has been elaborated by Cynthia Chase. See Paul de Man, "Shelley Disfigured," in Harold Bloom, Paul de Man, Jacques Derrida, Geoffrey Hartman, and J. Hillis Miller, *Deconstruction and Criticism* (New York: Seabury Press, 1979), 46, 61–62, 65–67; Cynthia Chase, *Decomposing Figures: Rhetorical Readings in the Romantic Tradition* (Baltimore: Johns Hopkins University Press, 1986), 5–6, 22, 85, 132, 198, 208.

25. On Molly's menstruation see Paul van Caspel, *Bloomers on the Liffey: Eisegetical Readings of Joyces' Ulysses* (Baltimore: Johns Hopkins University Press, 1986), 250, 255–57.

26. The "spontaneous afterimage," is one of Walter Benjamin's key examples of shock in the modern world. He develops this notion early in "On Some Motifs in Baudelaire," in his *Illuminations*. I shall have occasion to return to this notion, above all in chapters 3 and 7.

27. From its title alone, *Ulysse gramophone*, it is evident that Jacques Derrida's recent book on Joyce, which appeared after the present chapter was completed, takes up, among others, the issues of voice and music in relation to this author. See Jacques Derrida, *Ulysse gramophone* (Paris: Galilée, 1987), 79–86, 93–98, 103, 117–23.

28. See my *High Resolution: Critical Theory and the Problem of Literacy* (New York: Oxford University Press, 1989), 116–23, 128–31.

29. See Borges, "Tlön, Uqbar, Orbis Tertius," 7.

30. See such canvasses as *Around the Fish* (1926), *Departure of the Ships* (1927), and *Mask of Fear* (1932).

THREE. KAFKA AND MODERN PHILOSOPHY

I dedicate this chapter to Richard Macksey, whose work on the relationship between eating and words was a direct inspiration.

1. Ludwig Wittgenstein, *Tractatus Logico-Philosophicus*, trans. D. F. Pears and B. F. McGuinness, intro. Bertrand Russell (London: Routledge and Kegan Paul, 1969). In the text, I cite propositions by number.

2. I think here particularly of René Magritte, *The Ladder of Fire I* (*L'Échelle du feu I*) (1933) and *The Fair Captive* (*La Belle Captive*) (1947). Other images in this vein include *The Ladder of Fire* (1939), *Threatening Weather* (*Le Temps menaçant*) (1928), and *The Heart of the Matter* (*L'Histoire centrale*) (1928).

3. For the impossible figure see E. H. Gombrich, "The Evidence of Images," in *Interpretation: Theory and Practice*, ed. Charles S. Singleton (Baltimore: Johns Hopkins University Press, 1969), 35–68.

4. See Franz Kafka, *Amerika*, trans. Willa Muir and Edwin Muir (New York: Schocken Books, 1974), 196–200, 247–58.

5. Jacques Derrida, *Of Grammatology*, trans. Gayatri Chakravorty Spivak (Baltimore: Johns Hopkins University Press, 1976), 8, 12.

6. See Jacques Derrida, "Plato's Pharmacy," in his *Dissemination*, trans. Barbara Johnson (Chicago: University of Chicago Press, 1981), 63–64.

7. Martin Heidegger, *Identity and Difference*, trans. Joan Stambaugh (New York: Harper and Row, 1969), 69, 137–38.

8. My primary methodological paradigm for this chapter—an exploration of textual allegory and analysis based on various tropes of orality—was work on Petronius and Proust by Richard Macksey. During the spring of 1974, Macksey delivered a presentation entitled "Eat Your Words" to a conference on "Hard Language" organized by Bruce Jackson and Diane Christian at the State University of New York at Buffalo. This paper defined the field of the present chapter.

9. Wittgenstein himself thematizes the issue of fatness and thinness in language. In *Last Writings on the Philosophy of Psychology* (in paragraphs 795 and 796), he asks, "Given the two words 'fat' and 'thin'—would you rather be inclined to say that Wednesday was fat and Tuesday thin, or that Tuesday was fat and Wednesday thin?" See Ludwig Wittgenstein, *Last Writings on the Philosophy of Psychology*, ed. G. H. von Wright and Heikki Nyman (Oxford: Basil Blackwell,1982), 1:102e.

10. Wittgenstein, *Tractatus*, 7.

11. I refer, of course, to Milan Kundera, *The Unbearable Lightness of Being*, trans. Michael Henry Heim (London: Faber and Faber, 1984).

12. See Werner Heisenberg, *Physics and Philosophy* (New York: Harper, 1958), 51–56, 62–63, 81–82, 98–101, 125, 139–42, 160–62, 167–69, 175–79, 185–86, 197–98, 201, 204–5; Heisenberg, *Physics and Beyond* (New York: Harper and Row, 1971), 63–65, 68–69, 134–35.

13. See Sir Arthur Eddington, *The Nature of the Physical World: The Gifford Lectures* (1929) (New York: Macmillan, 1929), xiv–xv, 1–2, 8–10, 13, 27–29, 33–36, 47–52, 61–62, 66–68, 70, 74.

14. See, above all, Franz Kafka, *Letter to His Father*, trans. Ernst Kaiser and Eithne Wilkins (New York: Schocken, 1966). Two examples should illustrate my point: "In point of fact, in the group photographs taken at Franzensbad, for instance, you always looked big and jolly, among these sulky little people, a king on his travels" (71); "there were years in which, in perfectly good health, I lazed away more time on the sofa than you in all your life, including all your illnesses" (91).

15. In terms of landscape art, I think particularly of Robert Smithson and such productions as *The Spiral Jetty*, Great Salt Lake Utah (1970) and *Broken Circle—Spiral Hill*, Emmen, Netherlands (1971). See *The Writings of Robert Smithson*, ed. Nancy Holt (New York: New York University Press, 1979). Christo has executed a number of projects involving the wrapping of buildings and other architectural structures and natural features. Among the most notable of these are *Wrapped Coast—Little Bay, Australia* (1969), *The Museum of Contemporary Art, Chicago, Wrapped* (1972), *Running Fence, Sonoma and Marin Counties, California* (1979), and *Key Biscayne Island* (1986). See Christo, *Complete Editions 1964–1982* (Munich: Schellmann and Klüser, 1982). With regard to artistic minimalism, the work of such artists as Richard Serra, Carl Andre, Bruce Nauman, Agnes Martin, and Robert Ryman stands out. Representative works would be the following: Serra's *Pipe Prop* and *Corner Prop No. 8*; Andre's *Straight Short Pipe Run* (1969) and *Aluminum Square* (1968); Nauman's *South America Triangle* (1981): Martin's *Stone* (1960) AND *Happy Valley* (1967); and Ryman's *Director* and *Report* (both 1983). See Peter Schjeldahl, *Art of Our Time* (London: Lund Humphries, 1984), vol. 1.

16. Even when one bears in mind John Cage's qualification that the sense of cacophony is highly subjective and based on musical habit, it nonetheless seems justifiable to postulate a great receptivity to cacophony in twentieth-century music than at other moments. Whether atonal music is cacophonous or not is of course a matter of musical taste and background. In recent work, Cage's *Ryoanji* and Pierre Boulez's piano sonatas stand out in this regard. In terms of musical minimalism, such works as Philip Glass's *Einstein on the Beach*, Charles Amirkhanian's *Dutiful Ducks*, and Terry Riley's *Cadenza on a Night Plain* have achieved an exemplary status.

17. The Borges story in question is "Tlön, Uqbar, Orbis Tertius" (17–36). My discussion of this text, particularly with regard to marginality, is in the section entitled "Cone and Compass" in chapter 5.

18. Gottlob Frege, "On Sense and Reference," in *Translations from the Philosophical Writings of Gottlob Frege*, ed. Peter Geach and Max Black (Oxford: Basil Blackwell, 1952), 52–78.

19. See Bertrand Russell, *The Philosophy of Logical Atomism*, ed. David Pears (La Salle, Ill.: Open Court, 1985), 56. The centerpiece of this book is a 1918 essay of the same title, that was important in defining the starting point, issues, and stakes of logical analysis.

20. Stuart Barnett, a graduate student enrolled in my fall 1987–88 seminar, "Wittgenstein and Deconstruction," suggested that the overall traits of the vocal opposition in the Kafka story might well extend into Wittgenstein's relation to his predecessors. The paragraphs on Frege and Russell here bear out his intuition.

21. Frege, *Translations*, 70.

22. The possibility of a metaphoric dimension in Wittgenstein's discourse was first broached to me by Barbara Harlow, now at the University of Texas, in private conversations in Buffalo between 1973 and 1975. The end of this essay is therefore considerably indebted to her insights.

23. The issue of translation is, quite simply, decisive to twentieth-century literature, in part because of the strong element of *bricolage* in modernist esthetics; in part because it extends the imperialism implicit in Hegelian and post-Hegelian intellectual frameworks. Benjamin suggests the complexities of translation in "The Task of the Translator," in his *Illuminations*, trans. Harry Zohn, ed. Hannah Arendt (New York: Schocken, 1969), 69–83. Joyce, above all in *Finnegans Wake*,

rejoices in the hybrids that interlinguistic punning affords. The language of this novel might be said to be an occasional Esperanto, a universal language of comparative applications. Characteristically, Wittgenstein surrounds the complexities attending translation by a somewhat pained and depressive mood.

24. For Jacques Derrida's discussion of iterability, see "Signature Event Context," in Glyph 1, ed. Samuel Weber and Henry Sussman (Baltimore: Johns Hopkins University Press, 1977), 179–80, 183, 186–93; and "Limited Inc," in Glyph 2, ed. Samuel Weber and Henry Sussman (Baltimore; Johns Hopkins University Press, 1977), 175, 182–91, 198–217, 225–26, 235–37, 242–48, 250–51. Rodolphe Gasché, in his Tain of the Mirror: Derrida and the Philosophy of Reflection (Cambridge, Mass.: Harvard University Press, 1986), 212–17, includes iterability among the infrastructures by which Derrida both extends and dismantles the philosophical tradition from which deconstruction sets off.

25. I refer here to Kafka's "Crossbreed [A Sport]" (CS, 426–27), "Cares of a Family Man" (CS, 89–139).

26. For the spontaneous after image, see Walter Benjamin, "On Some Motifs in Baudelaire," in his Illuminations, 157, 175, 179, 184, 186–88, 191.

27. Wittgenstein, Tractatus, 7.

28. The visual is an extremely important component of Wittgenstein's thinking. The painter whose work most closely parallels the Wittgensteinian investigations is, to my mind, Paul Klee. I think particularly of those images composed neither of invisible strokes nor of specific points but of small squares. I would argue that these squares, larger than points but smaller than integral representational shapes, occupy a function in the painted surface analogous to that played by elementary propositions within logical space. Klee delights in analyzing larger shapes, say a boat or a house, by means of these differentiated but homologous shapes. In addition, he incorporates a metadiscursive language of indication, pointing, and directionality—with the arrows that he often inscribes on his painted surfaces. Klee may well be the exemplary twentieth-century painter of logical analysis and language games. I think particularly of such works as Around the Fish (1926), Classical Garden (1926), Departure of the Ships (1927), Arrow in the Garden (1929), Classic Coast (1931), Distant Landscape (1931), Equals Infinity (1932), and North Room (1932).

29. Among twentieth-century writers, Borges abounds in suggestive instances of synesthesia. See F, 20, 22–24, 27, 57, 61, 112–15 (the texts cited here are "Tlön, Uqbar, Orbis Tertius," "The Circular Ruins," and "Funes, the Memorious").

30. See Jacques Derrida, Speech and Phenomena, trans. David B. Allison (Evanston: Northwestern University Press, 1973), 68, 78–80, 82–83, 85–86.

31. Above all in Tain of the Mirror, 13–78.

32. For the notion of by-play, see Andrzej Warminski, "Prepositional By-play," in Glyph 3, ed. Samuel Weber and Henry Sussman (Baltimore: Johns Hopkins University Press, 1978), 98–117.

FOUR. THE CIRCLE OF EXCLUSION

1. Similarly, Gardena invests the wrap comprising one of Klamm's tokens, without which she "couldn't have held out" (C, 103) during the twenty years since the affair, with a uniqueness imperceptible to anyone else (at least to K. and the reader): "To K. it seemed to be an ordinary woolen wrap" (100).

2. Under the well-known image of two identical doors distinguishable only by

the heading HOMMES   FEMMES in Jacques Lacan's "L'Instance de la lettre dans l'inconscient" in his *Ecrits* I, Collection Points (Paris: Seuil, 1966), there is the following caption: ". . . où l'on voit que, sans beaucoup étendre la portée du signifiant interéssé dans l'expérience, soit en redoublant seulement l'espèce nominale par la seule juxtaposition de deux termes dont le sens complémentaire paraît devoit s'en consolider, la surprise se produit d'une précipitation du sens inattendue: dans l'image de deux portes jumelles qui symbolisent avec l'isoloir offert à l'homme occidental pour satisfaire à ses besoins naturels hors de sa maison, l'impératif qu'il semble partager avec la grande majorité des communautés primitives et qui soumet sa vie publique aux lois de la ségrégation urinaire" (256–57).

3. In the figure of Klamm a third point is added to the dyad underlying the production and movement of *The Trial*, Kafka-K. The new dimension, the triangle completed by Klamm, sets the duplicity of the categories established by *The Castle* even further in relief.

4. Three examples should suggest the widely polysemous use of the word *Verkehr* throughout the novel. First, it connotes traffic in its physical sense, an onrush of people or things: "the passage was becoming animated, traffic [*in Verkehr*] seemed to be beginning" (*C*, 365–66). It also describes the formal transactions of business or negotiations: "Again he had this sense of extraordinary ease in intercourse [*Verkehr*] with the authorities" (76). But the sexual connotation of this intercourse is no less explicit: "Frieda, who has had relations [*verkehrt*] with Klamm for a long time, doesn't possess a single keepsake from him" (103).

5. See Erich Heller, "The World of Franz Kafka," in his *Disinherited Mind* (New York: Harcourt Brace Jovanovich, 1975), 197–231. Heller argues convincingly and mercilessly against imposing naïve allegories on Kafka's fiction, particularly against theological allegorization of *The Castle*. His willingness to observe a gnostic or Manichean influence on Kafka's fiction as opposed to a grounding in Judeo-Christianity acknowledges the duplicity underlying Kafka's theological metaphors, the same duplicity that characterizes his psychological constructions. Yet there are specific plays on theological attitudes, mostly Judaic, that must be taken into account. In his blanket denial of theological allegory in Kafka's work, Heller refuses to do this. Yet Kafka's theological games are integrally related to the tricks that he plays within the sphere of the phenomenological and psychological subject.

6. The anti-Semitic quality of this ostracism is made overt on p. 268, where Olga explains to K. that her family possessed no land to sell in order to compensate for income lost in the village's boycott of her father's shoemaking business.

7. Perhaps the most striking *Gitter* in Kafka's fiction is the one defining both the Hunger Artist's imprisonment and his esthetic and critical separation from society. See Kafka, "A Hunger Artist" (*CS*, 268–77).

8. K., for example, fails to see the parallel between Klamm's propositioning Frieda and Sortini's propositioning Amalia, a similarity that he admits only at Olga's insistence.

9. The most extended elaboration of the machine metaphor in Kafka's fiction is to be found, of course, in the execution machine of "In the Penal Colony." In both cases the ultimate breakdown of the machinery is inevitable.

10. On this point, *The Castle* is clearly at variance with *The Trial*.

11. Søren Kierkegaard, *Either/Or*, trans. David F. Swenson and Lillian Marvin Swenson, rev. Howard A. Johnson (Princeton, N.J.: Princeton University Press, 1971), 1:4–6.

12. Kafka's reading of Kierkegaard is amply documented by Klaus Wagenbach in

Franz Kafka: Eine Biographie seiner Jugend (Berne: Franke, 1958), 115, 257–58. Both Wagenbach and Wilhelm Emrich, *Franz Kafka: A Critical Study of His Writings,* trans. Sheema Zeben Buehne (New York: Ungar, 1968), 516, date Kafka's discovery of Kierkegaard and reading a large segment of his works early in 1918. Emrich speculates that this is a good four years before the composition of the main part of *The Castle,* an opinion presupposing a biographical influence of Kafka's crisis over Milena on the novel. This opinion is supported by Brod, who records that Kafka read him the beginning of the novel on 15 March 1922 and believes (although he cannot document) that this date could not be far removed from the actual composition. See Max Brod, *Franz Kafka: Eine Biographie* (Frankfurt am Main: S. Fischer, 1962), 226–27.

13. Two other examples indicating how Bürgel's discourse refers to K.'s situation as much as, if not more than, to the subject at hand are the following: "'How long will you be able to put up resistance?' one wonders" (*C,*348), asks Bürgel rhetorically, describing the officials' weakening resistance to nighttime petitioners, but just as aptly characterizing K.'s losing battle against sleep. Similarly, the intruder pictured by Bürgel is every bit as much K. as it is some hypothetical case: "He has, after all, in his own opinion probably only for some indifferent, accidental reasons—being overtired, disappointed, ruthless and indifferent from overfatigue and disappointment—pushed his way into a room other than the one he wanted to enter, he sits there in ignorance, occupied with his thoughts, if he is occupied at all, with his mistake, or with his fatigue. Could one not leave him in that situation? One cannot" (349).

14. I disagree with Politzer's contention that K.'s profession of Land-Surveyor limits his concern to surfaces and hence implies the superficiality of what he discovers. See Heinz Politzer, *Franz Kafka: Parable and Paradox* (Ithaca, N.Y.: Cornell University Press, 1962), 222–23.

FIVE. THE TEXT THAT WAS NEVER A STORY

1. A good general introduction to Freud's thought regarding obsessional ideas is to be found in the theoretical section of the "Rat Man" case history (*SE,* 10:221–49).

2. See G. W. F. Hegel, *Phänomenologie des Geistes* (Hamburg: Felix Meiner, 1952), 141–50, or *Hegel's Phenomenology of Spirit,* trans. A. V. Miller (Oxford: Clarendon Press, 1977), 104–19. For a reading of this passage in terms of the tropes that Hegel developed to account for his own discourse, see Henry Sussman, *The Hegelian Aftermath: Readings in Hegel, Kierkegaard, Freud, Proust, and James* (Baltimore: Johns Hopkins University Press, 1982), 54–56.

3. This ambiguity in characterization may be said to structure such major works as "Description of a Struggle" and "A Hunger Artist." Kafka rehearses its potentials in "First Sorrow." For a full treatment of "Description of a Struggle" as an exercise in scenic construction based on a play between intersubjective and intrasubjective conflict, see Henry Sussman, *Franz Kafka: Geometrician of Metaphor* (Madison: Coda Press, 1979) (dist. Johns Hopkins University Press), 61–74.

4. Freud develops his notion of the uncanny in a 1919 essay, "The 'Uncanny,'" whose major instance of this phenomenon derives from E. T. A. Hoffmann's tale "The Sandman." Initially, Freud situates the uncanny at the end of primary narcissism, when a child's self-image of benevolent omnipotence is partially eclipsed by its opposite. Freud realizes, however, the inadequacy of a developmental explanation in accounting for the full literary potentials of doubling (*SE,*17:232–45).

5. Of all critics, Benjamin has provided the best account of the allegorical gestic language in Kafka's fiction, an illustration of his broader notion of shock. For Kafka's gestic language, see Walter Benjamin, "Franz Kafka," in his *Illuminations*, trans. Harry Zohn, ed. Hannah Arendt (New York: Schocken, 1969), 118–26. For the notion of shock, see Benjamin, "On Some Motifs in Baudelaire," in ibid., 161, 163, 175–80.

6. See Jacques Lacan, *Ecrits: A Selection* (New York: Norton, 1977), 146–78, and Lacan, *The Four Fundamental Concepts of Psychoanalysis* (New York: Norton, 1978), 42–52.

SIX. KAFKA IN THE HEART OF THE TWENTIETH CENTURY

1. See Claude Lévi-Strauss, "The Structural Study of Myth," in his *Structural Anthropology*, trans. Claire Jacobson and Brooke Grundfest Schoepf (New York: Basic Books, 1963), 209–12, 216–19, 229–31.

2. For the specific texts in question, see Jorge Luis Borges, *Labyrinths*, ed. Donald A. Yates and James E. Irby (New York: New Directions, 1962), 193–95, 236. I owe this final turn in the argument to Johann Pillai, who kindly edited this chapter.

3. For a full sense of the decisive role played by hypothesis in the structure of Kafka's fiction and of the link between hypothesis and metaphor, I am indebted to Brent Whelan and the lectures he presented as part of a cotaught course on fiction at the Johns Hopkins University in 1977–78.

4. Contemporary writers on science fiction and fantastic literature tend to define these genres thematically, that is, by some condition, such as estrangement or the unexpected, that prevails within the fictive world that the literary work represents. According to Tsvetan Todorov, the fantastic work internalizes the hesitation experience by the character (as a reader surrogate) at the uncanny circumstances represented. My approach here defines science fiction methodologically and linguistically, according to the rigor with which textual qualities, attaining the status of hypotheses, are tested. It is interesting to note the conjunction of Kafka and Borges in the work of several of these writers. Suvin and Brooke-Rose both attempt to go beyond thematics in their treatments of the genre. See Darko Suvin, *The Metamorphoses of Science Fiction* (New Haven, Conn.: Yale University Press, 1979), 8–15, 29–30, 59. Also see Christine Brooke-Rose, *A Rhetoric of the Unreal* (Cambridge: Cambridge University Press, 1983), 72–82, 333–34; and, Robert Scholes, *Structural Fabulation: An Essay on Fiction of the Future* (Notre Dame, Ind.: Notre Dame University Press, 1975), 45–49, 100–104.

5. Such a work as E. T. A. Hoffmann's "Sandman," with its model of a clockwork woman, raised vital modernistic questions concerning the nature of subjectivity and its relationship to mechanical processes. The most far-reaching impact of this fictive scenario was on American literature, although Freud recognized the psychoanalytical implications of mechanization within the subjective sphere. Such texts by Edgar Allan Poe as "The Pit and the Pendulum" and "Maelzel's Chess-Player" arise in a distinctly Hoffmannian atmosphere, although it is primarily in *Eureka* that the latter author reaches the plateau of science fiction as I intend the term here and as it is practiced by Kafka, Borges, and Calvino: an exploration of the dimensions of representation and discourse carried to the point of scientific insistence and form. *Eureka* describes a universe in terms of linguistic repetition, concentration, and dispersion. Even as the genre of science fiction

formalizes itself, in such a text as H. G. Wells's *Time Machine*, the exploration of the analogy between linguistic, cognitive, and empirical processes remains constant. The hyperextension of time that Wells hypothesizes in this novel provides for a questioning of temporal assumptions strikingly similar to Borges's own inquiry.

6. I have elsewhere examined the systematic exploration of metaphor throughout Kafka's fiction and the theoretical implications of this process. See Henry Sussman, *Franz Kafka: Geometrician of Metaphor* (Madison, Wisc.: Coda Press, 1979), (dist. Johns Hopkins University Press), 27–34, 114–19, 153–60.

7. Note, for example, that Borges' story, "The Rejected Sorcerer," appears in the March 1960 number of *Fantastic Universe Science Fiction*.

8. For an excellent treatment of the interdependency of reading and writing in Borges' work, see Emir Rodríguez Monegal, "Borges, the Reader as Writer," in *Prose for Borges*, ed. Charles Newman and Mary Kinzie (Evanston, Ill.: Northwestern University Press, 1974), 96–137.

9. The key text in terms of Freud's discussion of condensation is *Jokes and their Relation to the Unconscious*, although this term also figures in the scheme of the dream-work in *The Interpretation of Dreams*. See *SE*, 5:592–97, 648–53; 8:18–29, 41–45.

10. For an analogous vocabulary of textual tropes in Kafka's writing, see Sussman, 128–43. For a discussion of some of the primary textual tropes characteristic of modernism, which emanate from Romantic theory, see Henry Sussman, *The Hegelian Aftermath: Readings in Hegel, Kierkegaard, Freud, Proust, and James* (Baltimore: Johns Hopkins University Press, 1982), 19–22, 27–49.

11. For a definition of the fantastic in literature in terms of ambiguity, hesitation, and the inscription of this hesitation in the text, see Tzvetan Todorov, *The Fantastic: A Structural Approach to a Literary Genre* (Ithaca, N.Y.: Cornell University Press, 1975), 31–38, 41–46. In exploring the connections between the fantastic and fantasy, Rabkin identifies certain traits that would be quite at home on Tlön: the unexpected, the *nonsequitur*, variance of perspective. See Eric S. Rabkin, *The Fantastic in Literature* (Princeton, N.J.: Princeton University Press, 1976), 8–10, 14–18, 74–81.

12. Children's literature often tangibly reifies the "other" worlds of enchantment or horror encountered by its characters by means of tokens or traces carried over from the fantastic realm to the real one. It thus furnishes many models for Borges's cone and compass. A most striking example consists of the twigs and cup brought back by the prince in the Grimms' "Shoes That Were Danced to Pieces" as proof of the twelve dancing princesses' nightly escapades. Cf. Jacob Grimm and Wilhelm Grimm, *Grimm's Fairy Tales*, illus. Josef Scharl (New York: Pantheon, 1956), 596–600. The tragic power of such items as eyeglasses and bushes over Nathanael in E. T. A. Hoffmann's "Sandman" derives precisely from their ability to bridge what Freud would call primary and secondary processes.

13. For the fullest and best exploration to date of the complex interactions between Borges' life and writing, see Emir Rodríguez Monegal, *Jorge Luis Borges: A Literary Biography* (New York: E. P. Dutton, 1978).

14. All theological (not to mention ideological) history may be regarded as a series of departures in which the new position is exegetically generated: a subsequent crystallization is read within and around the margins of a prior text. History proceeds by textual appropriation and *reading in*. The New Testament writes itself into the margins of the Old, finding there not only a justification but also a foreknowledge and anticipation of Jesus as well. This dynamic is analogous

to the relationship between the Old and New worlds, in history as well as litera-ture. Some of the key statements in the textual interplay at the origins of Chris-tianity, a succession thematized and reversed in "Death and the Compass," include the following (all citations are from the King James Version): "For unto us a child is born, unto us a son is given: and the government shall be on his shoul-der: and his name shall be called Wonderful, Counsellor, The mighty God, The everlasting Father, The Prince of Peace" (Isa. 9:6); "Thus saith the Lord; A voice was heard in Ramah, lamentation, *and* bitter weeping; Rahel weeping for her chil-dren refused to be comforted for her children, because they *were* not" (Jer. 31:15); "Then was fulfilled that which was spoken by Jeremy the prophet, saying In Rama was there a voice heard, lamentation, and weeping, and great mourning, Rachel weeping *for* her children, and would not be comforted, because they are not" (Matt. 2:17–18); "Now when Jesus had heard that John was cast into prison, he departed into Galilee; and leaving Nazareth, he came and dwelt in Capernaum, . . . That it might be fulfilled which was spoken by Esaias the prophet, saying, the land of Zebulun, and the land of Nephthalim, *by* the way of the sea, beyond Jor-dan, Galilee of the Gentiles" (Matt. 4:12–15).

15. For a discussion of this term, see Martin Heidegger, *Identity and Difference*, trans. Joan Stambaugh (New York: Harper and Row, 1969), 29–33, 36–41, 92–97, 100–106.

16. In "The Circular Ruins," Borges retells the Judeo-Christian myth of creation, but in terms of a literary rather than onto-theological genesis. The wizard, who is as anonymous when consumed by flames at the end of the story as when he first appears from nowhere, makes two attempts to create a human being. The first effort, a "dialectical" act of selecting one individual from both a pedagogical and a logical class of imaginary children, fails. This Gnostic creation story is consum-mated by an organic imaginary creation, one proceeding from an embryo to a fully developed individual. Immediately after the wizard's abortive, "dialectical" attempt at creation, he falls into a sleep described as a "viscous desert." Viscosity in Borges figures the concentration and density of poetic language, as does the figure of the cone. See *F,* 59.

17. For the best placement of Borges in a broad philosophical context, see John Sturrock, *Paper Tigers: The Ideal Fictions of Jorge Luis Borges* (Oxford: Oxford University Press, 1977). Sturrock treats such crucial issues as idealization in Borges' writing (61–76), discontinuity and disorder (108–22), and play (141–47).

18. See Ferdinand de Saussure, *Course in General Linguistics*, trans. Wade Bas-kin (New York: McGraw-Hill, 1966), 65–71, 73.

19. Cf. Ernest Fenollosa, *The Chinese Written Character as a Medium for Poe-try*, ed. Ezra Pound (San Francisco: City Lights Books, 1983), 9–10, 13–20. Such a pas-sage as the following one is indeed close to Borges' characterization of the languages of Tlön: "The Chinese have one word, *ming* or *mei*. Its ideograph is the sign of the sun together with the sign of the moon. It serves as verb, noun, adjec-tive. Thus you write literally, 'the sun and moon of the cup' for 'the cup's bright-ness.' Placed as a verb, you write 'the cup sun-and-moons,' actually 'cup sun-and-moon,' or in a weakened thought, 'is like sun,' i.e., shines. 'Sun-and-moon cup' is naturally a bright cup" (18).

20. See Jorge Luis Borges, *Other Inquisitions, 1937–1952*, trans. Ruth L. C. Simms (Austin: University of Texas Press, 1965), 101–5.

21. See Saussure, *General Linguistics*, 9, 14–15, 17–19, 76–78.

22. To cite merely one of many possible examples, in *Of Grammatology*, Derrida

explores the methodological and theological biases implicit within the model of phonetic script that characterizes virtually all Indo-European languages. He links the priority given to speech and voice in phonetic languages to such major metaphysical attitudes as immanence, presence, and immediacy (temporal, spatial, and logical) that pervade Western thought throughout its development. A Derridean approach must raise serious questions regarding the centrality of imagination as an otherworldly and almost transcendental construct in Borges' work. But the alternate status of Tlön is closely akin to the debunking of Western attitudes so deeply entrenched as to be nearly transparent, a position that constitutes one of the major contributions of deconstruction. See Jacques Derrida, *Of Grammatology*, trans. Gayatri Chakravorty Spivak (Baltimore: Johns Hopkins University Press, 1976), 8–13, 17, 43, 74–76, 144–49, 280–86.

23. For a critical treatment of Borges' literary politics, see Alicia Borinsky, "Repetition, Museums, Libraries: Jorge Luis Borges," in *Glyph 2*, ed. Samuel Weber and Henry Sussman (Baltimore: Johns Hopkins University Press, 1977), 88–101.

24. For a treatment of the notion of chance as it applies to Borges' writing, see William Beatty Warner, *Chance and the Text of Experience* (Ithaca, N.Y.: Cornell University Press, 1986), 142, 299–302.

25. *Always already* (*toujours déjà*) is a term by which Derrida demonstrates the futility of establishing temporal priority, originality, and causality. The temporality of language is such that articulation has always already taken place, so that the initiating moments of genealogies, historical fictions, and logical processes are merely hypothetical wishes. See *Of Grammatology*, 14, 66–67, 199, 215, 244, 266–67.

26. For an important article on this story, one approaching Borgesian expansion from the point of view of geometrical symbolism, see Robert C. Carroll, "Borges and Bruno: The Geometry of Infinity in *La Muerte y la Brújula*,' *MLN* 94 (1979): 321–42.

27. The name of "Dandy Red" Scharlach, like many names in Borges' fiction, is heavily determined. It plays on Shylock, the merchant of Venice, the German verb *lachen*, "to laugh," and the color scarlet. It may not be accidental that the last syllable in the name of Lönnrot—Scharlach's adversary but also partner in reading—is *rot*, the German word for red. Elias Lönnrot (1802–84), by the way, was a Finnish folklorist whose efforts at collecting the folktales and ballads of his people emulated the activities of the Grimms in Germany. See *Grimm's Fairy Tales*, 852.

28. In the course of the foregoing discussion alone, there are no less than three significant signifiers with umlauts: *Tlön, hrönir,* and *Lönnrot.* Since there is no unusual emphasis placed on the Germanic languages or culture in Borges' work, one must ask oneself why this particular notation—and the very slight phonetic disfiguration that it entails—attains such prominence in spite of its typographical slightness. One metaphor that Søren Kierkegaard selects for irony consists of the diacritical marks in Hebrew that transform the identities and meanings of letters and words *almost* silently and invisibly. "I am as drunken as the Hebrew *shewa*, weak and silent as a *daghesh lene;* I feel like a letter printed backward in a line," exhalts the esthete (*Either/Or*, trans. David F. Swenson and Lillian Marvin Swenson, rev. Howard A. Johnson [Princeton, N.J.: Princeton University Press, 1971], 1:22). Borges' umlauts effect the small but uncanny change of irony. They bring about an upheaval in perspective by means of minimalist devices.

SEVEN. THE MODERN/POSTMODERN

1. Of course, this performance could just as well be described as language above standard specifications or more than optimal. If I select the more negative formulation, this is in keeping with an overarching postmodern esthetic of indifference.

2. Rodolphe Gasché, *The Tain of the Mirror: Derrida and the Philosophy of Reflection* (Cambridge, Mass.: Harvard University Press, 1986).

3. Clive Hart, *Structure and Motif in Finnegans Wake* (London: Faber and Faber, 1962), 79, 83.

4. Adaline Glasheen, *A Second Census of Finnegans Wake* (Evanston, Ill.: Northwestern University Press, 1963), 81.

5. Hart, *Structure and Motif,* 87–95.

6. Noam Chomsky, *Cartesian Linguistics* (New York: Harper and Row, 1966), 24, 29–30, 35, 40, 59, 63–64, 73.

7. Glasheen, *Second Census;* John Gordon, *Finnegans Wake: A Plot Summary* (Syracuse, N.Y.: Syracuse University Press, 1986); James S. Atherton, *The Books at the Wake* (New York: Viking, 1960); Joseph Campbell and Henry Morton Robinson, *A Skeleton Key to Finnegans Wake* (London: Faber and Faber, 1947); Roland McHugh, *Annotations to Finnegans Wake* (Baltimore: Johns Hopkins University Press, 1980).

8. See Jacques Derrida, "From Restricted to General Economy: A Hegelianism without Reserve," in his *Writing and Difference,* trans. Alan Bass (Chicago: University of Chicago Press, 1978), 268–77.

9. As I prepare to conclude this study, the rhetoric of modernity and its afterimages remains compelling to me in a double sense: both as a sliding frame of reference, not time-specific in scope, hence incorporating *Tristram Shandy* and other radical performances throughout the history of literature; and as a confluence of experiments and distortions giving twentieth-century literature certain of its distinctive qualities. The failure to resolve this double vision constitutes not so much a conceptual or interpretative limitation as an acknowledgment of the volatile and often self-negating activity prevailing at the horizons of possibility. This dissonance may in fact be what we know best about the borderline of improvisation.

10. For Gasché, the movement toward indifference does not constitute a conceptual relaxation or giving up but rather arises in a very specific context under precise conditions. See Rodolphe Gasché, "In-Difference to Philosophy: De Man on Kant, Hegel, and Nietzsche," in *Reading De Man Reading,* ed. Lindsay Waters and Wlad Godzich (Minneapolis: University of Minnesota Press, 1989), 259–94.

11. This crucial novel's characters are as much conceptual positions as they re subject surrogates. Its chapters are very often illuminations of their titles, which just as often assume propositional form. While extending its traditional genre, then, *The Man without Qualities* is also a field for the interaction and divergence of logical propositions. Any novel that included such chapters as "If there is such a thing as a sense of reality, there must also be a sense of possibility" (chap. 4), "The effect of a Man Without Qualities on a man with qualities" (chap. 17), and "The assertion that even ordinary life is of a Utopian nature" (chap. 84), must be regarded, at least in part, in a logical-analytical vein.

12. See Franz Kafka, "A Common Confusion" (*CS,* 429–30). Also see Italo Calvino, "t zero," "The Chase," and "The Night Driver," in *t zero,* trans. William Weaver (New York: Harcourt Brace Jovanovich, 1976), 95–111, 112–27, 128–36.

13. Italo Calvino, *If on a winter's night a traveller*, trans. William Weaver (New York: Harcourt Brace Jovanovich, 1981).

14. See Freud, *SE*, 7:152–53, 184–87, 192–93, 197–98; 9:168–75; 10:8, 127, 200, 220; 17:80–84, 130, 132. Also see Allen S. Weiss, "The Other as Muse," in *Psychosis and Sexual Identity: Toward a Post-Analytical View of the Schreber Case*, ed. David B. Allison, Prado de Oliveira, Mark S. Roberts, and Allen S. Weiss (Albany: State University of New York Press, 1988), 72–75.

15. Søren Kierkegaard, *Either/Or*, trans. David F. Swenson and Lillian Marvin Swenson, rev. Howard A. Johnson (Princeton, N.J.: Princeton University Press, 1971), 1:49, 61–63, 67–69, 100, 133–34, 289–93; 2:6, 32–33, 96, 136–37, 161, 214–15, 258–64.

16. See Derrida's discussion of the relation between the "frontispiece" and chant 6 of Lautréamont's *Chants de Maldoror*, in "Outwork," in Derrida, *Dissemination*, trans. Barbara Johnson (Chicago: University of Chicago Press, 1981), 35–45.

17. See Roland Barthes, *A Lover's Discourse, Fragments*, trans. Richard Howard (New York: Hill and Wang, 1984), 18, 75–77.

18. See Ezra Pound, *Guide to Kulchur* (New York: New Directions, 1970), 63–70, 266; Ernest Fenollosa, *The Chinese Written Character as a Medium for Poetry*, ed. Ezra Pound (San Francisco: City Lights Books, 1983), 3, 6–9, 14, 17.

19. In terms of the postmodern mood, see, for example, Antonin Artaud, "The Umbilicus of Limbo" and selections from "The Nerve Meter," *The Theater and Its Double*, and "A Voyage to the Land of the Tarahumara," in *Antonin Artaud: Selected Writings*, ed. Susan Sontag (New York: Farrar, Straus, and Giroux, 1976), 59–76, 79–90, 215–78; Georges Bataille, "The Solar Anus," "The Jesuve," "The Pineal Eye," "The Labyrinth," and "The Sacred Conspiracy," in his *Visions of Excess: Selected Writings, 1927–1939*, ed. Allan Stoekl (Minneapolis: University of Minnesota Press, 1986), 5–14, 73–90, 171–81; Maurice Blanchot, "Literature and the Right to Death" and "Two Versions of the Imaginary," in his *Gaze of Orpheus and Other Literary Essays*, trans. Lydia Davis (Barrytown, N.Y.: Station Hill Press, 1981), 21–62, 79–90.

20. This is documented, for example, by G. H. von Wright, in his "Biographical Sketch," in Norman Malcom, *Ludwig Wittgenstein: A Memoir* (Oxford University Press, 1984), 10–11.

21. Postmodern drama, whether its inception is taken to be Antonin Artaud's *The Theater and Its Double*, Samuel Beckett's *Waiting for Godot*, or Robert Wilson's productions, is striking in the manner in which it pauses over a relative dearth of images.

22. For a fuller discussion of Kafka's "Burrow" and its theoretical and stylistic implications, see Henry Sussman, "The All-Embracing Metaphor: Reflections on Kafka's 'The Burrow,'" in *Glyph 1*, ed. Samuel Weber and Henry Sussman (Baltimore: Johns Hopkins University Press, 1977), 100–131; reprinted in Sussman, *Franz Kafka: Geometrician of Metaphor* (Madison, Wisc.: Coda Press, 1979) (dist. Johns Hopkins University Press), 147–81.

23. Heidegger, writing on the pre-Socratics, specifically Heraclitus, situates the happening (*Ereignis*) of language as Being in an allegorical clearing (*Lichtung*). For Bernhard as well as Heidegger, the clearing becomes the site of something inadmissible and profound related to the recognition of language. It is Bernhard, however, who explores the terror of this happening, the potential breach it opens in the Derridean guardrail around his life. See Martin Heidegger, "Aletheia (Heraklit, Fragment 16)," in his *Vorträge und Aufsätze* (Pfullingen: Günther Neske, 1954), 276–82.

24. Gasché, *Tain of the Mirror*, 143–44, 155.
25. Ibid., 186–224, 152.
26. Ibid., 165.
27. Ibid., 174–75.

Index

Index